# The Temples of Golden Light

## Awaken, Shift & Love Yourself

Linda Jarrett

BALBOA.
PRESS
A DIVISION OF HAY HOUSE

Balboa Press books may be ordered through booksellers or by contacting:

Balboa Press
A Division of Hay House
1663 Liberty Drive
Bloomington, IN 47403
www.balboapress.co.uk
1 (877) 407-4847

Because of the dynamic nature of the Internet, any web addresses or links contained in this book may have changed since publication and may no longer be valid. The views expressed in this work are solely those of the author and do not necessarily reflect the views of the publisher, and the publisher hereby disclaims any responsibility for them.

The author of this book does not dispense medical advice or prescribe the use of any technique as a form of treatment for physical, emotional, or medical problems without the advice of a physician, either directly or indirectly. The intent of the author is only to offer information of a general nature to help you in your quest for emotional and spiritual well-being. In the event you use any of the information in this book for yourself, which is your constitutional right, the author and the publisher assume no responsibility for your actions.

Any people depicted in stock imagery provided by Getty Images are models, and such images are being used for illustrative purposes only. Certain stock imagery © Getty Images.

Cover Design by Alice Readman

Print information available on the last page.

ISBN: 978-1-9822-8085-7 (sc)
ISBN: 978-1-9822-8087-1 (hc)
ISBN: 978-1-9822-8086-4 (e)

Balboa Press rev. date: 08/30/2019

# Contents

Foreword..................................................................vii
Preface ................................................................. ix
Acknowledgements ................................................. xiii
Introduction ..........................................................xv

Chapter 1   What Are the Temples of Golden Light? ..................... 1
Chapter 2   The Main Temples of Golden Light ........................... 7
Chapter 3   Europe ................................................... 25
Chapter 4   The Americas.............................................56
Chapter 5   Australasia and Oceanic ................................85
Chapter 6   Asia.....................................................103
Chapter 7   Rest of the World.......................................127
Chapter 8   Healing.................................................149
Chapter 9   Children and Animals....................................165
Chapter 10  Meditation and Relaxation ..............................180
Chapter 11  Meditations to Connect with the Twelve Main
            Temples and the Main Animal Healing Temple .......198

Appendix 1 .........................................................221
Appendix 2 .........................................................227

# *Foreword*

When Linda asked me to write the theme music for her Temples of Golden Light CDs and downloads, I knew it was really important for me to personally experience this incredible energy in order to connect with and ground its musical resonance. So I attended some of her workshops and easily followed her beautiful guided meditations as she linked the whole group to this profound and strong vibration.

With each breath, I could feel myself ascending into the higher planes of light and healing. As we connected through Linda's clear and loving guidance with different power points on the earth, I experienced the etheric temples above as vast vibrating structures, sometimes filled with rainbow colour and crystal energy, other times simply with pure golden light which seemed to bathe the cells of my body. I was filled with tranquillity, with an inner peace, but with a strength and wisdom too, and on occasion I was able to completely let go, as though I was lying in a beautiful healing space where I was held, loved, and cherished. Indeed, I *was* being held and loved, and infused with healing rays of light.

Occasionally, I would intuit an angelic guide or guides working with me, and I always returned from my temple visit calmer and retuned. There was a feeling of absolute security, an inner knowing that all was well and as it should be. Often there was also a feeling of joy; I particularly felt this at the Stonehenge Temple as I intuitively gazed down from my meditation in the temple above and perceived the extraordinary power vibrating the henge below.

The Temples of Golden Light are a truly great gift, and I would personally like to thank Linda for bringing them into our spiritual awareness. It is a reflection of her great personal gifts that she is able to do this in the tranquil and gracious way she does everything.

Because the temples surround the earth, they can be accessed and used by anyone, anywhere, anytime. As you read this book, simply follow your own intuition, link with your favourite temple, and drink in the essence, as I strongly believe that the more we can connect with and utilise this energy, the higher we will be able to raise the vibration on our planet.

As Linda always says, 'Love and Golden Light to you all.' You will certainly experience this as you read and work with this beautiful book.

Shirlie Roden
singer, songwriter, sound healer

# *Preface*

The Temples of Golden Light are a gift from source to rebalance Planet Earth with goddess energy and raise the vibration through ascension. As these are etheric temples, each may be visited during meditation, contemplation, or one's sleep-state for healing, relaxation, upliftment, inspiration, cellular renewal, and release of any energy blocks stopping you from moving forward. The temples will give you guidance and protection. They are filled with love and total light.

The Temples of Golden Light are sacred goddess temples. Three goddesses watch over them: Lady Nada, twin flame of Jesus Christ; Goddess Jacinta, who works with the rainforests and nature on Planet Earth; and Goddess Lathinda, who comes from another universe called the Universe of Golden Light. They are surrounded by the rainbow angels who are able to heal all of your chakras at the same time, under the guidance of two new archangels: Archangel Metaziel and his twin flame, Archangel Honoriel.

The 144 Temples of Golden Light align to all of the pure energies within this wonderful universe and to the gods/goddesses of love and light of source. The Temples of Golden Light are surrounded by four universal global golden seraphim angels of the highest order representing north, south, east, and west of our beautiful planet. Being a gift from source, the temples may bring about miracles. The aim of the Temples of Golden Light is to heal humanity and Mother Earth herself, bringing peace and harmony to a new earth.

Linda Jarrett is an author, writer, spiritual teacher, healer, meditation teacher, clairvoyant, and light language channel. She is honoured to be the ambassador for the 144 Temples of Golden Light. She has channelled this work to be able to help people to heal themselves. You can create a new, positive, harmonious life by linking with the Temples of Golden Light; this will bring about balance and peace. For more information on Linda's work, please visit her website at www.templesofgoldenlight.com If you wish free distant healing, please direct-message Linda through her Temple of Golden Light Facebook page.

Linda has recorded meditations to help you connect to the many Temples of Golden Light:

- Temple of Golden Light Meditations
- Temples of Golden Light Meditations 11
- Temples of Golden Light 111
- Rainbow Angel Meditations
- Garden of Relaxation Meditations
- Unicorn Meditations

These are available at www.templesofgoldenlight.com Also on the site, you can order affirmation creams for well-being and chakra balancing. There are eighteen different creams:

1. Balance
2. Believe
3. Abundance
4. Clarity
5. Unblock/Release
6. Tranquillity
7. Earth Star
8. Enlightenment
9. Self-Confidence
10. Love
11. Harmony
12. Heart
13. Manifest
14. Empower
15. Joy
16. Forgive
17. Magical
18. Inner Peace

Each cream aligns with a different Temple of Golden Light to facilitate balancing, clear all your chakras, and bring forward a powerful clearing and affirmation of your choice. Simply apply the cream to your wrists twice daily.

# Acknowledgements

I would like to thank my family and friends for their love, encouragement, and understanding as I wrote this book. Special thanks to Christopher Jarrett, Alice Readman, Shirlie Roden, Sarah Tosey, Jooles Griffiths, Jonathan Moore, Gabriella Powell, Natasha Aitchison, Christina Hunt, Heidi Taylor, and Steve Nobel.

# *Introduction*

My spiritual journey began when I was only twenty-four years old. This was the age at which I started to be clairvoyant, as a consequence of a personal loss which was the catalyst for great change in my life. I lost my second child, a baby called Melanie who died at the age of eight months. Soon after, doors opened for me to connect with the many angels, earth guides, celestial beings, and ascended masters that are around us all providing constant and loving support.

As I went about my daily life, working in a number of commercial roles and bringing up a young family, I managed to find time to explore and understand this gift of clairvoyance. I started training in healing and meditation, and it was not long before I had trained as a reiki master, karuna reiki master, angel healer therapist, and meditation teacher. I attended courses on personal development, awakening, and enlightenment. As my practice as a healer evolved, I became aware of the rainbow angels. These are angels that specialise in healing with the vibration of colour, and they offer great gifts of balance, relaxation, and inspiration. It was through this practice that I became aware of the powerful presence of the many Temples of Golden Light placed around the world for our spiritual benefit. I felt very drawn to the beauty and power of the temples.

In 2011, I began channelling the Temples of Golden Light. It took me three to four months to identify the etheric blueprint for the first temple. It was a new process for me, and I received guidance between my periods of meditation on how to refine the work I was doing. I was told that I would be the ambassador for the temples, which is when I realised that the task I'd been given was huge, but I accepted the challenge and slowly came to know where all the temples were placed around the globe. I felt blessed to be channelling all the necessary information to help spread golden light around the world for everyone's benefit. It took me two years of sitting quietly on my own to channel all 144 temples.

I then decided, in order for my work to be considered more authentic, to ask four of my regular ladies who came to my meditation groups and workshops to sit with me every week for six months while I again channelled the different temples. Over this period of time, they told me what they experienced, felt, sensed, knew, or saw in their mind's eye. Very often, they felt the same energy and had similar experiences as I had, which helped to verify my own channelling.

I made notes from these sessions and began to write this book slowly, chapter by chapter. Each temple took me on a magical journey. I connected with all of the pure energies on our planet—including Native American, Aboriginal, Maori, Mayan, Inca, and Aztec energies—as well as many star systems, other planets, angels, archangels, celestial beings, and pure white formless beings of light, all of which, with Planet Earth, are helping us to raise our vibration.

And so the 144 Temples of Golden Light were born. Many people in meditation groups and workshops have visited the temples over the last few years, and it is amazing how many remarkable consistencies I have witnessed in how the temples are experienced. I am in awe of them all, as nothing is comparable to their love, peace, happiness, grace, and healing power. They have all been activated to light up our world, and now is the time for the temples to be doing their work.

I usually connect through meditation to a temple to activate its energy. I do not often need to visit a city to activate the temple. Yet sometimes, I do find myself travelling to a city where there is a temple, and I realise that my job is to clear the energy beneath the temple. Sometimes I am aware that temples are activated as I arrive. Certainly, I love the way the light starts to clear the city or area near the temple. Sometimes it rains, which means that the energy in the etheric above is clearing. Other times, the reaction has been more dramatic.

In travelling to a wide range of countries where the temples are situated, I have had some very interesting experiences that you will read about later in the book. When I visited Palermo in Sicily, for example, I discovered that I had been guided to visit the city because old Mafia negative energy was keeping the temple from shining its light. All the other temples helped to clear the area beneath the

Palermo temple of its heavy energy. It took three days to clear. On the fourth day, the city was cleansed by water. It rained solidly for three hours and the city was flooded, as if there had been a monsoon. The water rose to three feet in some areas, and cars came to a halt. The light now shines upon Palermo brightly.

I have chosen to write this book to help you with your ascension process. The more earthlike Temples of Golden Light operate from the fifth dimension, and those with higher energy are in the seventh dimension. By connecting with them, you will raise your vibration, which will help your spiritual growth. The temples are places of great healing and harmony, and each has unique individual attributes, which will enable you to embrace and nurture your inherent spiritual abilities. I hope that by connecting with the temples, you will find inner peace, contentment, grace, and healing.

I am so thankful for my journey with its twists and turns, highs and lows. All the lessons, guidance, and experiences have brought me to a place in my life where I can truly appreciate all that has happened with the deepest of gratitude and a joyful heart. I offer you this book so that you may also come to know the beauty and healing power of these amazing etheric temples scattered around the planet.

Love and Golden Light,
Linda Jarrett

# Chapter 1

## *What Are the Temples of Golden Light?*

The Temples of Golden Light form a powerful grid of golden light to heal the cities and regions of the earth below. The oceanic temples heal the area of the particular ocean where the temple is situated. The temples have been placed within the etheric over ley lines or sacred sites so that the energies are then stronger and more intensified. This placement makes the temples more powerful when it comes to clearing negative energies.

The temples are for personal healing and spiritual growth. You will receive healing on all levels—emotional, mental, physical, and spiritual. The temples are at least fifth-dimensional in energy and enable people to raise their vibrations to help them move towards the fifth dimension and beyond. You will experience a magical transformation when you connect to the Temples of Golden Light. You will be able to embrace changes around you and shift energetically into a different place, realising this change is for your higher good.

The temples can and will facilitate miracles on a personal level. They work for the highest good of humanity and will teach you how to work with Mother Earth and not against her, as well as how to help heal Mother Earth. They will show you how to live in harmony with humanity, animals, and sea creatures. They are capable of bringing about world peace. We are creating a new world of love, peace, joy, happiness, and heavenly order.

One day, the vibration will be so light and will have lifted so much that angels may even be seen holding our hands. That will certainly be a wonderful sight. The angels will help humanity overcome many fears of living. They will help heal many issues that people have held on to for far too long. Emotional issues, mental issues, and physical disharmonies will all be healed. When people let go of disharmonies, they raise their vibration towards enlightenment.

One of the aims of the temples is to create unity all around the world. The grid they form provides a conduit of healing energy to help raise the vibration of humanity and Mother Earth. They will heal all in their pathway, especially those who connect with the temples by meditation, contemplation, and thought intention.

All the Temples of Golden Light are filled with goddess energy: purity, beauty, compassion, and understanding. They contain statues, flowers, furniture, mirrors, gardens, and everything imaginable to make your visit comfortable and worthwhile. In some temples, there is a deafening silence, and time stands still. Everything flows in an orderly fashion in these temples, gently pulsating.

The temples have individual purposes such as enlightenment, healing, peace, and prayer. They are places of pure peace, serenity, contentment, joy, well-being, and happiness. In most temples, there are rooms for meditation and contemplation, as well as healing sanctuaries with musical chambers that heal through sound. Some have schools and colleges for teaching and learning, such as schools of enlightenment, study groups, therapy groups, counselling, new-technology groups, and classes on how to raise your vibration to meet the energy of the new Golden Age. There is a temple for everyone—even you.

The temples vary considerably in size. The smallest is the size of St Paul's cathedral in London, whereas the largest covers most of the city of Istanbul in Turkey. Typically, they have a roof with a large dome or several domes. The domes are usually golden and sometimes show different colours. Some temples have many levels, and it is possible to reach higher dimensions all the way to source level.

The Temples of Golden Light incorporate energy from the area in which they are situated, and temples across different regions of the world can share similar characteristics. For example, those in the United States often have Native American energy. In the Asian Himalayan temples, the energy is particularly peaceful, in keeping with such a spiritual part of the world. In Europe, the temples often feature the energy of angels, while the temples in the etheric of the oceans have a wonderful and unique water-based energy connecting to the energy of the dolphins, whales, and other sea creatures.

The Temples of Golden Light in the etheric above Africa tend to be traditional and churchlike. These qualities fit with the region, as the African temples are only beginning a slow transition from the third to the fifth dimension, which will help raise the vibration of the heavier energy in this location. Similarly, the temples in the Middle East play an important role in lifting any energies in this region that are less than light and often strongly male.

The temples differ in other ways, too. They can be ethereal or grounded, such as to Middle Earth or to tree spirits. They may be on one or multiple levels, whereby the energy and vibrations rise and come closer to source light. They may be highly angelic or may feature celestial beings or ETs from this universe or other universes, all here to help Mother Earth.

The Temples of Golden Light have much work to perform, and for this reason they are the temples for the next two thousand years. Goddess energy is needed to balance our planet's energy—the love energy much needed here at this time. The 144 temples hold the energy of all pure beings of light from this planet, this universe, and the seven universes surrounding our universe. They are all ultimately overseen by three goddesses:

- Lady Nada, the twin flame of Jesus Christ
- Jacinta, a Mayan elder who connects to earth, nature, and the rainforests of this world
- Lathinda, who comes here from a higher vibrational universe to help with your spiritual growth, development, and awareness

The three goddesses complement each other, as each one carries different gifts of enlightenment. Ultimately, they dictate what happens in the temples. All decisions are made by the three goddesses. Some of the smaller temples are overseen directly by one particular goddess, while the bigger temples are watched over by all of them.

The goddesses come from the love and light of God to say that anything can be achieved when you love someone—husband, partner, brother, sister, mother, father, children, or any other family members or friends. We are all one on a soul level, whether we know it consciously or not. Only here when we incarnate do we separate from our real source, our real soul family. We have chosen to move through the veil of amnesia. Sometimes we can have no clue as to what we are doing here or even what our purpose is.

This planet is very dense compared to other planets and star systems within this universe, and that can be hard for some people who are sensitive. When you meditate, you connect with your soul and your soul family, and therefore you do not feel so alone. You also connect to your guardian angels, earth guides, and other guardians of light that are with you to help you.

The goddesses connect to all the known goddesses on this planet: Mother Mary, Mary Magdalene, Quan Yin, Isis, Pallas Athena, and Kali, to name a few. All the temples are surrounded by four immense, global, golden archangels representing north, south, east, and west for our planet. Each individual temple is surrounded by its own group of rainbow angels that work to balance chakras and help people and animals to heal in order to move forward into yet more light and understanding. These rainbow angels are led by Archangel Metaziel and his twin flame, Archangel Honoriel. Lord Buddha and his helper, Lord Maitreya, are also involved, and Lord Buddha has personally blessed the temples.

All the Temples of Golden Light are watched over by Divine Mother, who monitors their energy to make sure everything is of the purest light for all.

## Ascended Master Lord Hilarion

All ascended masters connect to the temples, but it is the ascended master Lord Hilarion who holds directorship of all 144 Temples of Golden Light. There are twelve ascended masters in charge of the twelve esoteric rays that shine down on our planet. Master Hilarion is considered the *chohan* (lord) of the fifth ray. He embodies the qualities of healing, truth, science, and concrete knowledge, and he also works with the laws of alchemy, which is the science of divine healing. He projects as his colour the green or emerald ray within the twelve esoteric rays, and he will help you to access the divine healer within.

Master Hilarion is believed to have lived his last incarnation as St

Hilarion in Cyprus, and his life before that was as the apostle Paul of Tarsus. Remember the conversion of Saul on the road to Damascus when Jesus appeared to him in a great light? Saul fell to the ground, blinded, and did not see, eat, or drink for three days. The blinding of Saul and the renaming as Paul was an act of conversion, and Paul became a preacher of great righteousness. Hilarion helps people to master themselves and helps to purify souls. He is a member of the Great White Brotherhood. Hilarion has a retreat in the etheric over Crete in Greece, known as the Temple of Truth, along with Pallas Athena, a female ascended master of great light. Together they hold the flame of divine truth and light. The light is the ultimate source of all healing.

## Connecting to the Temples of Golden Light

You can connect by meditation or set the intention to connect in your sleep-state. Think about the temple just before you go to sleep, and you will visit that temple—it's simple. Assuming that your soul wants to be healed, you may need to work with a few of the Temples of Golden Light in order to be totally healed. Complete healing depends on how much baggage you need to release and how much anger and resentment you are still holding on to for reasons personal to yourself.

Certain Temples of Golden Light clear the solar plexus chakra, other temples clear the heart chakra, and so on, facilitating a clearing of the whole body. Even the cellular memory is cleared. There are temples that teach us how to live with the planet and connect to Mother Earth. There are temples that heal children, animals, and sea creatures, such as dolphins and whales.

When connecting to any of the Temples of Golden Light, remember you have for many lifetimes lived and sat under our sun, moon, and stars. For many lifetimes, you have walked upon this earth, and we are actually one with each other and our universe. Now you have raised your energy so much that you can access the Temples of Golden Light. These are the temples for the New Earth. The temples connect to source light and as such are filled with much love and light of source. When you meditate on any of the temples, you will receive peace, serenity, light, and divine guidance.

The following chapters outline the different qualities of the individual Temples of Golden Light. First, I describe the twelve main temples, and then I go into detail about all 144 temples in order of where they are in the world. To find out more about the Temples of Golden Light which are particularly suitable for helping to heal the heart, emotions, or the physical body, or to heal children and animals, please see chapters 8 and 9.

# Chapter 2

## *The Main Temples of Golden Light*

There are twelve main Temples of Golden Light in the etheric of Mother Earth. That's not the physical earth but the etheric of Mother Earth. All 12 temples hold different vibrations, and different qualities for example Istanbul temple is the largest and main healing temple, although all 144 Temples of Golden Light are healing temples, but give different healing energy according to the area the temple has been placed around the world. New York as well as healing holds the quality of Believe, Athens Abundance, Antarctica Tranquillity, Sedona Clarity, Pacific Ocean One Unblock and Release, Machu Picchu Enlightenment, Stonehenge Groundedness, Uluru Self-Confidence, Agra Spirituality, Phoenix Harmony, and Paris France, Heart qualities. These twelve temples are larger than the other temples and are extremely powerful. Together, they form a powerful energy grid that connects all 144 Temples of Golden Light. They are schools of learning and are surrounded by cities of light. They are presented in this chapter in order of size, from largest to smallest; the number in parentheses after the name of each temple is its number within the full set of 144 temples:

- Istanbul, Turkey (1)
- New York, New York, United States (40)
- Athens, Greece (36)
- Antarctica (122)
- Sedona, Arizona, United States (43)
- Pacific Ocean One, off the Hawaiian Islands, United States (85)

- Machu Picchu, Peru (60)
- Stonehenge, England (4)
- Uluru, Australia (78)
- Agra, India (97)
- Phoenix, Arizona, United States (44)
- Paris, France (8)

Each temple is described in more detail in the pages that follow.

## Istanbul, Turkey: The Main Temple of Golden Light
*Listed in Europe | Surrounded by a city of light*

Situated where east meets west, the main temple is located on a very important ley line in the etheric over Istanbul and is surrounded by a city of light. This is an enormous temple covering the whole of the city—an area that I think was part of the bygone civilization of Atlantis. It is a city within a city, as source light comes directly into the temple.

When I first connected to this temple, I was amazed by its size, and I found the energy so peaceful. In the centre of the beautiful temple is a tower of crystal light, opening out and unfolding into a lotus flower. This is the direct source light connection. In another great hall there is a huge golden pyramid linking out from this universe and beyond to the seven universes that surround our universe.

Istanbul's sacred temple is in the centre of a gigantic web of golden light, the grid of light that links all Temples of Golden Light across the globe. Inside, it is full of vibrant colours. It is like being in a sumptuous, luxurious palace in heaven where everyone is friendly and prepared to give you time to talk, think, meditate, contemplate, or just be one with our beautiful universe. As the temple is so large, there are many sections, including areas of silence, universities teaching many subjects, educational classrooms, and healing chambers. It is a place of enlightenment and an educational learning temple that holds the wisdom of all healing modalities, ancient and new. You can develop spiritual gifts here—for example, clairvoyance, healing, and channelling.

All of the ascended masters, known and unknown, meet here

in this temple, including El Morya, Lord Lanto, Confucius, Lord Hilarion, Jesus Christ, Paul the Venetian, Serapis Bay, St Germaine, Rakosky, Quan Yin, Lady Nada, Pallas Athena, and Aphrodite, to name a few. You simply connect through meditation or when you go to sleep (in this case, you need to set the intention first).

Once you have connected with the main temple, you will be guided to another temple or temples that can help you the most to release, heal, and move forward—to learn or understand experiences or understand the reason why you came here. Part of the plan is that we have no memory of any past lives. This is the planet of free will. In order to move ahead and raise our vibration, we must gain some knowledge of why we are here.

As we progress from life to life, we get to a point where we have done most or all of our karma. Therefore, our soul will start to let us in on some of its secrets as to where we have lived on the planet, why we chose that life, and who we were with. This is why we can resonate with certain countries, people, or places.

The main temple has a higher temple, and these twin higher and lower. The higher temple emits ascension light codes constantly; these are DNA light codes, namely diamond crystal light codes that help you manifest and create your dreams, desires, and goals; golden light codes that give you peace, calm, and harmony; diamond golden light codes that help you integrate the higher energies coming through from source given to our planet; and rainbow crystal light codes that will help you on your ascension pathway. Another temple that will help you download light codes is the Antarctica Temple of Golden Light.

Sometimes we meet someone who helps us to understand ourselves, although I believe our greatest teacher is our soul. You may even meet soulmates and your soul family or your twin flame—all wonderful people experiencing life just the same as you.

### New York, New York, United States: Temple of Believe
*Listed in the Americas | Surrounded by a city of light*

New York City has the second largest Temple of Golden Light after the Istanbul temple. It is a very busy temple of tremendous light—a gift to New York since 9/11. The temple is situated in the etheric to the side of the Statue of Liberty, above Ellis Island.

The New York Temple is a magnificent golden temple with golden domed roofs and a star on top that acts as a beacon of light. It is tall, large, and rounded in shape, and it is one of the more elaborately decorated temples. Working on many levels, it connects to many different energies and to celestial beings from Pleiades, Sirius, Andromeda, and Venus, as well as angels, archangels and their twin flames, and indigenous people from our world, including Native Americans, Aborigines, Maori, Eskimos, and the older Mayan, Inca and Aztec people. The illumined ones of immense pure light holding the highest integrity and greatest love for our planet reside here, although they are not usually seen or spoken about.

All of the known ascended masters meet here. The male ascended masters include St Germaine, Hilarion, Paul the Venetian, Rakoczy, Serapis Bay, El Morya, Lord Lanto, Jesus Christ, St Francis of Assisi, Dwyul Kwul, Lord Maitreya, Mohammed, and Confucius. Female ascended masters include Pallas Athena, Lady Portia, Quan Yin, Mother Mary, Mary Magdalene, Princess Diana, Mother Teresa, White Buffalo Calf Woman, Goddess Isis, and Goddess Kali.

Decisions are made at this temple for the highest good of our planet. This is where you can meet the three goddesses who oversee the temples, since Lady Nada, Jacinta, and Lathinda all have an office here. You have to book in to see them personally, so you need to set a time in your night sleep-state. They have the ability to change karma, as they sit on different karmic boards. Dispensations can be given and changes can be put in place with all people.

Nothing is impossible and everything is possible when working in the light and holding the highest integrity and love for all. Help for healing on all levels is given by the goddesses, surrounded by the amazing rainbow angels and Archangel Metaziel and his twin flame, Archangel Honoriel, who work under the direction of Archangel Metatron.

## Athens, Greece: Temple of Ascension
*Listed in Europe | Surrounded by a city of light*

The Athens Temple of Golden Light is overseen by all twelve Grecian gods and goddesses shining down on humanity. It is an amazing temple of tremendous bright light and love for all of humanity. This is the third largest Temple of Golden Light, located right over the centre of Athens in the etheric above the Acropolis.

It is a temple within a temple that has been created in true Grecian style: gold and white with beautiful marble pillars connecting outwards to this universe and the surrounding universes. This is the sacred temple of Pallas Athena, surrounded by a city of light. Greece is a leading force in moving forward into the new Golden Age, and this is a pivotal temple where council meetings are held.

The following Grecian gods and goddesses oversee the Athens Temple of Golden Light:

- **Pallas Athena**, goddess of intelligence, skill, peace, warfare, battle strategy, handicrafts, and wisdom. She was the patron of the city Athens (which was named after her). Her symbol is the olive tree, and she is commonly shown accompanied by her sacred animal, the owl.
- **Aphrodite**, goddess of love, beauty, desire, sexuality, and pleasure. Although married to Hephaestus, she had many lovers, including Ares and Adonis. She was depicted as a beautiful woman.
- **Apollo**, god of music, arts, knowledge, healing, prophecy, poetry, archery, and manly beauty. He is the son of Zeus and the twin brother of Artemis.
- **Artemis**, virgin goddess of the hunt, wilderness, animals, young girls, and childbirth. She is the daughter of Zeus and twin sister of Apollo.
- **Demeter**, goddess of grain, agriculture and the harvest, growth, and nourishment. Demeter is a daughter of Cronus and Rhea and sister of Zeus.
- **Dionysus**, god of wine, parties, festivals, and chaos. He is the consort of Ariadne.

- **Hera**, queen of the gods and goddess of marriage, women, childbirth, heirs, kings, and empires.
- **Hermes**, god of travel, boundaries, communication, trade, language, and writing. He is the son of Zeus and Maia.
- **Hephaestus**, god of fire, metalworks, and crafts. He is the husband to Aphrodite.
- **Hestia**, virgin Goddess of the home and chastity. She is sister to Zeus and daughter of Rhea and Cronus.
- **Poseidon**, god of the oceans, seas, and rivers. He is a son of Cronus and Rhea and brother to Zeus and Hades. He rules one of the three realms of the universe as king of the sea and the waters.
- **Zeus**, king and father of the gods, the ruler of Mount Olympus, and god of the sky, weather, thunder, lightning, law, order, and justice.

Deep healing with the rainbow angels takes place at the Athens Temple of Golden Light, which inspires to you to reflect, be introspective, and look within.

**Antarctica Temple of Golden Light**
*Listed in Rest of the World and in Meditation and Relaxation |
Surrounded by a city of light*

The Antarctica temple is the fourth largest Temple of Golden Light after Istanbul, New York, and Athens. The silence within this temple sounds like the muffled silence when it has snowed. It is a teaching and healing temple which connects to the whole of this universe, including the star systems Pleiades, Sirius, Andromeda, and all of the planets. The temple gives out a beacon of light that is so powerful it resonates out into the universe. The light is passed from star system to star system and planet to planet and then on to the seven universes that surround our planet.

This is a huge crystalline temple with a multifaceted diamond light coming through a large crystal lotus flower that opens and then slightly closes inside a pyramid in the centre of the temple. You can imagine how powerful this must be. The crystals give out signals and special encodings, and they talk to each other. They can download DNA that will help humanity to change. People will become more loving and kind.

The DNA codes, namely the diamond crystal light codes, help people manifest and create; the golden light codes help bring about peace, calm, and harmony; the diamond golden light codes help humanity integrate the new energy being released onto our planet; and the rainbow diamond crystal light codes help people on their ascension pathway. All these light codes are released onto humanity when the crystals open and close. This is a slow process; the crystals are powerful and therefore the process needs to be gentle. It is important to trust the love of the universe to guide us through this next step of the Golden Age.

Everything happens at the right time when you will find yourself in the right place. This temple is all about balance and alignment, and it will help to regulate the waters of our planet, bringing about new beginnings, new birth, and rebirth. People need to change; change is important and necessary for all to move forward. People are to be at one with source to live in the moment, the now, and not worry about money. The universe will look after you, providing that you trust, believe, and have faith. It is possible within this temple to let go of one's baggage and be released from burdens, gaining a wonderful sense of relief.

This temple holds crystalline energy and brings forward a new healing vibration. The rainbow angels surround this temple. Also connected here are universal golden-winged angels of ascension and many other celestial beings of light and love.

Antarctica is earth's southernmost continent, containing the geographic South Pole in the southern hemisphere and surrounded by the Southern Ocean. For comparison, Antarctica is nearly twice the size of Australia, and almost all (98 per cent) of the continent is covered by the Antarctic ice sheet. Antarctica is colder than the Arctic; animals that survive here include penguins, seals, orcas, blue whales, fur seals, and three birds, of which the snow petrel is the most common.

The Arctic Temple and the Antarctica Temple are twin temples of the southern and northern hemispheres of our planet.

## Sedona, Arizona: Temple of Universal Light
*Listed in the Americas | Surrounded by a city of light*

Sedona is an amazing Temple of Golden Light, filled with powerful energy. There are many levels to the temple, and Native Americans work on the first level. They know how to heal naturally with herbs, and if you are interested, they will provide information about your health, your diet, or your lifestyle.

The temple reaches right out into this universe that is called Nebadon. It connects with all known and unknown star systems, galaxies, and planets, in this dimension and other dimensions. Many spaceships land and take off from a hub and docking station platform within the temple. New technology will be brought forward from this temple; it is a very important temple overseen by an enormous golden angel that protects it.

For those who have seen the film *Men in Black*, there is a scene where the two central characters are in a big warehouse filled with so many different beings—star people and ETs all in one place all together. This is what the Sedona Temple of Golden Light would look like to an outsider. There is a vortex of energy which appears to spin on its axis and can be cloaked when required. It is a huge temple filled with a maze of offices and corridors leading off to many places.

Commander Ashtar has an office here. He is a master and commander of the star fleet's spaceships that travel through our universe, galaxies, and other universes and multi-universes protecting everyone from the dark forces. The Sedona temple is run with military precision. Nothing goes unnoticed. There are chambers for sleep-state regeneration and places for walk-ins to wait for a physical body. There is a new rainbow fleet with new ETs that now work helping our planet. Please remember that all beings that come here must gain permission to enter this universe from the Galactic Federation of Light.

There is a healing room with a large emerald crystal on the ceiling in one of the healing sanctuaries. Archangel Raphael and Mother Mary heal everyone here. In summary, Sedona is a massive temple beaming golden light right across the United States and out into this universe.

## Pacific Ocean One
*Listed in Australasia and Oceanic | Surrounded by a city of light*

There are twelve Oceanic Temples of Golden Light beneath our oceans. These temples create a vast network of golden light linking to the other 132 temples and together acting as a web of light in and around the globe to bring about healing and peace for humanity and Mother Earth. The oceanic temples are overseen by the god called Poseidon by the Greeks and Neptune by the Romans.

The Pacific Ocean One temple is the largest and the main oceanic temple, and it is in the centre of a city of light. It is situated near the Hawaiian Islands and the west coast of the United States, directly aligning with the Temple of Golden Light in the etheric over San Francisco, California. The temple is filled with the energy of Atlantis and Lemuria, and indeed, it looks like an Atlantis temple. It has seven pillars and seven glass-domed roofs. The energies of Atlantis and Lemuria blend as one energy, giving the temple a very soothing feel. There is the energy of the dolphins, whales, sea turtles, sea lions, elephant seals, seals, porpoises, penguins, and all sea creatures, particularly koi carp, who hold a high place in the sea world, as well as seahorses, shellfish, and starfish.

In this temple, everything is important, as everything here is felt vibrationally. The beings are sensitive. They feel every drop of water vibrationally. The energy inside the temple is very loving and caring. Beauty is seen in everything. Gentle angelic energy is present in the form of water angels or mer-angels. Of course, water is a very important part of our planet. It represents the ebb and flow of life. We human beings are made up largely of water, and our emotions remind us of this.

Important decisions are made at the council meetings held here, and this temple plays an important role in controlling the waters of our planet, as not all of the tectonic plates have moved yet, and when they do, this has to be monitored. The energy of this temple rises up from the depths of the waters within the etheric of our oceans and right out into the universe. This is the sixth largest Temple of Golden Light. As with all of the temples, it has a healing pool that you may bathe in whilst meditating or visiting in your sleep-state.

## Machu Picchui, Peru: Temple of Golden Energy
*Listed in the Americas | Surrounded by a city of light*

This is a golden, very large Temple of Golden Light in the etheric right over the top of Machu Picchu, Peru. Every vibration on this planet and in this universe links to this temple. It aligns to the star people, celestial beings, angelic realm, ascended masters, and christed extraterrestials of light connected to Commander Ashtar.

New technology will come forward from this temple. Inside, there is a landing station for spaceships, and it is important to understand that the Christed ET's are here to help and not to hinder us. This temple is on many levels and is surrounded by a city of light. It is above ley lines. In the centre is a huge golden pyramid the size of the Eiffel Tower in Paris which people can step into and meditate in, thus connecting to this and outer universes. Your crown chakra will be cleared and cleansed in this temple, allowing you to start a fresh new life with new beginnings.

Decisions are made here, as this Temple of Golden Light connects to a galactic federation that resides within the temple. Twelve beings of light and love sit on the galactic board. They have the highest loving intentions for humanity's highest good. Nine of these are universal beings that are connected to other universes of light and love that surround this universe. It is a meeting place of minds, ideas, and inspiration.

Machu Picchu is a Temple of Golden Light of sonic vibrations. As it is a high vibrational temple, you need to be ready to visit. It is only for those already initiated into mastership.

## Stonehenge, England: Temple of the Universe
*Listed in Europe | Surrounded by a city of light*

Stonehenge is a prehistoric monument in Wiltshire, England, a short distance from Avebury. Avebury is known as the higher heart chakra. Stonehenge is one of the most famous sites in the world—it is the remains of a ring of standing stones set within earthworks. Sometimes thought of as a Mayan calendar and originally built in Wales, it was vibrationally moved to the present site.

This Temple of Golden Light is in the etheric directly above Stonehenge, emitting a radiance of energy around the globe and beaming this golden light out into space. Stonehenge's Temple of Golden Light has many levels and is a multidimensional vortex to different dimensions connecting to many different energies, rather like the TV series *Stargate*. From here, you can be transported to different star systems or stars energetically. The temple aligns with the star constellations of Pleiades, Sirius, and Andromeda, all within Orion's Belt.

It is a very large temple surrounded by a city of light, holding the energy of all known beings on this planet and this universe and connecting to every positive energy on our planet. Inside is one of the many schools held within the Temples of Golden Light. This is a learning school for new technology, as it connects to many celestial beings of light and certain ETs of the light.

In this temple resides a galactic council of twelve members, and when they meet, the temple is cloaked. It is a meeting place of like-minded people. Here, if you have a mind to, you can learn how our planet and universe were formed. Classes cover all aspects of technology.

The temple connects to the A lines on which the spaceships are allowed to travel. Below the A lines on the physical Earth are the ley lines, known throughout history as powerful energy lines. When meditating on this temple, please be aware that much information and knowledge will be given to you, increasing your understanding of why we are here and how you can help Mother Earth.

## Uluru, Australia: Temple of the Star
*Listed in Australasia and Oceanic and in Healing | Surrounded by a city of light*

Uluru is a very large temple, the Aboriginal star temple, holding a beautiful energy of bright light surrounded by a city of light. It is filled with beings of light, natural medicinal plants, and nature. On top of the temple is a massive star beaming outwards to other star systems.

To find out how to heal naturally, connect with this Temple of Golden Light and learn how the Aborigines healed with natural medicine, old ways, and old remedies. Natural healing remedies are much better for our bodies, as they have no side effects. You will learn how to respect earth's energy and respect other people, gaining qualities of peace, virtue, and honour.

Uluru is right under the Milky Way star system. The roof of the temple in the etheric is open so that you can see the wonderful sky with plentiful stars to view. It is a natural temple, shimmering with rainbow colours—a temple to teach you of the wonderment of our earth and how to explore it. This temple is on a ley line connected to serpent energy. Uluru is considered one of the great wonders of the world; it is a large magnetic mound located on a major planetary grid point much like the great pyramid in Egypt.

Uluru is also known as Ayers Rock. It is literally an island mountain, an isolated remnant left after the slow erosion of the original mountain range in the southern part of the Northern Territory in central Australia. The nearest town is Alice Springs, 208 miles away. Uluru is a sacred part of Aboriginal creation mythology or dreamtime—reality being a dream. It is of great cultural significance to the Anangu, the Aboriginal people of the area. Uluru has many caves, some decorated with rock art depicting dreamtime myths. When you connect to this Temple of Golden Light, you will be taken through meditation into dreamtime.

## Agra, India: Temple of Golden Radiance
*Listed in Asia and in Healing | Surrounded by a city of light*

Agra's is a very large Temple of Golden Light, surrounded by a city of light, situated in the etheric close to the Taj Mahal in Agra, India. The city of Agra is on the banks of the River Yamura, paradoxically rich in life, in the northern state of Uttar, Pradesh. The Taj Mahal was built by Prince Shah Jahan and dedicated to his loving wife, Mumtaz, as a mausoleum in 1653. Prince Jahan was an incarnation of the ascended master Lord Kuthumi.

This is a splendid, ornate, decorative, and palatial Temple of Golden Light, and inside are many diamond-coloured crystals. The temple connects to the Indian gods/goddesses Brahma, Shiva, Vishnu, Krishna, Ganesh, Lakshmi, Kali, and many more, making this a beautiful sacred Temple of Golden Light. It is a busy temple with many healing sanctuaries and prayer rooms. Your soul can fragment over many lifetimes as a result of difficult situations, such as dying in shock. This temple has a special sanctuary that can bring your fragments back together and make you whole again.

In the centre is a golden lotus flower that connects to source light and acts as a vortex of energy, giving out a wonderful golden radiance that covers much of northern India, clearing and cleansing the earth below. Everyone wears white when entering this temple. It is overseen by the Divine Mother and surrounded by rainbow angels.

### Phoenix, Arizona: Temple of the Future
*Listed in the Americas and in Healing | Surrounded by a city of light*

The Temple of Golden Light in Phoenix is another very large temple which looks and feels quite futuristic. This aligns to many star people of celestial light and connects to Commander Ashtar. It is the eleventh largest temple and has a spaceship docking station. Strongly connected to the Arcturians, fifth-dimensional beings here to help our planet ascend, the temple is filled with many Christed ETs trying to help us ascend rather than destroy ourselves. The Arcturians work as one, and they do not speak, as they have no need. They are telepathic with each other. They can read people's energy and auras and work on a higher vibration.

We are not alone in this universe. It would be unwise to think that. Why would we think that we are so superior as to be alone? We are definitely not alone, and one day, humanity will realise this. The ETs are trying to help us, not take control over us. They only wish to help us and Mother Earth, because what we do here on earth affects the rest of our universe.

As with a few other temples, this temple will bring a new healing modality—a new vibrational healing tool brought through from the higher realms to help us heal. This will facilitate miracles when people are ready to heal. This is a very light, bright Temple of Golden Light which connects to Mother Earth's heart centre, up and out into the universe, pulsating prisms of light, opening up and closing down like a crystalline lotus flower.

## Paris, France: Temple of Golden Light One
*Listed in Europe and in Healing | Surrounded by a city of light*

Paris is known as the City of Lights or the Illuminated City. Widely considered a romantic place, it has many statues of angels and cherubs. Paris is architecturally very well preserved, and the Eiffel Tower is by far the city's most famous monument, together with the Louvre, Notre Dame, and Sacré Coeur.

This beautiful temple is situated in the etheric behind the Sacré Coeur and is overseen by Mother Mary and Jesus Christ, along with many angels and archangels, particularly Archangel Raphael and his legions of angels. It is one of the high-vibrational Temples of Golden Light connecting to the Divine Mother and the angels on high. The large, ornate golden temple looks like a high Catholic church, with many chapels inside connected to different saints.

The temple is surrounded by a city of light, and inside is a healing chamber of light with a rose quartz crystal couch to lie on. The angels will wrap their wings of love around you to help you clear and cleanse your chakras and aura and bring you into balance, to feel healthy and full of vitality. You are a powerful being of light. Your soul has the power to heal you, and your body will regenerate itself every twelve months if you let it and give it the right tools to work with. So be kind to yourself, as you deserve the best and to be healed of all physical ailments and disharmonies. Ask for the temples' help. Follow your divine guidance and accept all of the abundant ideas and opportunities coming your way.

## Cities of Light

Energetically, a city of light is a high-vibrational city of glowing golden light that connects to pure source light. These cities are places where the masters meet alongside angels and high-vibrational celestial beings of love and light. They are all seventh-dimensional, and decisions are made here to help humanity to solve problems. This energy filters down through the higher dimensions to here on earth, so that lightworkers know what to do to help people raise their vibration and help Mother Earth. The cities of light look futuristic; the buildings are different from here.

There are thirty-three Temples of Golden Light surrounded by cities of light, and these are particularly high-energy temples. These temples are especially effective for healing, whether physically, emotionally, mentally, or spiritually. There are healing sanctuaries and many meditation rooms and places of silent retreat. There are great places of learning and studying, having within them universities, colleges, and schools with every possible subject taught there, as well as halls of creativity and music academies.

I first discovered the cities of light one day while I was meditating upon the main temple in Istanbul, Turkey. I was astonished to see in my mind's eye a wonderful city of golden light where the energy felt so peaceful, calm, and tranquil. I decided to work with this new energy with my meditation group to explore what they would see, feel, sense, or know about these cities of light. After again linking with the city of light surrounding the main temple, I took people in the group on a guided journey, asking them to visualise themselves sitting on a magic carpet moving around the city of light. They loved this experience of flying high above and around the city of light.

We saw the rooms for study, such as universities of enlightenment and those for healing, where sound therapy and colour vibrational healing were taking place. I believe what we all witnessed will be the healing of the future.

The following are the thirty-three cities of light surrounding thirty-three temples of golden light; the number in parentheses after the name of each temple is its number within the full set of 144 temples:

- Istanbul, Turkey (1)
- Glastonbury, England (3)
- Stonehenge, England (4)
- Paris, France (8)
- Rome, Italy (16)
- Venice, Italy (17)
- Stockholm, Sweden (27)
- Athens, Greece (36)
- New York, New York, United States (40)

- Mount Shasta, California, United States (41)
- San Francisco, California, United States (42)
- Sedona, Arizona, United States (43)
- Phoenix, Arizona, United States (44)
- Salt Lake City, Utah, United States (46)
- Boston, Massachusetts, United States (58)
- Machu Picchu, Peru (60)
- Buenos Aires, Argentina (67)
- Uluru, Australia (78)
- Margaret River, Perth, Australia (79)
- Sydney, Australia (82)
- Pacific Ocean One, off the Hawaiian Islands, United States (85)
- Pacific Ocean Two, off La Paz, Bolivia, and Lima, Peru (86)
- Mediterranean Ocean, off Valencia, Spain (95)
- Agra, India (97)
- Amritsar, India (98)
- Bangalore, India (100)
- Sri Lanka (101)
- Lahore, Pakistan (102)
- Beijing, China (109)
- Bali, Indonesia (121)
- Antarctica (123)
- Moscow, Russia (126)
- Cairo, Egypt (139)

I feel privileged to mention that many souls of light are connected to the Temples of Golden Light that are surrounded by cities of light, including John Lennon, George Harrison, Whitney Houston, Elvis Presley, Prince, Michael Jackson, Bach, Johann Strauss, Beethoven, and Mozart, plus many more enlightened souls as well as the ascended masters of the light.

If you visit the Temples of Golden Light and cities of light in your sleep-state or through meditation, it will greatly change your life for the better, helping you to transmute old energy patterns into new and turning them into energy that is positive, vibrant, abundant, and happy. It will help you release old negative thoughts and behaviour patterns and help you create abundance and manifest that which you need or want, so that you receive a financial gift from the universe to create what you would like to do with and in your life.

Lifting your vibration is what is needed right now, as our planet is ascending and lifting her energy. We must join Lady Gaia in her ascension. All those who move with her will bring more light into their four body systems and at the same time help all those around them to understand what is happening to them. Mother Earth is ascending. Whether we like this or not, this is what is happening, so we must change with her and ascend too or we will be left behind. The rest of this universe is watching and waiting to see how we deal with this, as what affects this planet affects the rest of this universe and the seven universes that surround our own.

As the temples surrounded by cities of light are energetically high up in the etheric of the earth, they will help us to ascend. Connect with the main Temple of Golden Light in Istanbul, and you will be directed to the most appropriate temple for you. It is really that simple. Be open to the universe, and you will be amazed at what happens, in a positive way. Nothing is impossible when you work with the universe. You will realise the infinite possibilities that you become open to on all levels: as above, so below.

The temples within the cities of light heal not only you and your family and friends but animals and sea creatures as well as Mother Earth. You simply need to connect and ask the temples for help. If karmically this is not allowed, you will still be helped and healed as much as possible.

Let me explain what I mean by 'karmically not allowed': When you were in the spirit world before you were born, you made a contract that you were born to fulfil. In this contract, you may have chosen to be ill for your learning experience or for someone else's. All sides of experiences have to be endured, which means that you may be paying back karma in this life. If healing in the Temples of Golden Light is 'karmically not allowed', this will be because you have not yet fulfilled your contract. Once you fulfil your contract, you are free again to live as you wish.

The Temples of Golden Light within the cities of light do not just heal on a physical level. They heal on an emotional, mental, and spiritual level. The temples will help you let go of any issues you came into this life with. They will help you to have focus and clarity of mind and to be happy and content, seeing your work as positive and good. They will help you to appreciate yourself and all those around you, giving you courage and strength when needed. The temples will help you to work from your heart, your intuition centre, as your heart knows your truth. Your mind presents you with possibilities and choices, but your heart knows the truth and can allow you to grow spiritually at your own gentle pace, giving you guidance.

As already outlined, the Temples of Golden Light and cities of light are teaching, learning, and healing places of great light. They cover a broad spectrum of education, as all learning is connected to the new Golden Age. It is done with gentleness and compassion. You simply need to meditate on the temples and the cities of light, and all will be revealed.

You will learn how to deal with each other's misunderstandings and how to become discerning and listen to each side of a problem, and all this will be done in love. Guidance will be given through meditation. Love is the key to the new Golden Age. 'Love, love, love', as the Beatles said in one of their earlier songs, 'all you need is love'. It is so true. When you give love, you will truly receive it back tenfold.

The cities of light will help you in all areas of your life. You will learn to connect with your own soul and your soul family, your divine spirit brothers and sisters. You will find positivity through negativity.

All human beings naturally think negative thoughts. This is the way we have been programmed for thousands of years. It is time to change that, don't you think? It is time to realise who you are and how powerful you are; time to be happy and content; time to connect with your inner child; time to share your life with others who are on the same wavelength; time to move forward, into yet more light.

Do not fear the darkness, as all light workers transform darkness into much light. Our DNA is changing; it is upgrading, and we are becoming conscious of the evolutionary potential we all truly possess. You are a guardian to this beautiful planet, and the cities of light can help you to create a new world of unconditional love, peace, happiness, and abundance.

# Chapter 3

## *Europe*

There are thirty-nine European Temples of Golden Light, and I have travelled with my husband, Chris, to a number of the countries where these are situated. On many occasions, we have had strange or unusual experiences. One was when we flew to Istanbul and stayed for a few days. The only flights I was able to arrange involved flying into an airport on the European side of Istanbul and out of a different airport on the Asian side of the city.

We walked around the whole of the centre of Istanbul in three days. I was guided to do this, and I think Chris felt as if we had walked for miles. Well, we probably had, but it seemed very important. We visited Hagia Sophia, Blue Mosque, Sultan Ahmed Mosque, Topkapi Palace, and the Grand Bazaar. We also went on a large boat on the Bosphorus River. I realised, but only after we arrived home, that I was connected to the Temple of Golden Light all this time. Esoteric light was coming through me, and I was anchoring this light wherever we walked. I had acted as a catalyst for the temple to be activated.

The most unusual aspect of our visit happened the day after we arrived back in England. We saw on the TV news footage of riots on the Bosphorus Bridge in Istanbul, and we were stunned as we watched this, as our visit there had been so peaceful. Looking back, I believe the universe was trying to tell me something through an incident that happened as we were leaving the country. I noticed a Turkish lady at the boarding gate apparently getting on our plane. She appeared to be talking to herself, and as we boarded, I felt uncomfortable. I sensed that she would sit behind me, and sure enough, that is what happened.

She took ages placing her carry-on luggage in the overhead locker and was causing others behind her to become impatient. Increasing numbers of passengers asked her to sit down, but she remained standing. I was feeling very uncomfortable, as I could feel her energy, and for some reason I started to cry. I felt that I was clearing her in my capacity as a healer without even looking at her or touching her. Eventually, an air hostess appeared and asked the woman to sit down, as we were about to take off.

As the plane left the runway, I heard shouting behind me. The Turkish lady was shouting at all the passengers around her, and I realised that she must have been suffering from a mental illness, bless her. She was making faces and taking photos with her mobile phone of other passengers and shouting at them at the same time. Three air hostesses tried to calm her down, but they were not successful.

Then a lovely young man appeared from the front of the plane saying that he was a doctor and asking if he could help. I turned around to look, and he winked at me. The next thing I knew, the pilot announced over the intercom that we were returning to Istanbul airport, where someone was going be removed from the plane. This was fifty minutes into our flight, and by the time we turned around, landed in Istanbul, refuelled, and took off again, we were running two hours late. At the time, I remember thinking, *What was that all about?*

In hindsight, I realise that the temple was being activated by my arrival in Turkey, and as light exposes negativity, situations under the surface needed to be dealt with. When I returned home, I could feel that the temple was fully activated and that its radiance was causing some chaos and unrest. This is not unusual, as I will explain further on.

The following are the Temples of Golden Light in the etheric across Europe:

1. Istanbul, Turkey
2. Bodrum, Turkey
3. Glastonbury, England
4. Stonehenge, England
5. Snowdonia, Wales
6. Edinburgh, Scotland
7. Dublin, Ireland

8. Paris, France
9. Lourdes, France
10. Berlin, Germany
11. Cologne, Germany
12. Amsterdam, Holland
13. Madrid, Spain
14. Seville, Spain
15. Lisbon, Portugal
16. Rome, Italy
17. Venice, Italy
18. Sicily, Italy
19. Geneva, Switzerland
20. Zurich, Switzerland
21. Vienna, Austria
22. Salzburg, Austria
23. Savinja Alps, Slovenia
24. Budapest, Hungary
25. Oslo, Norway
26. Mo i Rana, Norway
27. Stockholm, Sweden
28. Helsinki, Finland
29. Tallinn, Estonia
30. Warsaw, Poland
31. Bratislava, Slovakia
32. Prague, Czech Republic
33. Zazanlak, Bulgaria
34. Zagreb, Croatia
35. Belgrade, Serbia
36. Athens, Greece
37. Crete, Greece
38. Paphos, Cyprus
39. Kiev, Ukraine

## 1. Istanbul, Turkey: Main Temple of Golden Light
*Listed in Main Temples | Surrounded by a city of light*

This is an enormous temple covering etherically the whole of the city of Istanbul. Source light comes through directly into the temple, changing all those within and dissolving blockages in all your chakras. This opportunity ignites your spiritual growth and your healing journey on all levels, helping you to gain inner peace and allowing the realisation of your highest and fullest potential.

This temple is the lead temple of all 144 Temples of Golden Light placed around the globe. It holds the energy of all pure beings of light from this planet, this universe, and the surrounding universes. Once you have connected with the main temple in the web of the golden light temples, you will be directed to the temple or temples that will be able to help you the most.

This temple has a lower aspect and a higher aspect. It twins with a higher Temple of Golden Light, much higher up in earth's etheric. The higher temple holds different key codes of light that can change your DNA.

### Rainbow Angels

Rainbow angels surround all of the Temples of Golden Light. They work with all of the colours of the rainbow: red, orange, yellow, green, blue, indigo, and violet, plus the pastel colours pink, aqua, coral, peach, lemon, and mint green, working with different vibrations, as we are all different and unique. The rainbow angels work under the guidance of Archangel Metaziel and his twin flame, Archangel Honoriel, who are new archangels to this planet and who oversee all 144 Temples of Golden Light. They come from another universe which holds a higher vibration than this planet.

The rainbow angels are here now to help us shift into a new phase of enlightenment and to help us raise our vibration. They are able to be here now as the vibration on our planet is lifting. They act as a conduit, helping to hold all the temples together in a grid. They are here to help ease our journey with Mother Earth into the golden age of golden light.

### Rainbow Angels Poem
*Written by Julie Griffiths*

The beautiful beams of sunlight appear in so many ways.
The magical colours they throw on our
earth bring smiles on rainy days.
When a beam of sunlight shines from
above, it's the purest whitest light.
If it catches a raindrop on its journey to earth,
you will capture a wonderful sight.
As the sunbeam combines with the raindrop,
the truth that you may not know
Is that wonderful miracle of colourfulness
shows itself as a new rainbow.
The magic of sunbeams in raindrops creates shades of familiar hues,
With red, orange, yellow, green, indigo, violet, and blue.
Above clouds, above sky, above the universe,
way up high just as far as can be,
You'll find beautiful rainbow angels and their colourful energy.
You may sense this in quiet and silence, in
a peaceful and spiritual place.
You may see rainbow orbs swirling around
you in your special sacred space.
Be aware that their energy heals you; take
time just to welcome them near.
Be grateful for all that they give you; just
know that your words they can hear.
In their mission to bring love, light, and healing
to all beings and all of the earth,
We each in our way can support them, if
we return to the purity of birth.
When we are born, we are pure loving beings,
full of innocence, peace, and good.
If we could all but live in this purity, in our
hearts and our lives, live in truth,
We would know that the angels have printed
their stamp all over our soul,

And would know that we heard and we listened,
and we helped make our universe whole.


## 2. Bodrum, Turkey: Temple of Peacefulness

The Bodrum temple is small and golden. It is overseen by a large golden master angel with huge golden wings. It is a temple built etherically like a Turkish castle, very light energetically, connecting to Pegasus the winged horse with many heart-healing angels. Surrounded by rainbow angels and white doves, it is a temple of amazing peace to help you find balance and harmony in your life.

This temple sorts out your problems for you, guiding you gently to receive an answer, as all problems and concerns have a solution. Deep within this temple is a coloured crystal fountain that is continuously changing colour, giving out healing energy. It is mesmerizing to watch. In the garden is a very large maze for those who would like to take a walk.


## 3. Glastonbury, England: Temple of the Heart One
*Listed in Healing | Surrounded by a city of light*

Glastonbury is the heart chakra of the world and has been since 2012. This is why the temple is over Glastonbury. It connects to Avebury, which is known as the world's higher heart chakra. Glastonbury's early history is linked with its dominant landmark the Tor: a sacred, holy hill since ancient times. Glastonbury is famous for the Glastonbury Abbey and Chalice Well, an ancient spring at the foot of the Tor, with beautiful gardens that have special energy.

Legend claims that Joseph of Arimathea and Mary Magdalene visited Glastonbury with the Holy Grail. The place has special traditions, being the home of King Arthur and Lady Guinevere, who were buried there. It is home to the medieval saints Benedict, David, Bridget, Dunstan, and Patrick.

This Temple of Golden Light lies on a special ley line and connects to Middle Earth. As such, it is a very earthy, magical temple connecting to Camelot, King Arthur, and Lady Guinevere, and to the Templar

Knights, the Knights of St George, the Elemental Kingdom, fairies, and unicorns. In fact, it is surrounded and protected by unicorns that can take you to different realms and to different parts of this universe and another universe, if you wish. The temple also connects to Archangel Michael and his legions of angels, giving you protection, courage, and strength.

Master St Germaine (known in an older life as Merlin the magician) oversees this temple with his purple flame of transmutation. The Glastonbury Temple of Golden Light twins with the Stonehenge Temple of Golden Light. The temple is as tall as the Tor and energetically reaches out for hundreds of miles around. The temple is surrounded by a city of light. As the heart chakra of the world, this temple metaphorically enables hands to be linked around the world, removing darkness by the glowing light of God/Goddess.

What this temple does is help ground you to Mother Earth, connecting you to her heart chakra, aligning you with pure love and trust for our planet, and helping you to gain family values and traditions. If you need to focus on anything in your life—whether family, health, relationships, or career—this is the temple to connect with, as it will bring you towards your heart's desire. It will ground you with stability, hope, and fortitude. Simply focus on the Glastonbury Temple of Golden Light for love, balance, and insight. This temple will help you see things more clearly and bring clarity to any situation.

## 4. Stonehenge, England: Temple of the Universe
*Listed in Main Temples | Surrounded by a city of light*

Stonehenge is a prehistoric monument in Wiltshire, England. It is the remains of a ring of standing stones set within earthworks, sometimes thought of as a Mayan calendar. This Temple of Golden Light is in the etheric directly above Stonehenge, emitting golden radiance around the globe.

Stonehenge's Temple of Golden Light has many levels and is a multidimensional vortex to different dimensions connecting to many different energies, rather like the TV series *Stargate*. From here, you can be transported to different star systems or stars energetically. The temple aligns with the star constellations of Pleiades, Sirius, and

Andromeda, all within Orion's Belt. In this temple resides a galactic council of twelve members, and when they meet, the temple is cloaked.

This is a learning school for new technology, and it is ideal to visit for people who would like information on how our planet or universe was formed or who have a scientific mind. It covers all aspects of technology, and it connects to the A lines on which spaceships are allowed to travel.

## 5. Snowdonia, Wales: Temple of Healing All Animals
*Listed in Children and Animal Healing*

Snowdonia is a mountainous region and a national park in northern Wales. The temple itself is situated etherically to the west of Snowdon near the railway track that goes up the mountain. It is one of six animal healing temples overseen by St Francis of Assisi, the Italian saint. Known as the ambassador of peace and for his love of animals, he comes from Assisi in Perugia, Italy.

This is a small but very powerful temple of healing light. It is purely for the healing of animals and is surrounded by four large king unicorns who guard the temple, as well as by the winged horse Pegasus. Franciscan monks help out here. It holds an earthy energy with a castle-like feel to it, and there are many carvings on the walls of doves, eagles, hawks, and owls. In the courtyard, there is a splendid fountain enhanced by the light of the unicorns. This temple is a healing sanctuary for all animals, including goats, sheep, horses, donkeys, deer, and cows.

## 6. Edinburgh, Scotland: Temple of Peace and Contemplation

This Temple of Golden Light is in the etheric over the centre of Edinburgh. It holds the light for this area and is a small teaching temple. It has an energy like that of a monastery, giving it a sense of stillness and peace. You will learn to have respect for each other; to feel appreciation, joy, and acceptance of the little things in life; how every little thing is important; and how to do service work. You can transform your life and awaken.

Surrounded by rainbow angels and overseen by Archangel Michael and his legions of angels, this Temple of Golden Light is a beautiful healing temple of peace and contemplation. Inside are many meditation rooms filled with rainbow colours shining through the windows. Archangel Michael will give you strength, courage, bravery and protection.

If you feel you have etheric cords connected to someone or many other people, do this exercise: Visualise a white circle of light in your mind and ask Archangel Michael to cut the cords from you and the other person. You need to do this three times. If you visualise many people, then group them all together and ask Archangel Michael to cut all the cords from your chakras to their chakras. When you have done this, simply see all of the people walking away from the circle of light feeling happy and filled with joy.

## 7. Dublin, Ireland: Temple of Prayer

The Dublin Temple of Golden Light is in the etheric over the entrance to the sacred site called Newgrange, located in the present-day county of Meath on the east coast of Ireland. The Boyne Valley Mounds at Newgrange were built around 3200 BC. This temple is surrounded by rainbow healing angels and connects to the elemental kingdom, particularly the leprechauns, pixies, tree spirits, gnomes, goblins, dwarves, elves, salamander fire fairies, flower fairies, and earth elementals. Together, they bring happiness, laughter, silliness, jolliness, light-heartedness, and fun.

This temple is very earthy, rustic, and traditional, with a touch of the Old World. It is happy and full of warm feelings, just like sitting next to a warm log fire in the winter. You leave your concerns and worries outside before you enter into this peaceful, churchlike, very simple family temple that is overseen by many saints, including St Patrick, Jesus Christ, and Mother Mary. It is a temple of prayer as well as a healing temple, with a lovely healing sanctuary.

When you are feeling sad and lonely, please pray to the goddess to help you. You will find all of the answers in the prayer chapel within this Temple of Golden Light. Never underestimate the power of prayer. I channelled this prayer whilst connected to this temple:

Oh Lord, I ask thee for help, as I am weak.
I ask for divine guidance, for life looks bleak.
I ask for peace and to be shown love.
I wait for your answer from above.
I know you can give me courage and strength.
I have hope and faith to go the length.
My soul is searching everywhere.
You hold the answers over there.
The universe, our home, is full of treasure.
Love me and keep my life full of pleasure.
I now trust you, so please trust me
To do my best as I let all things be.

## 8. Paris, France: Temple of Golden Light One
*Listed in Main Temples and in Healing | Surrounded by a city of light*

Paris is known as the City of Lights or the Illuminated City. Widely considered a romantic place, it has many statues of angels and cherubs. Paris is architecturally very well preserved, and the Eiffel Tower is by far the city's most famous monument, together with the Louvre, Notre Dame, and Sacré Coeur.

This beautiful temple is situated in the etheric behind the Sacré Coeur and is overseen by Mother Mary and Jesus Christ, along with many angels and archangels, particularly Archangel Raphael and his legions of angels. This is one of the high-vibrational Temples of Golden Light connecting to the Divine Mother and the angels on high. The large, ornate golden temple looks like a high Catholic church, with many chapels inside connected to different saints.

The temple is surrounded by a city of light, and inside is a healing chamber of light with a rose quartz crystal couch to lie on.

## 9. Lourdes, France: Temple of the Golden Heart
*Listed in Healing*

The small town of Lourdes is nestled in front of the French Alps. It is one of the world's most important pilgrimage sites. The Lourdes Temple of

Golden Light is small but aligns to the absolute heart of God/Goddess. This is a very bright-light temple and is overseen by a magnificent angel of golden light and by St Bernadette herself. You can ask St Bernadette for a dispensation to heal your heart and to heal anyone you know— adults, children, and animals. She may telepathically give you a message or gift, and you may sense St Bernadette's energy as she blesses you.

There are no words, no thoughts, no speaking; you are simply being, and you will connect with the oneness of the universe and Mother Earth's heart centre. This is a wonderful ethereal Temple of Golden Light which links to God's heart. This is the nearest you will get to paradise and total bliss. Whilst connected to this Temple of Golden Light, I channelled these words:

> I am that I am, I am all that there is, and all that is to be and all that has passed. I am absolute love of source. Within me there are endless infinite possibilities. I am overflowing with love for you. You can do whatever you want to do; you have the power, so use it for your highest good. Speak your truth and walk your path in joy, in divinity, and in happiness of source. I am God/ Goddess, the light of source; I can show you wondrous things and abundance. You know me and I know you.

You may ask for your abundance, whether it involves money, love, a relationship, change of job, new home, health, or family issues; this temple is overwhelming with the love that God/Goddess has for you. You will release old energy patterns, old issues, and old mindsets whilst meditating or connecting with this temple in your sleep time. Your higher self knows what is best for you, so as you connect with this temple, release everything that you no longer need or want. Afterwards, you will feel peaceful and rested.

## 10. Berlin, Germany: Temple of the Crystal and Rainbow Children
*Listed in Children and Animals*

Situated in the etheric near the cathedral in the centre of Berlin, in an area called Mitte by the River Spree, this Temple of Golden Light is light and bright. It is filled with fun, laughter, and happiness. It is one of the eighteen children's temples overseen by the Divine Mother and is filled with the energy of the angels of peace and healing rainbow angels. The children in the temple are crystal children, rainbow children, and indigo children. They teach adults the art of enjoyment and how to play.

## 11. Cologne, Germany: Temple of Grounding

The Cologne Temple of Golden Light is very earthy. It is full of pure energy, connecting to Middle Earth and the realm of Camelot. Cologne Cathedral is the city's most famous monument and a highly respected landmark for residents. The temple is situated north of the city in the etheric on the outskirts of Cologne, over pine forests. It is castle-like, with many domes.

When you enter this Temple of Golden Light, it is like walking into a church here on earth that is decorated with golden statues and stained glass windows, but it has a higher purpose and a purer energy than on earth. Here the trees and plants talk, and the temple also connects to the unicorns. It is a temple which is excellent for grounding.

In the temple, you can pray for yourself as well as others. You can pray for global peace and ask for forgiveness and divine guidance. The Cologne Temple of Golden Light has a sense of well-being and a sense of peace, balance, and equanimity, and you will receive all these qualities as soon as you enter the temple through thought, intention, or meditation. Sit and light a candle if you wish. Now connect, and instantly you will be there.

Allow yourself to rise to any challenges in your life. Let yourself feel the love, peace, and balance in this wonderful Temple of Golden Light right now. You feel comfortable, cosy, warm, looked-after, and protected.

## 12. Amsterdam, Netherlands: Temple of Convergence

The Amsterdam Temple of Golden Light has been placed directly over the centre of the city. It is a cleansing temple connecting to dolphins, whales, and all the oceans and seas. Surrounded by rainbow angels, it is a calming place, very connected to water and the oceanic Temples of Golden Light.

Amsterdam has many historic canals running through it dating back to before the seventeenth century. Amsterdam's name derives from the Sanskrit word *Antardham*, which means 'region below sea level'. The Dutch people are expert at reclaiming land and have been doing so since the tenth century. The country is often called the Venice of the North, as about ninety islands link to more than twelve hundred bridges.

Amsterdam is very elemental; there are many elemental beings in the etheric of Amsterdam and the Netherlands. The temple connects to the elemental kingdom on the first level. The Amsterdam Temple of Golden Light is for teaching; you will learn how to help yourself and others. Inside the temple is a special wide tower where people can go to pray for the earth to be helped to lift her energy. You will be helped to focus on your chosen pathway in life or maybe to change your pathway. Here you will receive realisation and become awakened. Within the Temple of Golden Light is a spa or bathing area, rather like a Roman bath. This will cleanse and clear you as you bathe in golden light, rejuvenating your cells.

To connect with this beautiful Temple of Golden Light, simply close your eyes and meditate. Visualise yourself bathing in a relaxing spa or bathing area inside the temple. Feel yourself floating as you relax into the water, de-stressing yourself of life's hectic energy. Relax and let go. Call on the rainbow angels for healing and divine guidance.

## 13. Madrid, Spain: Temple of the Divine Flame of Love
*Listed in Healing*

The Madrid Temple of Golden Light is in the etheric towards the north of this capital city of Spain, high up in the etheric. It is a temple that is incredibly peaceful and serene, with beautiful artwork inside and a painted ceiling just like the famous Sistine Chapel. Very tall and elegant, it is a beautiful golden temple with a painting of all of the disciples. As a centrepiece, there are diamonds and emeralds on a golden cross.

The energy of this temple is filled with the love of the angels, including cherubs, Jesus Christ, Mother Mary, and Mary Magdalene. You feel as if you have walked through a divine flame of love. It is also connected to the energy of many Spanish saints, including St Teresa of Avila. They all will help you to forgive and to heal emotionally. Even old, stored, stuck energy can be released when you connect to this temple.

As you enter, you get a wonderful sense of graceful, refined earth energy, letting you know that all will be well in your life. There are many study groups held here. You can gain scientific knowledge, and I have been shown many books. Through this temple, people can reach God if they listen to the teachings. You will learn honour, truth, dignity, and good morals.

If you wish your path to be illuminated, you only have to ask once, and this will be granted. You will be shown light, protection, and truth. Any concerns or worries you have will be dispelled within this temple, as all prayers are answered, all problems are solved, and total grace is given.

Archangel Raphael's energy is felt in this beautiful temple of sacred energy, love, and peace, and all who visit will receive a message or gift of divine blessings. Issues of the heart and solar plexus are helped here. It is very much a family Temple of Golden Light, visited by parents, children, and all family members. The sick, homeless, and lonely are encouraged to receive healing, to heal their lives, and to live in a more positive, abundant way.

## 14. Seville, Spain: Temple of Strength

Seville is the resting place of Columbus, known to be an aspect of St Germaine. Seville is physically the home of Carmen, Figaro, and Don Juan, a romantic city with winding streets and cafes. The Temple of Golden Light lies in the etheric on the outskirts of the city and is recognised for its qualities of strength and fortitude. It is a white-and gold-coloured temple designed in typical Andalusian style with wooden carvings and an Old World feeling inside. In the middle of the temple, there is a large contemplation hall with a centrepiece waterfall surrounded by rocks in honour of the love of God/Goddess. It is a very spacious temple, with beautiful etheric gardens to be enjoyed by people visiting.

This temple holds the energy of Jesus Christ and the Divine Mother and honours all known religions and creeds. The Seville temple connects to Joan of Arc, known for her qualities of bravery. The temple is overseen by Archangel Michael, holding his sword of holy truth, and his powerful legions of angels. He is known for his qualities of strength, courage, and bravery, and he helps all those who ask for help with sincerity and honesty. So connect with this temple now if these are the qualities that you need. Archangel Michael will also help you cut the etheric cords between yourself and others to whom you no longer wish to be connected.

This is a peaceful, serene temple full of energy. It is light-hearted and happy, enjoying the celebration of life. It is a sacred temple standing for integrity, honour, and truth. If you need to find strength, courage, or bravery, connect with this Temple of Golden Light, and you will receive help. It is also a family temple, sharing friendship and linking hands across the water. With its many rooms for healing and prayer drawing hope out of sadness, it is a very uplifting place to be. It is a temple that teaches you how to live in each 'now' moment. When you connect to this temple, it is like you are taking a day out of life.

This temple, like Madrid's Temple of Golden Light, connects to St Teresa of Avila and many other Spanish saints, male and female.

## 15. Lisbon, Portugal: Temple of Peace
*Listed in Healing*

The Lisbon Temple of Golden Light is so very calm. Situated in the etheric on the outskirts of the city, this large temple exudes serene peacefulness. It is a cleansing, clearing temple; you enter heavily laden with sadness and come out much lighter, leaving behind heavy energy. The temple helps clear solar plexus and heart issues. The solar plexus works with the heart chakra, the throat chakra works with the sacral chakra, and the crown chakra works with the base chakra.

Archangel Zadkiel and his divine feminine twin flame, Archangel Amethyst, help all in this temple. This temple also works with the

Christed angels. They have white wings with golden tips, and they work with issues of forgiveness and the heart. The temple's energy helps people to clear away all sadness. It's time to let go of anything that is holding you back.

This temple is all about feeling interconnected with everyone and everything, all at the same time. Our souls connect with everyone else's on a higher level. Imagine yourself and then, around you, imagine the shape of an enormous arc. This is your soul, and when you see or speak to someone, straight away you are connected with their souls on a higher level. At a higher level, we are all one. So it is about time we became connected here on the earth level. Take time to experience this feeling of being interconnected by visiting this temple in your sleep-state. You will feel balanced, rejuvenated, and refreshed when you wake up.

## 16. Rome, Italy: Temple of Light
*Listed in Healing | Surrounded by a city of light*

This temple is in the etheric over the centre of Rome. It is a large golden temple surrounded by a city of light overseen by a huge golden master angel. It has an earthy churchlike feel to it and is filled with very large lit candles. Smaller areas are also filled with glowing tea-light candles. The temple has ceilings just like the Sistine Chapel but bigger, with paintings of Jesus, the angels, and many other biblical characters. Inside are many rooms for singing, and choirs of angels can be heard.

This is one of the temples of the Apostles of Christ, where they meet personally and make important decisions regarding their work here on earth. When the apostles are in a meeting, the temple is cloaked. It is a temple that heals on a physical body level, healing all adults, children, and animals, including sea creatures. It holds the love and energy of Mother Mary, Jesus Christ, Mary Magdalene, and St Francis of Assisi, as well as Archangel Raphael and the rainbow angels.

Working with heart issues and disharmonies of the physical body; healing issues of 'poor me' and victimhood consciousness; and forgiving the sins of all who think they have sinned, this temple teaches you to think of not *I*, but *we*. You can ask for grace in your life and for blessings to be bestowed upon you and your family. Ask also for absolution and to be shown your own beauty from within, as God/Goddess will show you your own divine spark of God/Goddess that is within you. This is a beautiful Temple of Golden Light, healing the physical body and heart and helping you to awaken and receive enlightenment.

## 17. Venice, Italy: Temple of Loved Ones
*Listed in Healing | Surrounded by a city of light*

This is a large ethereal temple of golden light over the Rialto Bridge extending to St Mark's Basilica. When you enter the Venice temple, it has a magical, serene feel. It is very ornate, with paintings, mirrors, and statues and a huge golden sphere in the centre of the temple. It is, in fact, a gateway to heaven, as this temple connects people to their loved ones who have passed over. It is the only one of the 144 Temples of Golden Light that enables you to connect with these loved ones.

The temple also helps you to forgive any family member or friend who has ever hurt you and allows them to forgive you too, for forgiveness is the key to happiness and wholeness. Healing takes place in this temple by sound and vibration, healing your heart and emotions through musical tones.

We usually think of gondolas, canals, and waterways when we think of Venice. Meditation to this Temple of Golden Light includes seeing yourself in a gondola gliding along the canals of this beautiful city with your guardian angel. You are likely to sense angelic energy. You become connected to source; you see cherubs, doves, and golden light as you step up through the clouds on a golden stairway to heaven.

The temple connects to Jesus Christ, Mother Mary, Archangel Raphael, and legions of their angels. On the higher levels, this is a temple of bliss. It is an incredibly peaceful, calm temple—a meeting place for your loved ones, family, and friends—held together by God/Goddess energy of divine love.

## 18. Sicily, Italy: Temple of Healing All God's Creatures
*Listed in Children and Animals*

This is the main animal healing Temple of Golden Light and is exclusively for the healing of animals. It is a small temple, about the size of St Paul's Cathedral in London, and it is overseen by St Francis of Assisi, patron saint of all animals. St Clare of Assisi and St Anthony of Padua (patron saint of animals and children in Italy) work alongside St Francis. This temple is filled with the energy of Jesus Christ and Mother Mary, and it is surrounded by four large king unicorns and protected by the winged horse Pegasus.

In front of the temple are statues of lions and unicorns, and behind it is an enchanted forest. This temple is filled with love from the elemental spirits, fairies, and tree spirits. The large waiting room is itself a healing sanctuary. It is filled with golden statues of cats, dogs, horses, and other animals, and there is a strong connection to Sirius.

This wonderful healing sanctuary is situated in the etheric near the harbour, over Palermo. The city used to be heavy with old Mafia energy, but a few years ago, I visited Palermo with my husband, and over several days, I managed to clear all the negative energy. A beautiful light now shines brightly over the city.

## 19. Geneva, Switzerland: Temple of Groundedness
*Listed in Children and Animals*

This is the only Unicorn Temple of Golden Light, situated to the north of the city in the etheric in front of snow-capped mountains, Geneva's Temple of Golden Light is very close to the earth and is filled with the pure sacred energy of Mother Earth's heart centre. If you wish to ground into Mother Earth, connect to this temple. It is surrounded by two mountain chains: the Alps and the Jura. Geneva is a global financial centre as well as a worldwide centre for diplomacy and was where the Geneva Conventions were signed.

Geneva has a very grounding, earthy temple connecting to Middle Earth and Camelot. Four large unicorns and the winged horse Pegasus guard this unicorn Temple of Golden Light, and many other unicorns help within and around it. The unicorns are ascended horses; they are wondrous beings of tremendous light filled with so much love for humanity. When you call on them, they will help you immediately.

A happy temple, it connects to the fairies and elementals, which gives it a woodland feel and brings through the tree spirits of the natural kingdom. The air is filled with butterflies and dragonflies. This temple heals animals as well as adults and children.


## 20. Zurich, Switzerland: Temple of Earthy Qualities

The Temple of Golden Light over Zurich is surrounded by golden cherubs and aligns to the many-coloured rainbow angels, bringing healing with the twelve colours of creation and giving love and light on all levels. It is constantly emitting golden light, covering a huge area greater than Zurich itself. The temple itself is small, about the size of St Paul's Cathedral in London, and it has a churchlike structure and feel to it. It will balance your chakras and give you peace and enough strength to carry you forward into new pastures, overcoming all obstacles.

The Zurich temple could be a starting point for many to appreciate the divine qualities of the144 healing Temples of Golden Light, bringing peace to those with strong beliefs. It is a temple of hope and strength—a solid Temple of Golden Light, adhering to strong, solid beliefs based on morals, truth, and justice. Remember, do not waste words on people who deserve your silence. Sometimes the most powerful thing you can do is say nothing at all.

This is an earthy temple of realism and being able to see situations clearly. It is a temple of cutting through daydreaming—a temple of getting things done and being factual. The attitude of this Temple of Golden Light is that we are here, so let's get on with the job in hand. We are one unity consciousness, so let us realise this and get on with uniting humanity and the world globally with loving thoughts. Let us love ourselves and all around us. Let us unite in sisterhood and brotherhood. We are one; let us see the world globally covered in love and golden light.

## 21. Vienna, Austria: Temple of Sound One

Vienna is the largest city of Austria. It is regarded as a city of music and said to be the city of dreams. The majestic Vienna Temple of Golden Light is over the centre of this large city, etherically placed by St Stephen's Cathedral and the Vienna State Opera House. It twins with Salzburg, Austria's other Temple of Golden Light. It is primarily a temple to heal your voice and soul. Overseen by Johann Strauss and the rainbow angels of sound, the temple helps to release burdens, sorrows, and shadows by sound healing. It is also a temple of forgiveness, where joy and Christed energy help you unlock your inner child.

As you enter, you will hear music—angelic tones of celestial sound—and you will be guided to a particular room for sound healing. The key to sound healing is to find your own personal tone. Once you have this, you can start to heal any of your issues.

It is amazing how quickly you can heal yourself and balance your chakras by sounding your tone—the tone of your soul. If you feel that this Temple of Golden Light is the right temple for you at this time, connect with it now. Make a sound to clear your voice, and sing at the top of your voice with the intention of healing yourself.

## 22. Salzburg, Austria: Temple of Sound Two

Lady Nada personally oversees Salzburg's Temple of Golden Light. She is one of the three goddesses who oversee the 144 Temples of Golden Light, and she is the twin flame of Jesus Christ. The temple looks quite castle-like, similar to the Vienna temple with which it is twinned, but it has a softer feminine energy.

Lady Nada is in charge of the seventh ray, and she asks you to comfort, console, and be God's hands and heart in helping all those around you to heal. This is a temple of forgiveness where burdens and wrongdoings are released and forgiven. Prayers are asked here for individuals for forgiveness and mercy, so by the grace of God you will be healed.

Rainbow angels of sound surround this temple, so allow yourself to sing and be free of any unhappiness. Some people may like to meditate upon this peaceful Temple of Golden Light if they have had an operation and need to rest. Before you leave here, you will be given a pink flower, a rose that symbolises Lady Nada.

Some of our chakras are connected to each other. For example, your heart chakra is connected to your solar plexus chakra, your throat chakra is connected to your sacral chakra, and your crown chakra is connected to your base chakra. This temple works to clear your heart chakra, so your solar plexus chakra will also be cleared of any negativity. This is a very restful temple, harmonising all your chakras with the simple technique of meditation.

## 23. Savinja Alps, Slovenia: Temple of Loving Light

Lady Nada also directly oversees the Slovenia Temple of Golden Light. There is an incredibly peaceful Atlantis energy here. The energy is very light and bright. This is a high-energy temple for those who already do service work—a light workers' and light bearers' temple. The temple is filled with crystals, particularly rose quartz crystals that lie in between tall marble pillars. Inside is a sanctuary that contains a healing pool holding the energy of the dolphins of Atlantis.

A temple of total love and rejuvenation where light workers and light bearers can come to rest and replenish their energy, it is only for those who are ready—and in fact, you can only come here by invitation. It is cloaked much of the time, as it is only seen by those who are ready to enter. It is a peaceful escape from life only to those who are worthy, a feminine temple of divine love. Information is downloaded here from the galactic council through one's teeth. It is a small temple for specialist souls of unconditional love, a haven of rest when energy is depleted or one needs rejuvenating.

## 24. Budapest, Hungary: Temple of Open Heart
*Listed in Healing*

Budapest is the capital and largest city in Hungary and occupies both sides of the River Danube. Buda on the west bank and Pest on the east became a single city in 1873. The Budapest Temple of Golden Light has an earth energy that you feel immediately when you arrive. It is very peaceful, with beautiful gardens and a large .

As you enter the temple, you are greeted by Archangel Chamuel and Archangel Charity and by golden seraphim angels who telepathically link with you. You become aware that inside, the temple is palatial and ornate, with large windows in grand rooms with chandeliers where you can meditate or simply sit in silence and be healed. People transform and change for the better when they come to this transformational Temple of Golden Light. The more often you visit, the more you will find yourself awakening, bringing heaven to earth.

The temple has many levels within it. At the top level, it aligns to Archangel Metatron, the Lord of Light. The main aim of this temple is to begin to open people's heart centre as well as to move old, stuck, earthbound souls over to the light so that they can move forward on their own journey of love and rejoin their soul group. There are many healing rooms, and they provide healing on a physical body level.

## 25. Oslo, Norway: Temple of Planting Seeds of Love

Oslo is the capital and the most populous city in Norway. It is a hub of Norwegian trade. Modern linguists generally interpret the original name, *Oslo* or *Aslo*, as either meaning 'meadow at the foot of the hill' or 'meadow consecrated to the gods'. This is likely because of the abundance of trees in the Oslo area. The Temple of Golden Light lies on the outskirts of this large city towards the north.

Pine forests fill the air around this Temple of Golden Light. It has a very strong earthy energy of elementals, trees, spirits, and forest energy. It is a large temple of much light surrounded by rainbow angels. This is the Temple of Planting Seeds of Love, and here you can learn how to live with nature, like the Amish and Mennonite people living on and with the earth and her purity.

You will learn how to work with Mother Earth, her seasons, and her land. You can learn how to live a community life in love, peace, and friendship. You can come here to de-stress, relax, and think. The temple has a beautiful healing sanctuary, a place of stillness and silence connecting to Mother Earth's heart centre. Learn to be open to the experience called life by connecting with this temple and living naturally, creating a rhythm within your life of honouring nature.

### 26. Mo i Rana, Norway: Temple of Divinity
*Listed in Children and Animals*

The Mo i Rana Temple of Golden Light is in the etheric in the middle of a huge pine forest. Surprisingly, it is quite tall, like a tower reaching up and out into the star systems of Pleiades and Sirius, linking with the Cat People and the Hathors from Venus called the Golden Ones. The connection to the earth is strong, as this temple connects to Middle Earth and Agartha, a city that is said to reside in the earth's core. It also links with the tree spirits as well as the elemental kingdom.

As you enter, you will connect with a talking owl and feel the earthiness of this temple. You can gently move up through the four levels, linking with all of our universe in its entirety. If you are holding on to any negativity energy, it will be changed to positive energy.

This temple gives out beams of pink light that look like the aurora of the Northern Lights, attracting celestial beings, star people, star seeds, and angels—all loving, gentle souls. It is an ethereal temple of divine love, peacefulness, quiet, stillness, and motionless energy. This temple is capable of many qualities, from healing to travelling in space. If you are ready, there are doorways here that can provide access to other worlds, rather like the TV series and movie *Stargate*. All in all, this is a splendid temple of magnificent and universal love.

Mo i Rana is a beautiful temple of healing, peace, and understanding. Inside is a children's healing sanctuary with big pink rose quartz crystals and many rainbow angels. If you feel drawn to visit this temple, adults too can be healed here.

### 27. Stockholm, Sweden: Temple of Wisdom
*Surrounded by a city of light*

Stockholm is Sweden's cultural, media, political, and economic centre. The temple is over the centre of Stockholm, slightly to the north of the city. This is a very light, bright temple energetically, having a connection to the star systems of this universe, particularly Pleiades, Sirius, and Andromeda. It connects to Archangel Ariel and his legions of angels to facilitate wisdom. When you enter, you will immediately become aware of thousands of angels.

This Temple of Golden Light is where will you learn to utilise your skills and where you can learn to change and awaken—to wake up or shake up. You can learn here how blessed you are and how to be grateful and appreciate what you have. As it is already known, the more grateful you are, the more you will receive abundance.

Archangel Ariel and his angels will connect you to this beautiful temple if you sit quietly and ask. He will help you in any way he can; you simply need to ask, and all will be well. Ask for your abundance by connecting to your universal abundance. See yourself receiving your abundance in all ways.

## 28. Helsinki, Finland: Temple of Crystal

The Helsinki Temple of Golden Light is high up in the etheric. It is filled with silver-winged angels and cherubs. It is overseen by a huge master angel who also has silver wings and is connected to Archangel Raphael and Mother Mary.

This temple has a High Church feel to it. If you can you imagine being in a room filled with hundreds and hundreds of lit candles, you will sense the energy inside. Part of the temple is devoted to being a school and a study centre.

The Temple of Crystal is a very powerful healing temple that aligns to crystal healing. There is a large rose quartz crystal floating in the centre of the main healing room, where you can learn about crystal healing. Rainbow angels can be seen walking in this temple and will hold your hand when asked. Situated etherically towards the back of the city, it is strongly connected to the ascended master St Germaine, known to have brought forward 'the violet flame of St Germaine'.

## 29. Tallinn, Estonia: Temple of Comfort One

The Tallinn Temple of Golden Light is a lovely, cosy, and homely temple with a churchlike feel to it. It is overseen by Master Rakosky, whom I believe to be an aspect of St Germaine, who is in turn an aspect of Merlin. Inside the temple, many candles are lit to honour spirit. This is a healing sanctuary filled with Christ energy and the energy of the Divine Mother, allowing you to feel nurtured whilst receiving spiritual nourishment. Here is a place where you can visit and speak to God/Goddess in prayer.

Also in this temple, you can study philosophy and a simpler way of life. Deep inside, there is a healing sanctuary that is lit with many more candles; it will balance your chakras as well as ease any disharmony you may feel. This is very much a family temple, honouring all forms of life. It is somewhere you can feel safe and secure.

This temple speaks of morals and honouring family life within the community. It has a caring and sharing philosophy, honouring thy neighbour as thyself, so to speak. It is a very comforting temple where one can find peace and tranquillity. Prayers for world peace are spoken in this temple. Here is one such prayer:

> Oh Lord, our Father, we ask for peace.
> May all the troubles on our planet cease.
> We are here to love and to be happy,
> Not here to be selfish and so unhappy.
> Mother Earth gives us strength when needed.
> Help us to listen for her call not to go unheeded.
> She is beautiful, and she can shine so bright.
> With our help, she can excel herself to be a great light.
> Please, heavenly Father, listen to our prayers.
> You can help us with our concerns and cares.
> Teach us to love the earth and be loved too.
> Please bring about peace, love, and truth.

## 30. Warsaw, Poland: Temple of Caring
*Listed in Children and Animals*

The Warsaw Temple of Golden Light is very light and angelic. It connects to Archangel Raphael, Mother Mary, and Jesus Christ. It is a beautiful temple with huge ceilings and paintings of angels, cherubs, and saints of Poland.

Poland has accumulated suffering from the First and Second World Wars, so much healing needs to happen here. Old memories need to go. Those memories fill the earth with negative energy and hold patterns of pain. The Warsaw temple will heal all this.

This is a soul rescue temple, saving stuck souls from wartime and taking them over to the light using a bridge that is permanently situated within the centre of this temple. Many souls from surrounding countries will be drawn to this temple. Changes for the good are happening in Poland, and this is a powerful, large temple holding much light for this area. This is also a large children's temple of tremendous light with a special healing sanctuary for children inside, healing all disharmonies.

The Warsaw Temple of Golden Light is a particularly large, busy temple covering huge areas and consisting of many levels. The temple offers healing by changing the DNA in every cell of your body and filling it with love. The love within you is now being activated to its fullest potential. God loves you, and God gives you whatever you pray for, so think well and discern clearly before you ask and pray in this temple of prayer.

## 31. Bratislava, Slovakia: Temple of Rainbow Fairies

The Bratislava Temple of Golden Light is in the etheric over a mountain range. A two-tiered earthy temple, it first connects to the elemental kingdom and the rainbow fairies, and then it moves up and becomes brighter, connecting to the rainbow angels of healing. This is a temple where energy that is less than light can be released.

People who have solar plexus issues are helped here, and healing is possible for people of war zones. One learns here to understand the other person's point of view. Things are pointed out to people about the way they think and feel. One is taught all about cause and effect. This temple has quite a Russian feel to it, connected to Russian influences.

This Temple of Golden Light will take you on a journey of discovery, which will be all about yourself—healing certain areas of distrust, pain, anger, and resentment. It is a vortex of light, healing different points of view within people. You will realise by connecting with the temple through meditation that this will be a very easy process to follow. You will experience a feeling of being grounded and then floating upwards through the temple, and by moving through many levels, you can reach the top.

## 32. Prague, Czech Republic: Temple of Angels

This large temple is more of a traditional churchlike temple, white and gold with domed roofs. It holds a Catholic energy, mostly of Mother Mary, Divine Mother. It is a very angelic temple which exudes golden light continuously, and many golden cherubs work here.

The Prague Temple of Golden Light is overseen by Archangel Michael, who holds his sword of holy truth, strength, courage, and bravery. This represents the cutting of old ties and cords of attachment, removing negativity with the old Prague and allowing the new Prague to come through with splendour; encouraging progress, prosperity, and healing; and helping all those in need of comfort and uplift.

Mindsets in Prague are being changed to blend with newer concepts and ideas. The message of this Temple of Golden Light is of healing to facilitate change and move forward, to let go of the past, and to move on to new pastures.

Prague itself flourished in the Gothic and Renaissance eras as the home to the Habsburg monarchy and its Austro-Hungarian empire. After the First World War, it became the capital of Czechoslovakia. The temple itself is in the etheric by Prague Castle and Charles Bridge.

## 33. Zazanlak, Bulgaria: Temple of Reflection

Zazanlak is a sacred area in Stara Zagora Province at the foot of the Balkan Mountain Range in Bulgaria. It is home to an earthy, quiet, peaceful temple of ethereal stillness that holds the light for this area. Archangel Uriel and his legions of angels of peace oversee this temple. It is a smallish temple created in an octagonal shape.

The temple is filled with candles of light to help you see your reflection by mirroring others around you. It will help you find your truth and look at fragments of yourself. Help is here for your journey through life, and you will learn how to appreciate and live in the here and now.

If you are not happy, you can have a review of your life to see if things can be changed. Changes can always be made to your life path if you are prepared to listen and change aspects of your life. You can certainly be helped to move forward if you have a quest for enlightenment. So reflect upon your life and ask yourself: is all as well as you would like it to be? If not, then reflect and meditate by connecting to the Zazanlak temple to find your answer.

To do this, use the following meditation: Sit quietly, close your eyes, and breathe in and out three times, breathing in love and breathing out gold. Start to feel the Zazanlak temple's energy. Feel the peace and stillness. Sense, feel, or see clairvoyantly a Temple of Golden Light. Visualise yourself sitting in the main hall of the temple meditating, and when you wake up, remember what you felt, sensed, saw, or simply knew, and smile.

## 34. Zagreb, Croatia: Temple of Healing Children and Your Heart
*Listed in Children and Animals*

The Zagreb Temple of Golden Light is in the etheric over the centre of the city, which lies in front of the Medvednica mountain range near the River Sava. It is filled with twinkling starlight and is connected to many angels, fairies, and star beings and to the Pleiades. Energetically, this is a light temple which is high up in the etheric of earth. It is a large temple that focuses on healing children as well as people with heavy hearts, removing past life issues and old programming. The energy shines out like small silver stars, healing all those within.

The temples all connect to the known archangels and their divine feminine counterparts, but this temple particularly works with Archangel Chamuel and his divine twin flame, Archangel Charity, both of whom work to heal your heart chakra. Archangel Metatron, known as the Radiant One, is in charge of all of the archangels and the whole of the angelic realm, and he will help you to heal and restore your nature and divine blueprint, so expect a miracle. You are the star, the creator of your destiny. Unfold your wings and learn to fly.

If you are interested in organic farming methods, you can meditate on this temple and learn how to farm naturally, putting back into the earth instead of taking out of the earth. This may sound strange, as it is in the etheric of earth and not the physical earth, but sometimes this is how we learn. We meditate and then, wow, we receive inspiration on any topic.

## 35. Belgrade, Serbia: Temple of Rest and Peace

Belgrade, an ancient city, is now the capital and largest city of Serbia. It is located at the confluence of the Sava and Danube rivers, where the Pannonian Plain meets the Balkans. Its Temple of Golden Light will help you aspire to be the best you can be, giving you grounding and basic building blocks to help you through your life.

The temple has a sacred churchlike feel to it, homely and welcoming. You will receive grace and forgiveness here. It is a temple where all is understood. You will be given guidance, counselling, and clarity and feel refreshed when you leave, knowing that you have the power to change your life.

This temple is filled with the energy of love, justice, and power. It is honoured by the presence of the god Thor, known as the god of justice. The ascended master El Morya connects to this temple with his qualities of divine will and love. It is helped too by many other ascended masters, known and unknown.

The Belgrade temple has many levels. On the top level is a universal galactic council and also a council of elders. From this temple will come information—lots of information and directives on how to plan our future and the future of our planet in peace and love.

## 36. Athens, Greece: Temple of Ascension
*Listed in Main Temples*

The Athens temple is one of the twelve main Temples of Golden Light. It is overseen by all twelve Grecian gods and goddesses shining down on humanity: Pallas Athena, Aphrodite, Artemis, Apollo, Zeus, Hermes, Hercules, Poseidon, Hephaestus, Hera, Hestia, and Demeter. This temple is over the centre of Athens in the etheric above the Acropolis, the sacred temple of Pallas Athena. It is an amazing temple of tremendous light.

## 37. Crete, Greece: Temple of the Stars

The Crete Temple of Golden Light is a beautiful ethereal temple that aligns to the Temple of Delphi in Greece, connecting this world to the star systems of our universe. Emitting healing energy, peace, and harmony, it changes all those who visit. It is frequented by celestial beings, star people, angels, and light bright beings from this universe.

Inside, there is a wonderful amphitheatre where you can feel a oneness with the universe, oceans, mountains, rivers, moon, sun, stars, and the many galaxies. You will realise that you are a divine spark of reality and remember who you are, as we are all one consciousness. From the Crete temple, you can learn about and be given the keys to the universe. You will connect to the many Grecian gods and goddesses and help to bring about change as we enter into the Golden Age. Pallas Athena oversees this Temple of Golden Light along with Artemis.

Many writers will visit this temple for teachings on writing and channelling. It is a small but powerful temple, filled with the feminine energy of divine love and surrounded by many rainbow angels. The rainbow angels ask you to love yourself and forgive all your past mistakes—to move on and live now. Your life is so precious and unique.

## 38. Paphos, Cyprus: Temple of Inner Light

A small, powerful Temple of Golden Light which links to Mohammed, Allah, Zoroastrian, and Jesus, the Cyprus temple has a different sacred energy. I think Cyprus is part of the old Atlantis, which also played a part in biblical days, as this was where Lazarus lived and was brought back from the dead by Jesus.

The Paphos temple is placed on a pivotal point within the grid of Temples of Golden Light. It anchors light for this part of the world, coming together to celebrate the love of God/Goddess and Mother Earth. A unification of faiths and creeds, it is a temple of spiritual growth and spiritual development, working from the heart of God, releasing heavy issues, and recognising that we are all one.

It is a feminine temple aligning to Mother Mary and carrying the energy of Goddess Aphrodite. Through the Divine Mother, it rebalances feminine energy. The temple is surrounded by rainbow angels of love and light, healing all those who enter.

## 39. Kiev, Ukraine: Temple of Awakening

The Kiev temple is a large Temple of Golden Light emitting radiant golden light to a huge area. It is a temple of awakening overseen by Archangel Metaziel and his divine twin flame, Archangel Honoriel. They are new archangels to this planet, coming from another universe to help us. They can now come here with their legions of rainbow angels, as the vibration has shifted and lifted on our planet.

This is a temple of awakening souls and is beautifully decorated inside. It is a temple of jubilation and joy, celebrating with the many awakening souls. Change is within. It is not the world that needs peace, it is people. When people in the world are at peace within, the world will be at peace.

As the great masters teach, enlightened souls do not ask anyone to believe anything. They simply point the way and leave it to the people to realise for themselves. The people here will realise the truth, and a new energy will emerge. Love with pure wisdom and creative power can overcome all limitations and resistance, ultimately setting us free. It is the true healing power.

# Chapter 4

## *The Americas*

In February 2015, I visited New York with my husband to connect to and activate the New York Temple of Golden Light. As I mentioned earlier, I do not usually need to visit a city to activate a temple, but I had to trust my guidance that this was the right thing to do.

We arrived to freezing conditions where it was -21C, the coldest we have ever experienced. We are used to English weather, which does not usually drop much below -3C. I had expected cold weather but not freezing weather. We took a taxi to our hotel and were immediately offered an upgrade, and we were told that breakfast would be free the next morning. I remember thinking, *We are in the right place. The universe is shining on us.*

The following day, we booked a tour to visit the Statue of Liberty. This is where the New York Temple of Golden Light has been placed. It is an ascended masters' temple that was gifted to New York after 9/11, and it is in the etheric to one side of the Statue of Liberty, quite close to the Temple of the Sun. We took the ferry to Ellis Island, and it started to snow. Despite the weather turning to blizzard conditions, it was a wonderful feeling standing by the Statue of Liberty, knowing that this temple was in the etheric above us. I connected with the temple, and the temple completed its activation.

Our tour guide for this day told us about his experiences the day the Twin Towers fell to the ground, and how it took him five years to return to this part of the city after losing his cousin. His story highlighted to us the massive impact of 9/11 on each and every person in New York and beyond, and how important the new ascended masters' temple is to the city. There is now a beacon of light that shines continually around the world that can be felt on the physical earth.

## United States

The following are the twenty US Temples of Golden Light:

40. New York, New York
41. Mount Shasta, California
42. San Francisco, California
43. Sedona, Arizona
44. Phoenix, Arizona
45. Denver, Colorado
46. Salt Lake City, Utah
47. Idaho Falls, Idaho
48. Portland, Oregon
49. Omaha, Nebraska
50. Dallas, Texas
51. Little Rock, Arkansas
52. Nashville, Tennessee
53. Atlanta, Georgia
54. Indianapolis, Indiana
55. Minneapolis, Minnesota
56. Chicago, Illinois
57. Detroit, Michigan
58. Boston, Massachusetts
59. Kauai, Hawaii

## 40. New York, New York: Temple of Believe
*Listed in Main Temples | Surrounded by a city of light*

The New York Temple of Golden Light is huge, tall, and elaborate. This is where you can meet the three goddesses who oversee all 144 Temples of Golden Light: Lady Nada, Jacinta, and Lathinda. They all have an office here, but you need to book in to see them personally. Set a time in your night sleep-state to meet them.

The goddesses have the gift to change karma, as they sit on different karmic boards. Dispensations can be given and changes can be put into place for all people. Everything is possible when working in the light, holding the highest integrity and love for all. Help for healing on all levels is given by the goddesses.

## 41. Mount Shasta, California: Temple of Truth
*Listed in Healing and in Meditation and Relaxation | Surrounded by a city of light*

Mount Shasta is a special, sacred place of immense peace and healing, and it is known worldwide. Native Americans originally inhabited it and believed it to be the centre of creation. Considered one of the most sacred mountains in the world, it is a focus for angels, spirit guides, spaceships, masters from the light realm, and the survivors of ancient Lemuria. It is known as the retreat of Archangel Gabriel.

The Temple of Golden Light lies in the etheric right over the top of the mountain and has a domed golden roof that opens up and out to the universe, where it connects to many Christed ETs. It is overseen by Commander Ashtar of the command fleet. Holding the Christed energy of peace and love, they travel through time and space. We are certainly not alone in this universe, as other celestial beings are here to help us, and they are of positive energy, not negative.

St Germaine, Archangel Gabriel, and Archangel Hope (Gabriel's divine twin flame) have connections with this temple, and there is a strong Native American energy here. It is a temple where people speak their truth with love whilst sitting in a circle. White Buffalo Calf Woman offers words of wisdom in her native tongue. Chief Running Bull and Chief White Eagle are known to come, sit inside, and give interesting talks on peace and love.

Healing is performed here, and a new healing modality will come through this Temple of Golden Light. Very troubled souls can come to receive healing to remove past life issues, and current life issues can be released when they are ready. It is a place of undoing and unravelling strong feelings that have caused disharmonies and discontent throughout life. You will only begin to heal when you let go of past hurts, forgive those who have wronged you, and learn to forgive yourself for your mistakes. People who need emotional healing should connect with this temple, and enlightenment will also be given.

## 42. San Francisco, California: Temple of Compassion
*Listed in Children and Animals | Surrounded by a city of light*

The San Francisco temple is in the etheric over water, alongside the Golden Gate Bridge. It is a beautiful compassionate temple understanding every aspect of human life. Deep inside the temple is a large healing room with a very large pale pink rose-shaped crystal emitting loving energy from its centre.

This very angelic Temple of Golden Light, surrounded by a city of light, works to heal your heart and to heal children of all ages, no matter how big or small their problem. Archangel Chamuel's and Archangel Charity's legions of angels will visit you and your children when you have healing here. Lady Nada, the twin flame of Jesus, works personally within this Temple of Golden Light, offering words of comfort, love, and compassion to help those in need.

This temple is all about your heart and healing your heart. Let go of hurt, resentment, heartache, emotional pain, and anger. Offer these to the light and release them. Heartache is often confusing and messy, and most people want to get out of it as soon as possible, so they shut down. Life becomes more tolerable, but they become more blinkered, closing their eyes to everyone's heartache, even their own.

Each person's journey through emotional pain will be different. Some heartaches bring us to despair, but these situations can also bring us into spiritual growth and deeper love. Our bodies need to release emotional pain, and we do this through feeling and expressing sadness, anger, and tears. If they do not release these feelings, people can become ill or even violent, creating disharmonies within their own bodies. Let it go, cry, shout, offload onto friends or family, but please let it go.

Meditation is perfect for releasing emotional pain, as it dissolves disharmonies and negative thoughts. You need to love people always, even if they are not giving you what you want, and then do not take their behaviour personally. If you feel hurt, you have to recognize that they are not hurting you because you are you, but because they are they.

Whether we have lost someone we love, such as a family member or friend; lost our health; or lost money, grief is how we heal our hearts of pain, heal our emotional body, and breathe life back into our ability to care and be inspired to love again. When you find yourself in the position to help someone, be happy and feel blessed, because God is answering that person's prayer through you. Our purpose here on Earth is not to get lost in the dark but to be a light to others.

## 43. Sedona, Arizona: Temple of Universal Light
*Listed in Main Temples| Surrounded by a city of light*

This is a large, impressive temple beaming golden light right across the United States and out into this universe. An enormous golden angel protects the temple. This powerful temple is on many levels, and Native Americans work on the first level, teaching how to heal naturally with herbs. There is a healing room with a large emerald crystal on the ceiling in one of the healing sanctuaries. Archangel Raphael and Mother Mary heal everyone who comes here.

The Sedona temple is a vortex of energy; it appears to spin on its axis and can be cloaked when required. It is a very important temple, and new technology will be brought forward from here. Commander Ashtar has an office here. He is commander of the star fleet's spaceships that travel through our galaxies, universe, and other universes and multi-universes, protecting everyone from the dark forces.

The Sedona temple is run with military precision. Nothing goes unnoticed. There are chambers for sleep-state regeneration and places for walk-ins to wait for a physical body. Planet Earth is a very popular planet to incarnate onto, as it is possible to experience so much in order to gain spiritual growth.

All souls have to wait for the right time to be reborn. Walk-ins are generally souls that do not want to be born as babies and move through childhood. Someone encounters an accident of some kind at some point in life, and that soul leaves the body and another soul comes into the same body. Very often people will notice a personality change, as a different soul is in the same body.

There is a new rainbow fleet with new ETs that now works to help our planet. Please remember that all beings that come here must gain permission to enter this universe from the Galactic Federation of Light.

## 44. Phoenix, Arizona: Temple of the Future
*Listed in Main Temples and in Healing | Surrounded by a city of light*

The Phoenix Temple of Golden Light is another very large temple which looks and feels quite futuristic. It is the eleventh largest temple and has a spaceship docking station. Strongly connected to the Arcturians, who are fifth-dimensional beings and here to help our planet ascend, the temple is filled with many other Christed ETs trying to help us ascend. As with a few other temples, this temple will bring a new healing modality—a new vibrational healing tool brought through from the higher realms to help us heal. This will facilitate miracles when people are ready to heal.

## 45. Denver, Colorado: Temple of the Eagle
*Listed in Children and Animals*

This Temple of Golden Light in the etheric over Denver is filled with Native American energy and overseen by White Buffalo Calf Woman and a Native American chief called White Eagle. It is a powerful healing temple for animals as well as for people, and you will feel a strong love for humanity. The temple has a lovely pure earthy energy; it is a place where you can feel the peace of the trees and nature from within.

Inside are four elders who each sit on a bench to represent the four elements: earth, wind, fire, and water. At the back of this beautiful temple is a large lake, and there are many harmless eagles that will communicate with you. If you can imagine powwows, peace pipes, and tepees, then you are in the right place. There has been much written about Chief White Eagle, for example; he is supposed to have said, 'The secret of strength lies in having a quiet mind, and if you can, think of yourself being constant, gentle, loving, and kind to every living person.' When you connect to this Temple of Golden Light, you immediately connect to Chief White Eagle, who has a great energy of love, compassion, humility, grace, and strength.

## 46. Salt Lake City, Utah: Temple of Shining Light
*Surrounded by a city of light*

The Salt Lake City temple is situated in the etheric towards the back of the city, in front of the top of the central mountain range. It is a very light, bright Temple of Golden Light, with many levels and an enormous star above it reaching out to the stars and the cosmos, shining its light for thousands of miles around.

The temple is a vortex of light, transmuting all negative energy and in particular that of anger. Many celestial beings of light and angels gather here at this beacon of light. The temple connects to Archangel Gabriel, the messenger of God, and his twin flame, Archangel Hope.

I suggest you connect yourself via meditation or by simply closing your eyes to experience how dazzling the light is in this temple. Start by imagining a large ethereal temple filled with many beings of light. We are evolving as humans, and therefore we can understand more easily what it is like to be in a body of light and to be able to radiate that light outwards.

On earth, Salt Lake City is home to the headquarters of the Church of Latter-Day Saints. Brigham Young, second president of the church, upon his arrival on 24 July 1847, said, 'This is the right place. Drive on.' He claimed to have seen a vision prior to the wagon train's arrival that this would be the place for the Mormon pioneers' new home. It then took forty years to build the Salt Lake City Temple in Temple Square in the physical on earth. It was dedicated on 6 April 1893.

## 47. Idaho Falls, Idaho: Temple of Heaven

Idaho Falls is a city in Bonneville County, Idaho, and the largest city in Eastern Idaho, where it lies on the Snake River. There is a Temple of Golden Light here situated near the Idaho Falls Mormon Temple in the etheric of Mother Earth. It is filled with Christed consciousness energy of love, light, compassion, wisdom, and understanding, and is surrounded by rainbow angels.

In the etheric above is a large white star, and the temple has a hidden entrance behind a beautiful, sacred, heart-shaped rose quartz crystal. Inside are three big crystal healing rooms, so naturally this is a crystalline healing temple. The many crystals give out a crystalline energy that is very good for clearing and cleansing people's auric field. A lotus-shaped crystal is the centrepiece inside one healing room, and this energy connects to the trees and plants around the area. This temple has a lovely earthlike feel to it, and as you connect, you will feel yourself being balanced energetically in mind, body, and spirit.

Also inside the temple is a Native American presence. Those of you who wish to sit here and meditate will be taken in a dream-state to a sacred place. The Native Americans work very closely with Mother Earth and her seasons. They teach those who wish to learn how to do sacred ceremonies honouring the seasons.

## 48. Portland, Oregon: Temple of Universal Light Two
*Listed in Children and Animals*

The Portland temple is situated in the etheric of Mother Earth over the centre of the city near the river. Portland is the largest city in the US state of Oregon, and it lies near the confluence of the Willamette and Columbia rivers. It was once was inhabited by two bands of Upper Chinook Indians. From the city, you can sometimes see Mount Hood, Mount St Helens, Mount Adams, and Mount Rainier.

This is a very large Temple of Golden Light, up high in the etheric of Mother Earth, connecting to the whole of this universe and the star constellations of Pleiades, Sirius, and Andromeda. From here, you can communicate with this universe and all of the planets: Venus, Mercury, Mars, Jupiter, Saturn, Neptune, Uranus, and Pluto. The temple itself is pure golden white light, with a communication system connecting to all beings.

From this temple, you can travel and see how others live in different universes. It has connections to wormholes and major vortices of spiralling energy, so you can be transported to other planets and star systems. (This is often demonstrated in television programmes like *Stargate* and *Star Trek*.) Be mindful of celestial beings when connecting to this temple. All celestial beings are harmless. They are here to help us, not harm us. They are helping to stop us from blowing ourselves up.

The beautiful Portland Temple of Golden Light is the penthouse suite of temples, energetically speaking. It connects to the universal network of light and sends a beacon of light around the world. It is a children's healing sanctuary surrounded by and filled with rainbow angels. It is also a major healing temple for the physical body. All physical disease can be healed by this temple, not only for children but for adults and animals too.

## 49. Omaha, Nebraska: Temple of Soul Journey
*Listed in Healing*

Omaha was founded along the Missouri River, and a crossing called Lone Tree Ferry earned it the nickname 'Gateway to the West'. Many Native American tribes lived here, including the Omaha, Ponca, Pawnee, Otoe, Missouri, and Ioway. The Omaha Temple of Golden Light is in the etheric over the centre or heart of the city. It is a medium-size earthy temple of unconditional love.

This temple works with the heart chakra—my heart to your heart, we are one. As our heart chakra twins with the solar plexus chakra, this temple helps clear and cleanse any negativity connected to these chakras, removing any old issues and trauma and helping you to open up to unconditional love.

The Omaha temple teaches people how to forgive and how important forgiveness is for their souls. If one passes over in anger, hate, or resentment, that will impede the journey of one's soul until forgiveness is sought and given on all levels. So you need to forgive everyone for everything they may have done or said to hurt you, and other people need to forgive you if you have done something to hurt or harm them. It is very important that this is done before one passes over into the world of spirit. When people are religious, this simple act of forgiveness is made easier, but not everyone these days is religious.

In this temple, one can learn about the Tree of Life, the Kabbalah, and learn about good karma and not-so-good karma. You will learn about your soulmates, your soul group, and your soul family, whether they are living on this planet at the moment or are in spirit, or are even living on another planet or star system. If your soul has fragmented due to a shock, you will be rebalanced. Meditate, and you will be given the answer. Take notice of signs and symbols around you.

We are all created by God and will go back to the source of God when ready. So be prepared to be on a journey in this life, if that is your soul's wish. You will be guided on your spiritual journey, and you will realise how to get to the top of the mountain.

## 50. Dallas, Texas: Temple of Unity

This is a small Temple of Golden Light which lies in the etheric over the centre of Dallas. There is a strong energy of Jesus Christ and the Apostles, John the Baptist, Mother Mary, and Mary Magdalene, although all the Temples of Golden Light are multifaith temples and acknowledge all faiths and creeds. This is a grounding temple, one that is very compassionate and understanding. A strong sense of unity is felt within the temple—a sense of brotherhood and sisterhood, hands holding hands, and hands across the water, across the land, and across the world.

Dallas's temple is an educational Temple of Golden Light, teaching people how to live in peace, how what you eat affects your body, and what wrong eating can do to you. When your body is healed, you need to learn how to eat correctly, as this will keep you in good health for the rest of your life. It is also a teaching temple on natural medicine, connecting to the Native American Chief White Eagle and White Buffalo Calf Woman.

It is well known that President John F. Kennedy's life ended in Dallas on 22 November 1963, and there is a memorial dedicated to his life and accomplishments on Elm Street.

## 51. Little Rock, Arkansas: Temple of Blessings
*Listed in Children and Animals*

Little Rock is the capital of the US state of Arkansas and is located on the Arkansas River. The temple there is primarily a children's healing temple but also heals adults. It is a lovely, small, cosy, warm, comfortable temple with a churchlike community feel, and it is on four levels. There are separate levels for the healing of children and adults, for prayer and counselling, and for meditation.

A beautiful temple filled with angelic energy, it connects to Jesus Christ and the Apostles, Mother Mary, and Mary Magdalene. It is surrounded by golden seraphim angels and rainbow angels. It is called the Temple of Blessings because it is a temple of prayer and healing.

The temple provides a bright and light sanctuary, somewhere you can go to be cleared and cleansed while you meditate. You will look at what you have in life and learn to appreciate the simple things. You will learn and understand that people care about you no matter what you did or did not do. You will learn about and be given unconditional love. God loves you and gives you whatever you pray for, so think well before you pray and ask for divine dispensation. The Lord loves those whose hearts are filled with purest divine love, so work with the creator and all will be well.

Every cell of your being is made up of love. This love is now being activated to its full potential. What you think, you create; what you feel, you attract; and what you imagine, you become. Your dreams are precious diamonds of the soul. Bring them into the light and allow your inner light to shine.

## 52. Nashville, Tennessee: Temple of the Skies

The Nashville Temple of Golden Light is very large—three miles wide—and nestles in the etheric of the mountains around Nashville. This temple connects to the Sedona Temple of Golden Light and as such connects to the whole of this universe and the seven universes surrounding it. This is a very high-vibrational temple, with a golden crystal in a central position to clear any negative energy.

The temple has the scientific ability to bring through new

technologies and inventions from celestial beings, such as futuristic cars running on energy that is natural and not petrol. It has a docking station for spaceships connecting to many different ETs and celestial beings of all shapes and sizes. Portrayals of such beings are often shown in science fiction television and movies, such as *Star Wars, Star Trek*, and *Stargate*. We are not alone in this universe—I can assure you of that. People who think we are have much to learn.

This temple connects to other universes by vortices of energy that connect to wormholes which lead through to the other universes, galaxies, and multi-universes. Access to the many wormholes is given to those who have permission to space travel to other worlds. From this temple, there is a structure which enables you to travel through space and time to other worlds to see how other beings live in their different universes. How interesting would it be to learn about other worlds, star systems, and galaxies?

It is an amazing temple of all God's peoples and their different energies. It is particularly appropriate for scientifically minded people to connect to this temple. When you visit this temple, your DNA will change overnight. Subsequently, you will see life more clearly as you become less agitated and irritated by life's goings on. This will then allow you to gain a clearer realisation of our place in the universe.

## 53. Atlanta, Georgia: Temple of Goodwill
*Listed in Healing*

The Atlanta Temple of Golden Light is the Temple of Goodwill, as it is filled with so much reverence and love for humanity. Atlanta was the birthplace of Martin Luther King, an American pastor, activist, humanitarian, and leader in the African American civil rights movement. Prior to the arrival of European settlers, the Creek and Cherokee Indians inhabited the area, which was called Standing Peachtree. Atlanta sits on top of a ridge south of the Chattahoochee River.

This is a smaller temple, about the same size as St Paul's Cathedral in London. Set in the open air under the stars, it offers comfort, peace, healing, and reassurance. There is an ethereal feel, and it is surrounded by many rainbow angels. It connects to Jesus Christ and the Apostles, Mother Mary, Mary Magdalene, Raphael the Archangel of healing, and Michael the Archangel of truth, strength, and protection. Prayers are said here on a global scale, and people can pray for divine guidance and for family members to be healed.

## 54. Indianapolis, Indiana: Temple of Wise Elders

The Indianapolis Temple of Golden Light is in the etheric south of the city. It links to the Denver, Colorado, Temple of Golden Light. The Indianapolis temple is dedicated entirely to the older wisdom of the Native American elders. It is a regular meeting place for twelve Native American chiefs, where heart-to-heart discussions are held about world affairs and other serious issues. Sometimes Native American chiefs for all tribes throughout history meet here. White Eagle is one of the chiefs.

Inside, you enter into another world. Think of tepees, peace pipes, mountains, huskies, totem poles, Native Americans, and their culture. It is indeed a place of great wisdom. Connect with this temple if you want to learn how to speak truthfully, enjoy life, be happy, have fun, and live simply enjoying the old ways. People are seen as one—a global family. You will learn about the spiral of life and the importance of deep thoughts.

Thoughts are essences of the mind, and then thoughts become words. The key word is love, as love that is pure wisdom and creative power can overcome all limitation and resistance and set us free. It is the true healing power that we can feel in our hearts. This love flows to us from the spirit, but it also shows us how to connect with it in our daily lives with others in order to heal our relationships, thus showing us that love is the greatest power there is.

## 55. Minneapolis, Minnesota: Temple of the White Buffalo Calf Woman
*Listed in Children and Animals*

A Native American lady called White Buffalo Calf Woman oversees the Minneapolis Temple of Golden Light. Here, the Native American and

Christ energy become one. The temple has many healing modalities, including a lovely sanctuary filled with rainbow angels for children who need healing.

The legend of the White Buffalo Calf Woman tells how the people had lost the ability to communicate with the creator. The creator sent the sacred White Buffalo Calf Woman to teach people how to pray with a pipe. With that pipe, seven sacred ceremonies were given for the people to abide by in order to ensure a future with harmony, peace, and balance.

Sacred ceremonies are held here to honour the seasons at the solstices and equinoxes. Other ceremonies include the sweat lodge for purification; the naming ceremony for children; the healing ceremony to restore health to mind, body, and spirit; the marriage ceremony for uniting the male and female; the vision quest for communing with the creator for direction and answers to one's life; and the sun dance to pray for the well-being of all the people. White Buffalo Calf Woman represents Mother Earth's love. Inside the temple is a huge healing sanctuary, with a massive rose quartz crystal.

You may also become aware here of Chief Scarlet Cloud, sometimes known as Chief Red Cloud, as well as tepees and the Sioux tribe. This is a medium-size temple where differences are solved and oneness is recognized. All negative energy is released to the white light of God.


## 56. Chicago, Illinois: Temple of Trust

Chicago is the third largest city in the United States after New York and Los Angeles. It has many religions: Christianity, Islam, Buddhism, Judaism, Hinduism, Sikhism, Jainism, and Bahai, to name a few. This temple is a meeting place for all races and creeds. The Temples of Golden Light are multifaith and honour all religions, as humanity is understood to be in a process of collective evolution and the need of the present time is for the establishment of peace, justice, and unity on a global scale.

The Chicago temple lies in the etheric towards the north of the city and is situated across seven levels. As you enter on the ground level, there is a modern-day church feel to this Temple of Golden Light. It is a very peaceful sanctuary of calm and peace offering an escape from the maddening world outside. Inside the middle of the temple is a crystalline fountain of energy. This fountain rejuvenates one's energy field and heals all chakras, giving balance and harmony as well as removing any tears and holes within one's auric field. Sometimes we need to change our mind to heal our body, as our wrong thinking is often the cause of disharmony.

Inside, it is possible to sense the energy of the angels of peace and love. Higher up, near the top level, you can hear choirs of angels and harp music enabling a feeling of oneness with Mother Earth and our universe. The temple is overseen by Archangel Uriel and is surrounded by the rainbow angels of healing.

## 57. Detroit, Michigan: Temple of Harmony

Detroit is the fifth-largest city in the United States and is very important musically, as it was home to well-known producers of Motown music and many musical artists. The grounded Temple of Golden Light there is one of the smaller temples, like that of Atlanta, Georgia. It is similar in size to St Paul's Cathedral in London. Part of the seraphim angels' wings, which are golden in colour, cover this temple, as the seraphim angels are bigger than the temple. It has golden corridors, painted coloured windows, and five different levels.

There is an earthy feel as you enter the temple. Then, as you move up through the levels, it becomes increasingly light, with an ethereal energy. There are many rooms in which to be quiet and still and to contemplate.

In this lovely temple of peace and serenity, people share problems. Remember, a problem shared is a problem halved. During meditation or sleep-state, people can receive counselling here for all kinds of problems. They also come here to heal themselves and to pray to heal the world.

This Temple of Golden Light is in the etheric over the Cathedral of the Most Blessed Sacrament in Detroit. There is acceptance and understanding of all known faiths and creeds in the Temples of Golden Light and no judgement of any kind, only love.

Detroit is very poor, so I offer some affirmations for abundance for this city and the people who connect to the Detroit temple. Of course, anyone can use these in their everyday life if they wish.

### *Affirmations for Abundance*

I am successful in having financial freedom and abundance.
I am glowing with positive money flowing into my life.
I am open to receiving positive forms of money and abundance into my life.
I am successful in my career and all areas of my life.
I am open to receiving and working in the job of my dreams.
I am full of positive abundance energy that radiates from within me.
I am a magnet and attract large sums of money.
I am open to shining brightly on everything that I am given in gratitude and trust.
I am truly grateful for all that I have.

## 58. Boston, Massachusetts: Temple of Golden Rays
*Listed in Healing | Surrounded by a city of light*

A very powerful temple with high energy, the Boston temple is a holy place of pure light, giving out peace, serenity, and calm. Golden rays of divine light shine down and through this temple, as if someone has switched on a bright light. Archangel Metaziel oversees this temple, which is surrounded by rainbow angels, whose presence is very strong. They provide healing to all those who come here in need. People are absolved of issues and helped to move on. They can reach enlightenment through this temple, which represents physical healing and balance in your life.

## 59. Kauai, Hawaii: Temple of Beauty
*Listed in Children and Animals*

This Temple of Golden Light lies in the etheric over Mount Wai'ale'ale near the centre of the island. Kauai's origins are volcanic; the island was formed by the passage of the Pacific plate over the Hawaiian hotspot. Kauai is geologically the oldest and the fourth largest of the main Hawaiian Islands. It is the site of Waimea Canyon State Park.

The temple is filled with beautiful Lemurian energy (from a time before Atlantis), which holds a very high, pure vibration of celestial light. It is a healing temple especially for children, but it also heals adults, animals, and sea creatures. It is connected to the sacred ways of honouring the moon, sun, stars, and Mother Earth by ceremony. The temple has many special qualities of beauty, sunshine, happiness, healing, honesty, truth, and simplicity.

Think of palm trees and soft music, and you will be there. Imagine yourself swimming near a dolphin, relaxing in the water, and feeling totally peaceful and calm. Allow the soft water to gently glide over your face and body, cleansing and clearing you of any negative energy that you feel is holding you back from moving forward. Feel love entering your whole being. When you pour love into what you do, you will always be filled with love.

## South America

The following are the twelve South American Temples of Golden Light:

60. Machu Picchu, Peru
61. Callao, Lima, Peru
62. La Paz, Bolivia
63. Rio de Janeiro, Brazil
64. Montevideo, Uruguay
65. Caracas, Venezuela
66. Santiago, Chile
67. Buenos Aires, Argentina
68. Havana, Cuba
69. San José, Costa Rica
70. Honduras
71. Mexico City, Mexico

## 60. Machu Picchu, Peru: Temple of Golden Energy
*Listed in Main Temples | Surrounded by a city of light*

This very large and golden Temple of Golden Light is in the etheric right over the top of Machu Picchu. Every vibration on this planet and in this universe links to this temple. It aligns to the angelic realm, the ascended masters, star people, and celestial beings. It is above ley lines, and in the centre is a huge golden pyramid the height of the Eiffel Tower in Paris.

Decisions are made here, as this Temple of Golden Light connects to a galactic federation that resides within the temple. Twelve beings of light and love sit on the galactic board that is held in the temple, and nine are universal beings. New technology will come forward from this temple.

Machu Picchu is a Temple of Golden Light of sonic vibrations. As it is a high-vibrational temple, you need to be ready to visit, as it is only for those already initiated into mastery.

## 61. Callao, Lima, Peru: Temple of Silence
*Listed in Children and Animals*

This is a smaller temple in the etheric over Callao, on the edge of the ocean not far from Lima and near the rainforests of South America. Peru is the home of Machu Picchu, the Incan citadel; the Amazon River; the floating islands of Lake Titicaca; and singular cultures. It also has snow-capped mountains, giant sand dunes, flocks of tropical birds, and volcanoes.

This is a multifaith goddess Temple of Golden Light with a churchlike feel to it. The energy is strongly grounding because of the rainforests and is enhanced by the energy of Jesus Christ and Mother Mary. Within the temple, you will experience stillness and total silence, knowing we are all one with no separation. This temple will help you sort your head out and allow you to process and integrate your thoughts. It will provide a temporary escape from ordinary life. This is an amazing temple where you can learn to heal yourself, your family and friends, and others around you.

The focus in this temple is primarily on healing children, and many healing rooms are here for this purpose. The rainbow angels will heal all children here.

## 62. La Paz, Bolivia: Temple of Change
*Listed in Children and Animals*

La Paz (meaning Our Lady of Peace) is located on the western side of Bolivia, about 3,650 metres above sea level. Bolivia was a part of the Incan empire, and La Paz is located in the valley of the Andes near the Illimani Mountains. The Temple of Golden Light is situated in the etheric above this city. An earthy, very grounded Temple of Golden Light surrounded by a lovely green mist, it is filled with the energy of Christ consciousness and the Divine Mother in a High Church way.

This is a temple for changing from the old to the new ways and for healing the mind, body, and spirit of children and adults alike. The temple is surrounded by rainbow angels and also connects to Archangel Michael, Archangel Faith, and their own legions of angels, providing strength, courage, bravery, and protection to those in need.

This temple is where earth meets heaven, as indicated by the vortex of light in the centre of the main hall of the temple—a huge pillar of light which connects to source. To connect to this temple, simply close your eyes and visualise yourself there in the etheric over La Paz. Visualise a medium-size temple of very bright light.

## 63. Rio de Janeiro, Brazil: Temple of Purity
*Listed in Children and Animals*

Rio de Janeiro is famous for the giant statue of Christ the Redeemer, *Cristo Redento*, which is located on the top of Corcovado Mountain and looks down upon the city. This is one of the new Seven Wonders of the World. The temple is in the etheric to one side of the statue of Christ the Redeemer.

This is a temple dedicated to children's healing and to helping all crystal children, indigo children, and rainbow children understand their purpose of being able to lift the energy of others all around them and to change situations. Many special Christed angels that can heal children oversee this temple. It is a high-energy temple aligning with Jesus Christ and the Apostles, Mother Mary, and many blessed saints of the pure in heart, together with healing angels of peace, love, happiness, and spiritual harmony. This temple connects to God's heart.

When you meditate to connect with this temple, visit the courtyard behind the temple. It is beautiful.


## 64. Montevideo, Uruguay: Temple of Joy

Montevideo is the capital of Uruguay and lies off the South Atlantic Ocean. It has a mild, humid, subtropical climate. The Temple of Golden Light is situated in the etheric above the Palacio Salvo building in the city. Montevideo is well known for its carnivals and festivals and is mainly Spanish- and Portuguese-speaking, with Roman Catholic, Protestant, Umbanda, and Jewish religions. Visit this temple if you wish to connect with positive thinking.

Dancing, happiness, fun, laughter—this is an earthy Temple of Golden Light, teaching you how to be happy. Take a day out of life and relax and have some fun. It is a busy temple with a carnival, festival atmosphere. The attitude of this temple is that life is too short, so make the most of it. Dance, sing, draw, and play.

When you connect with this temple, it will give you the feel-good factor, so cheer up and have some laughter today. This temple will awaken your soul to the simple pleasures in life. Think of rainbow colours to awaken your creativity, and imagine being in a lively processional carnival with happy music around you and everyone smiling and laughing with each other.


## 65. Caracas, Venezuela: Temple of Pure Love

Caracas is located in the northern part of Venezuela following the contours of the narrow Caracas Valley on the Venezuelan coastal mountain range (Cordillera de la Costa). The Caracas Temple of Golden Light is in the etheric in front of the mountain range behind the city. A grounding, earthy Temple of Golden Light, it has a churchlike feel to it. It is very peaceful, honouring all life and different creeds.

This is a temple of stillness where you can relax and let go. There is a quality of humility here within the temple, and nothing is too much trouble. Everyone is considered equally important, and nothing is too big or too small a job to be undertaken. Divine Mother energy is everywhere: loving, compassionate, and understanding everything there is to understand. It is a place where you can let go of issues and sadness and talk to God/Goddess.

To connect with this temple of beautiful golden light, imagine being in the centre of a circle surrounded by healing angels, and straight away you will feel the all-consuming love of God/Goddess. Meditate on this temple and rest here awhile. St Francis of Assisi and many other saints work within the temple helping all those in need.

## 66. Santiago, Chile: Temple of Forgiveness

The Santiago Temple of Golden Light lies in the etheric to the south of the Mapocho River. Santiago is a few hours from the mountains and the Pacific Ocean. The city goes back to the time of the Incan empire and still holds some of this energy in certain areas. The city lies in the centre of the Santiago basin a large bowl-shaped valley consisting of land surrounded by mountains.

The Santiago Temple of Golden Light connects to the rainforests of this world and is situated on different levels. The temple emits golden radiance continuously and holds a light for this area, calling all light workers to focus their own light here and help heal this part of the world. The temple is filled with Christed energy that holds the qualities of love and forgiveness.

This energy needs to be shared by the people of Santiago to allow them to move forward into yet more love and light. When you enter, you connect with the Divine Mother and Jesus Christ and feel the energy of Archangel Raphael and Mother Mary and their many legions of healing angels. Inside in the main hall is a crystal pyramid made of clear quartz, which enables you to connect to other galaxies as you move up through the levels of the temple. On the highest level sits a council of light beings who are filled with love and light.

Goddess Jacinta watches over this temple directly with her energy, and she holds classes for self-improvement and empowerment.

This is a universal temple connecting to galaxies, star systems, and other planets within our universe. All of the Temples of Golden Light will change your DNA codes and raise your vibration. All you need to do is meditate and connect with the Temples of Golden Light or visit them in your sleep time.

## 67. Buenos Aires, Argentina: Temple of Sound Healing
*Listed in Children and Animals | Surrounded by a city of light*

Buenos Aires is the largest city in Argentina, and its Temple of Golden Light is over the river called Rio de la Plata. In the first foundation of settlers, Pedro de Mendoza called the city Holy Mary of the Fair Winds. So typically, in keeping with the energy of this lovely city, Mother Mary herself oversees this temple, along with Archangel Raphael and his legions of angels. Also surrounded by the rainbow angels, this is a Temple of Golden Light that holds a very high vibration of angelic energy.

St Francis of Assisi connects with this temple, and as it is an animal healing temple, you can ask in prayer for healing for your or someone else's animal. Inside is a special sanctuary purely for the healing of animals. Healing sound therapy angels reside here and work in a special healing sanctuary, helping all those in need. Healing with sound vibration as well as colour vibration will be the healing modalities of the future.

There is also a place where counselling is held (in one's sleep-state) to help people with emotional problems. Everyone who visits this temple with a disharmony can be healed. One can be cleared, cleansed, and restored to a balanced energy just by meditating upon this temple.

## 68. Havana, Cuba: Temple of Hearts
*Listed in Healing*

Havana is the capital of Cuba, the largest island in the Caribbean. The Havana Temple of Golden Light looks like a huge mansion or country house which is in three sections. Archangel Metaziel himself oversees this medium-sized temple, along with his legions of rainbow angels.

In this Temple of Hearts, your heart will be developed, cleared, and cleansed. We have three heart chakras: the heart chakra, higher heart chakra, and cosmic heart chakra. This temple will help you develop your heart chakra centres as well as raise your vibration. You will be helped to clear your heart centre, and this sometimes takes special work, as forgiveness for your own actions and for others' actions towards you will need to be addressed.

Please be mindful when connecting to this Temple of Golden Light, as positive shifts in your life will take place whether you ask for this or not. You will begin to learn about unconditional love and how love surpasses everything. To some, this seems so difficult, and yet it is so very easy. As human beings, we always seem to have to complicate things. Often, it is only when we suffer physically, emotionally, and mentally, or when we seem to have lost everything or someone, that we surrender to God/Goddess.

Please know that God is love, and try to find love in your everyday life. We all have our own stuff going on within our own life, and a smile can lift the spirits of those around you, so do not judge others or criticise, as you do not know what they have been through to get where they are now. Remember the mirror reflection: what is going on around you can reflect you in some way, and also you can reflect other people around you.

## 69. San José, Costa Rica: Temple of the Heart Two

San José, meaning St Joseph, is the capital of Costa Rica. It is named in honour of Joseph of Nazareth, who was chosen as the parish saint after the Spanish immigration due to Christopher Columbus discovering the country. San José lies in the torrid zone and is in a tropical rainforest. The Temple of Golden Light is in the etheric towards the back of the city, in front of the mountains.

This temple is overseen directly by Lathinda, goddess of golden light. She is goddess of another planet and two star systems in another universe. Lathinda is an aspect of the Divine Mother, having total understanding and compassion. She loves all humanity and spreads golden light around the world.

The temple connects to Mother Earth's heart centre. It is a grounded earthy temple. Outside, at the back of the temple, there is a beautiful garden filled with flowers and trees that talk to you and come alive. An image like this was created in the film *Avatar*. The flowers are colourful and like fireworks. It is a happy temple where you will learn happiness as opposed to being miserable. You will learn to understand and appreciate the little things in life and how to see the beauty in others as well as yourself.

This is a very comforting, lovely, homely, cosy temple, giving a strong feeling of being loved and fully looked after. Sacred ceremonies are held here respecting the Divine Mother and Mother Earth. This temple will take you back to basics and community living. All is oneness, everyone and everything; all are of the one energy, the root of love, connecting to the heart of God/Goddess and to source. You will learn to trust, believe, and have faith in God/Goddess. Always believe something wonderful is about to happen.

## 70. Honduras: Temple of Solace
*Listed in Children and Animals*

This is another earthy, grounding Temple of Golden Light and is partly suspended in water. It is situated in the etheric of Puerto Castilla on the northern coast of Honduras. Honduras was home to several important Meso-American cultures, most notably the Maya, prior to being conquered by Spain in the sixteenth century. The Maya flourished here for hundreds of years.

Many children of a very high vibration work within this temple, healing other children as well as adults. As you enter, you will sense a feeling of love and peace, and you will be dazzled by the bright light. You will be accompanied by Christed energy and surrounded by the rainbow angels that heal all chakras.

This is a temple of enlightenment and empowerment—a temple that will help people change in a faster time than some of the other temples. Within the temple grounds in the etheric are many lovely gardens filled with the most beautiful flowers and plants of rare abundance.

## 71. Mexico City, Mexico: Temple of Comfort Two

Mexico City is located in the Valley of Mexico. It was created by the Mexica people, later known as the Aztecs, in 1325. The city was the capital of the Aztec empire. Its temple is a sanctuary of safety, peace, comfort, and joy in the etheric over the centre of the city above the Metropolitan Cathedral.

The Mexico City temple is surrounded by rainbow angels and filled with love of the Divine Mother. It has been placed here to bring light to the city. It is a huge beacon of light for thousands of miles around it as it connects to the grid of all 144 Temples of Golden Light. The light of the other temples currently holds this temple up, but one day soon the temple will be able to hold itself up in the light.

This city will move from turmoil to tranquillity in the very near future. It is as if God's eye is watching this city closely to remove any negativity that is there. So if you have a moment, please send light to this city. Thank you in advance for your help.

The temple is very large, with many golden corridors leading to golden doors opening to spaces for meditation and contemplation. Meditation represents loving kindness. This temple also facilitates rescuing souls that have departed but have not gone over to the other side, to the spiritual realms of existence. When people pass over to the other side, the light usually only comes down for about thirty days, unless there is an agreement that someone would like to stay longer. If souls do not move towards the light, they remain earthbound and need a light worker to create a bridge of light to help them over to the other side. This is called *soul rescue.*

## Canada

The following are the six Canadian Temples of Golden Light:

72. Ontario
73. Quebec
74. Lake Winnipeg, Manitoba
75. Vancouver

76. Great Bear Lake, Northwest Territories
77. Amundsen Gulf, Northwest Territories

## 72. Ontario: Temple of Cleansing

Niagara Falls is the collective name for three waterfalls that straddle the international border between Canada and the United States, specifically the province of Ontario and the state of New York. The three waterfalls are Horseshoe Falls, American Falls, and Bridal Veil Falls, which is the smallest of the three waterfalls and is located on the American side.

The Ontario Temple of Golden Light lies in the etheric very close to Niagara Falls, over water on the Canadian side near Goat Island. It is a very large temple of meditation and contemplation, of stillness and silence, with a different energy from many of the other temples. It connects to Mother Earth's heart centre and to the mountains, valleys, hills, lakes, and oceans.

The temple has tall columns inside and appears to be very simple and crystalline. The energy of this temple resembles the feeling of being in the middle of nowhere. It has a transparency about it—as if it has no beginning or end, as if there is no doorway in or out but you know it is there. The temple helps people to release and clear stored emotional energy. This temple is filled with the energy of Christ and the Divine Mother, and you will also be aware of the energy of dolphins and whales. To connect with this temple, you simply need to set the intention and you are here.

The temple connects to the energy of the Amish and Mennonite communities of people. Founded upon the religious teachings of the early Christian Church, the Mennonite faith is generally thought to have begun in 1525 in Zurich, Switzerland. The Amish also generated from Switzerland around 1693.

## 73. Quebec: Temple of Home

This temple is in the etheric of Happy Valley–Goose Bay, Labrador, Quebec. The Aboriginal peoples of Labrador include the Northern

Inuit of Nunatsiavut, the Southern Inuit-Metis of Nunatukavut, and the Innu.

A bigger Temple of Golden Light, this is an earthy temple which is exceptionally peaceful and still—very homely, cosy, and welcoming. If you have a problem, you can talk through your concerns here and always get help. You can come here and just be and learn to live in the moment. You can de-stress and be at one with Mother Earth. The affirmation is 'I am safe here.'

There are individual rooms where one can meditate and be welcomed by many counsellors and other teams of people offering help where needed. You will learn how to have fun in life and not be so serious. The temple has Divine Mother energy and is surrounded by rainbow angels. When you meditate on this temple, you will be aware of rainbow lights, as if you are seeing the Arctic's northern lights of many rainbow colours.

## 74. Lake Winnipeg, Manitoba: Temple of Stillness

The temple is in the etheric very close to the water over the northern part of Lake Winnipeg, a large lake in Manitoba, Canada, with its southern tip about 55 kilometres (34 miles) north of the city of Winnipeg. It is the largest lake within the borders of southern Canada. Lake Winnipeg and Lake Manitoba are remnants of prehistoric glacial Lake Agassiz. The lake is elongated in shape and is 416 kilometres (258 miles) from north to south.

The Manitoba Temple of Golden Light will take you back to basics. Be prepared to ask questions when connecting to this temple, because your questions will receive answers. You will gain knowledge of the circle of life. You will have a feeling of how beautiful nature is and how wonderful life is, and can be, and should be. Inside this temple, you can receive an appreciation of much in your life for you to be proud of and learn about the history of the world.

Connecting to Native American energy and the energy of the owls, this temple is so very peaceful. Rainbow angels surround all of the Temples of Golden Light. In this temple, on the highest level, you will connect directly to their energy.

## 75. Vancouver: Temple of Rainbow Angels
*Listed in Children and Animals*

This is a smaller Temple of Golden Light in the etheric near the Rocky Mountains over a quiet area of Vancouver. It is a churchlike temple with a beautiful stained glass window in the main hall and is more of a place of worship than other temples. This temple is for prayer, forgiveness, and compassion, as well as peace. It is a lovely animal healing temple of happiness and calm.

Inside is a rainbow angel healing school, a sanctuary of love and light where you will feel showered with their healing energy from the moment you enter. Rainbow angels heal all chakras together, and as many chakras work in twos, if one chakra is affected, then another will also be. It is important to heal all of the chakra systems to be complete and whole.

All animals have chakras, and they also have souls. They are looked after by a deva in charge of that particular animal group of souls. Animals are born here and come from their own planets to experience life. They are here to give love, help, and comfort to adults, children, and other animals.

You may like to meditate upon this temple when you feel you need complete peace. Visiting this temple is rather like visiting a retreat where you can switch off and rest. This is a high-energetic temple overseen by St Francis of Assisi, Jesus Christ, and the Divine Mother. It is surrounded by rainbow angels.

## 76. Great Bear Lake, Northwest Territories: Temple of Greatness

This Temple of Golden Light is in the etheric over Great Bear Lake in the Northwest Territories. Great Bear Lake is the largest lake in Canada. Denesuline is the language spoken by the Chipewyan people of Northwest Canada, the Aboriginal people of this area. It is part of the glacial Lake McConnell in the preglacial valleys reshaped by erosional ice during the Pleistocene. Great Bear Lake is covered with ice from November to July. I hope this gives you some idea of the energy that is beneath the temple but is also felt within the temple.

This is a peaceful temple with very still energy which is overseen by the Divine Mother and surrounded by lovely rainbow angels. There is a strong sense of hands of love and friendship, old and new, joined together across the water and united by God/Goddess. As well as the energy of water, you can feel and sense the energy of trees and of owls and eagles. Spiritual talks are given on how to live in unity instead of separation, regarding evaluation of life and what is important for survival, acknowledging we are one. You come here to learn and have a reality check about earth and the world we live in. You will be given tools to live in peace and harmony by connecting with this temple.

## 77. Amundsen Gulf, Northwest Territories: Temple of Radiance

Amundsen Gulf is located in the Canadian Northwest Territories between Banks Island, Victoria Island, and the mainland. The gulf is at the western end of the famous Northwest Passage, a route from the Atlantic Ocean to the Pacific. The entire gulf is in the Arctic tundra climate region. Beluga whales, seals, Arctic char, cod, and even salmon use the waters of the gulf.

The Amundsen Gulf temple is a small but very powerful Temple of Golden Light. The radiance of this temple covers the area for miles around northern Canada. It is literally a ball of golden light surrounded by rainbow angels connected to source. It is over water, bringing more peace and quiet to an already peaceful place.

This temple is holding the light for this area, like a few other Temples of Golden Light are doing for their particular part of our planet. In effect, certain temples are holding other temples up in the light while our planet shifts and changes. When Mother Earth has shifted, things will settle down, and the light will be distributed evenly.

# Chapter 5

## *Australasia and Oceanic*

I have been to Australia many times, as my eldest daughter lives in Perth. It is a beautiful country with contrasting scenery. On our last trip to visit my daughter, son-in-law, and three wonderful grandchildren, we took a short break to visit Margaret River, where one of the temples is situated. It is a lovely small town in the midst of vineyards. It is about the size of Glastonbury in England, with one main street through it.

This whole area is well known as a wine region and has a very high reputation worldwide for its produce. Less well known is the fact that under this area, in and around the town, are many crystal caves, which greatly enhance the atmosphere. Anyone who is sensitive can feel the crystalline energy coming up from beneath the ground around Margaret River and the surrounding area. You would be amazed by the tranquillity, peace, and calm of the place. This is why a Temple of Golden Light has been placed in the etheric directly above the centre of town.

These temples are divine places to visit and rest and are invitations directing people to their divine home. They help people remove the veil of attachment that lies over the heart. Margaret River is the kind of place where you would quite happily sit upon the earth under the sun during the day or gaze languidly at the moon and stars at night. I have never experienced such peace before.

Our adventures continued with a lovely day at Gnarabup Beach (an Aboriginal name), which has gorgeous sandy shores. I decided to go for a dip in the ocean, and I could feel the energy of one of the Oceanic temples situated in the Indian Ocean off the coast of Rockingham in Perth. This is a temple connected to the energy of the dolphins that has tremendous healing power on the emotions.

During this same trip, we also had time to visit Sydney. I was surprised by the energy of this city, as it was not nearly as light as Perth, but at the same time it felt earthier. When we arrived, we were happy to be upgraded to a nicer, more spacious room overlooking the Darling Harbour. This was something that we had not asked for or even expected.

Another happy synchronicity was that unbeknown to us, we had chosen to stay at the only time of year when for one week, there were firework displays each night, and we were delighted by this. After being in Sydney for just a day, I started to feel low. Being a clairvoyant, I kept seeing what looked like a huge clam seashell opening and closing slowly. I told my husband about this, as I could not understand why I was feeling this way. He put it down to the fact that we had been busy on our trip to Australia, but I felt there was more to it than this.

When we returned to Perth, we visited a medium/clairvoyant called Jeanette. She knew I had been to Sydney and proceeded to explain to me what had happened. Apparently, there is a portal of light over Sydney, but the portal had become so dim and mucky that it had become partially blocked, stopping some light from shining down onto the city.

Whilst I was in Sydney, I connected to the Temple of Golden Light over the city, and as I did so, light filtered through from the temple, and the portal shone brightly again. My previous feelings of sadness were because I was picking up on much of the negativity hanging over the city. Jeanette told me that I had helped the people of Sydney and the surrounding areas (including all the light workers) by clearing the portal so that the light could shine freely from the portal and the Temple of Golden Light in the etheric overhead. I was truly thankful to Jeanette for this information.

During our stay in Sydney, we visited the Blue Mountains just outside the city, where another Temple of Golden Light is situated. We also spoke to a number of Aborigines and found them to be lovely people with big hearts who feel so proud of their heritage.

## Australasia

The following are the seven Temples of Golden Light in Australasia, including New Zealand and Fiji:

78. Uluru, Australia
79. Margaret River, Perth, Australia
80. Brisbane, Gold Coast, Australia
81. Cairns, Australia
82. Sydney, Australia
83. South Island, New Zealand
84. Suva, Fiji

### 78. Uluru, Australia: Temple of the Star People *Listed in Main Temples and in Healing | Surrounded by a city of light*

Uluru is a very large temple, the Aboriginal star temple, holding a beautiful energy of bright light surrounded by a city of light. It is filled with beings of light, natural medicinal plants, and nature. On top of the temple is a massive star beaming outwards to other star systems. Natural healing remedies are much better for our bodies, as they have no side effects. You will learn how to respect the earth's energy and respect other people, gaining qualities of peace, virtue, and honour.

Uluru is right under the Milky Way star system. The roof of the temple in the etheric is open so that you can see the wonderful sky with plentiful stars to view. This temple is on a ley line connected to the serpent energy, as Uluru is considered one of the great wonders of the world. It is a sacred part of Aboriginal creation mythology or dreamtime, which is of great cultural significance to the Aboriginal people of the area.

### 79. Margaret River, Perth, Australia: Temple of Crystalline Energy *Listed in Healing and in Meditation and Relaxation | Surrounded by a city of light*

Margaret River is a town in the southwest of Western Australia, located in the valley of the eponymous Margaret River about 172 miles south of Perth, the state capital. It is known for its wine region. In and around Margaret River, there are hundreds of crystal caves, of which six are open to the public. The earth above these caves is extremely special in energy. Walking around the town of Margaret River, you are aware of the crystalline energy moving up through the earth, and this energy is transmitted to the Temple of Golden Light in the etheric above.

This is a lovely, cleansing, clearing, healing temple which holds powerful Aboriginal energy linking the Australian temples of Uluru, Cairns, Gold Coast, Sydney, and Margaret River. It is situated on many levels, starting with crystalline energy, Aboriginal energy, and then moving up higher to a very pure angelic energy. Goddess Lathinda oversees this temple personally. Inside, there is a powerful healing sanctuary holding the energy of earth crystals. A healing retreat is a welcome relief from everyday life and concerns. Meditate upon this temple when you want to rejuvenate your energy.

## 80. Brisbane, Gold Coast, Australia: Temple of the Inner Child

The Brisbane temple is a happy place filled with sunshine, laughter, and joy. There is an attitude that nothing is impossible and the sky really is the limit—and then the universe. Follow your dreams and wishes and play. Have fun on your journey through life. Do not be sad, be happy. It is all about you. Be who you are; play, play, and play; and remember to smile. Be proud to be you, and now step into your power. Love and be loved. All is well.

This temple is about helping people with inner-child work, which is about singing, drawing, laughing, playing, and anything else you can think of to make you happy. Do that something that you have wanted to do for a long time. Go on that holiday. You may like to have a taste of sea, sand, and sunshine, or climb that mountain. Do that course of learning—do whatever it may be—because life is too short. Just get on with it. Release all your negativity. Let it go. Do not walk around carrying old heavy baggage; it will do you no good in the long run. We are here to be happy, not sad.

This is a smaller earthy temple in the etheric on the outskirts of Brisbane, connecting to all the other Australian Temples of Golden

Light that then connect to the rest of the 144 Goddess Temples of Golden Light. The temple holds the energy of the Aboriginal people who were experts in the healing of all complaints with traditional plants and herbs. The temple is surrounded by rainbow angels.

## 81. Cairns, Australia: Temple of Golden Light Two
*Listed in Children and Animals*

This is another very Aboriginal temple with the pure energy of Australia. You will learn about the Aborigines and how they used to live. It is a small but powerful animal healing temple of love connecting to St Francis of Assisi. Inside is a spiralling staircase around which animals are treated with gentleness, respect, and compassion, helping them to recover from disharmony, whether that is from ill health or unkind treatment by humans. There is a crystal healing sanctuary for animals that need more specific healing. Animals have as much right as we do to live without fear, in good health.

This temple is worth visiting even if you do not have an animal in need. The spiral staircase takes those who are ready up to the higher planes of existence. It is the gentle way to the heavenly planes, connecting to the star systems Pleiades, Sirius, and Andromeda. This temple connects to all other beings within the universe, including the Hathors from Venus, the golden beings of light, and the star beings aligning with the Rainbow Star Fleet and the Rainbow Alliance, overseen by Commander Ashtar.

## 82. Sydney, Australia: Temple of Golden Peace
*Listed in Children and Animals | Surrounded by a city of light*

The Sydney Temple of Golden Light is in the etheric in front of the Blue Mountains, which are known for their Aboriginal connection. It is on a ley line that is connected to serpent energy. I have given this temple the name of Golden Peace as it is in such a peaceful area, a two-hour drive from the city.

The Blue Mountains are a mountainous region in New South Wales geographically situated in the central parts of the Sydney basin.

In the mountains are the Three Sisters, made of sandstone rock, one of the region's best-known attractions. The Sydney Temple of Golden Light lies in the etheric next to the Three Sisters rock formation.

The temple is overseen by the ascended master Paul the Venetian and surrounded by rainbow angels and then by a city of light. It is a very large temple and has the power to radiate its light for thousands of miles. Some of the larger temples can do this. The light radiates out over the Pacific Ocean up to the coast of New Zealand and some of its mainland.

This golden temple has a large star on top and six domed minaret roofs. Inside the main hall is a giant golden pyramid used to harness the energy of the universe, all held inside this huge temple. There is a large pink rose quartz crystal healing those within, and a healing sanctuary with the energy of Quan Yin, the female Buddha, to help anyone heal and move on after cleansing and clearing any negative energy. Sound healing sessions are also held here regularly. This temple is for the healing of children as well as adults and animals.

This temple will appeal to those who are truth-seekers and those who thirst for knowledge, especially of design, culture, natural medicine, healing, technology, and the spiritual. The garden of this temple is beautiful, with an enormous waterfall infused with colour and surrounded by trees of different energies.

## 83. South Island, New Zealand: Temple of Holding Hands

The South Island is the larger of the two major islands of New Zealand. Many earthquakes have hit South Island; the last time was 13 June 2011. Christchurch was rocked by a 5.7 magnitude quake followed by a 6.3 quake, and the city was evacuated, as it lies on a fault line.

This is a community temple, exuding the Maori energy only known to New Zealand. It is a temple of friendship and of supporting each other, of holding hands around the globe and across the water. It is very much about trust and how good people can be when they are caring and sharing. People help each other here, and you can learn how to do that too.

Practicing soul rescue is also done in this temple—that is, rescuing trapped souls and taking them over the bridge of light to the spirit world so that they are no longer stuck. It is a small, simple temple filled with the female energy of Goddess Jacinta, who oversees the temple.

It is also earthy, which is particularly apt, as New Zealand is known as Middle Earth because of its unspoiled nature, hills, valleys, mountains, and lakes. There is a lovely energy of stillness and silence. Inside is a sound therapy healing sanctuary surrounded by unicorns and rainbow angels. It is a wonderful Temple of Golden Light to connect to, and it reaches right up and out into the stars.

## 84. Suva, Fiji: Temple of Stars

Suva, the capital of Fiji, is the largest and most cosmopolitan city in the South Pacific. It is a harbour city built on a peninsula reaching out into the sea. The Temple of Golden Light is high in the etheric over the harbour of the city.

This temple is particularly high up the etheric, and it is here to help you learn about our universe. The Suva Temple of Golden Light is overseen by Archangel Gabriel. It holds the energy of Jesus Christ and connects to the star people. It is a happy temple with a carnival atmosphere that is uplifting and joyous.

The temple has large crystalline domed roofs that shimmer and sparkle with white light. Inside is a crystal waterfall reflecting all the colours of the rainbow. There are white healing rooms filled with rainbow-coloured lights. The temple is very light, and to some people this white light may be too much, as it is so very bright. Inside, there are sculptures of the goddesses who oversee the 144 Temples of Golden Light: Lady Nada, Jacinta, and the cosmic goddess Lathinda, whose energy fills the temple with love, honesty, integrity, and sincerity.

## Oceanic

I have channelled twelve Oceanic Temples of Golden Light which have been carefully positioned around the globe, connected to each other as a grid of healing energy to help humanity and Mother Earth. Together, they link to the other 132 temples. Oceanic Temples of Golden Light have a different energy from the rest of the temples in that they are overseen by Poseidon, the god of the oceans and rivers and king of the seas and waters. They strongly connect to the energy of the dolphins and whales, plus many other sea creatures, all here sharing our planet with us.

As water covers approximately two-thirds of our planet, it makes sense that some of the temples have been placed beneath the oceans, so that the whole of our planet is covered by a grid of Temples of Golden Light and no area is excluded. At this time of awakening, we need to cover the whole of our planet as well as the oceans. The temples under the water are large and powerful and can radiate light out over very large areas. Having some temples under the ocean acts to balance the temples in the etheric, although only twelve temples are needed for this. They have been strategically placed on certain ley lines around the world.

Where would we be without water? Can you imagine a planet without water? One of the most amazing sights is to see a full moon shining on the ocean at night. It is important to remember that water is very healing. Water is soothing, relaxing, and can heal our emotions. The oceanic temples can heal emotional energy, changing it from negative to positive. A couple of the temples are partly submerged below the oceans and partly visible above, holding the light for the area; these are the Arctic and Atlantic Ocean Two Temples of Golden Light.

The Arctic Oceanic temple is near Spitsbergen, north of the two closest earth temples at Mo i Rana, Norway, and Reykjavik, Iceland. I had an interesting experience in Reykjavik when I visited with a couple of friends a few years ago. My purpose was to anchor more light there, or that's what I thought at that time. This was before I channelled the temples. Clearly now, I realise that I went there to clear the area for the temple to be placed.

When we arrived, everything was fine. We stayed in a lovely hotel. On the third day, we decided to take a trip to the Blue Lagoon, which is a geothermal spa in southwest Iceland, midway between Keflavik airport and Reykjavik. The warm waters are rich in minerals like silica and sulphur, and bathing there is reputed to help people suffering from skin diseases. The Blue Lagoon is also home to a research and development facility which helps find cures for skin ailments using the mineral-rich waters.

We decided to take a swim in the lovely pool there, and I said to my friends, 'Let's anchor some light here.' The energy completely changed within a few moments. The sky went from a pale blue sunny day with people in the pool laughing and having fun to grey and dull, with the wind blowing gustily around everyone. Very soon, it was raining, and people started to leave the pool. Both my friends started to get frightened, but I felt we needed to stay in the water a few minutes longer. Shortly afterwards, we bolted out of the pool, quickly got changed, and went to the cafe for tea and cake. Still reeling from what had happened, we caught the coach back to our hotel, and I fell asleep.

When I awoke, I saw clairvoyantly an avatar named Sai Baba. I had been to his ashram in Puttiparthi near Bangalore in India and knew that he would normally only appear when asked for help. Although I had not asked him for help on this occasion, he showed me what had happened when I anchored the energy in the Blue Lagoon. With my inner vision, I could see a dark goddess with long dark hair rising up from the pool, and I saw that she was very angry because I had disrupted her manipulative, controlling energy, breaking up her hold there. Just as we do not like dark energy, the dark does not like the light. When I anchored light in the area, she was forced to leave that part of the planet.

The rain poured down from the sky all through that evening and the next day, when we were due to fly home. By this time, there was thunder and lightning, and the plane was delayed for three hours. We were stuck on the runway with hailstones hitting the window. My friends were frightened, and I was certainly relieved when the weather improved sufficiently for us to take off and return home. The Temple of Golden Light in the etheric over Reykjavik is now fully functioning and shining brightly down onto the earth and the people of Iceland, helping everyone to feel positive vibrations.

The following are the twelve temples beneath the oceans:

85. Pacific Ocean One, off the Hawaiian Islands, United States
86. Pacific Ocean Two, off La Paz, Bolivia, and Lima, Peru

87. Pacific Ocean Three, off Tokyo, Japan
88. Atlantic Ocean One, off Bermuda, outside the Bermuda Triangle
89. Atlantic Ocean Two, off Cape Verde, Gambia, Africa
90. Atlantic Ocean Three, off Rio de Janeiro, Brazil
91. Indian Ocean One, off Rockingham, Perth, Australia
92. Indian Ocean Two, off Colombo, Sri Lanka
93. Caspian Sea, off Azerbaijan
94. Arctic Ocean, off Spitsbergen north of Norway
95. Mediterranean Sea, off Valencia, Spain
96. English Channel, off Dover, England

## 85. Pacific Ocean One
*Listed in Main Temples | Surrounded by a city of light*

The Pacific Ocean One temple is the largest and the main oceanic temple, and it is in the centre of a city of light. It is situated near the Hawaiian Islands and the west coast of the United States, directly aligning with the Temple of Golden Light in the etheric over San Francisco in California. The temple is filled with the energy of Atlantis and Lemuria, and indeed, it looks like an Atlantis temple. It has seven pillars and seven glass-domed roofs. The energies of Atlantis and Lemuria blend as one energy, giving the temple a very soothing feel. There is the energy of the dolphins, whales, sea turtles, sea lions, elephant seals, seals, porpoises, penguins, and all sea creatures, particularly koi carp, who hold a high place in the sea world, as well as seahorses, shellfish, and starfish.

Of course, water is a very important part of our planet. It represents the ebb and flow of life. We human beings are made up largely of water, and our emotions remind us of this. Important decisions are made at the council meetings held here, and this temple plays an important role in controlling the waters of our planet, as not all of the tectonic plates have moved yet, and when they do, this has to be monitored. The energy of this temple rises up from the depths of the waters within the etheric of our oceans and right out into the universe. This is the seventh largest Temple of Golden Light.

## 86. Pacific Ocean Two
*Surrounded by a city of light*

This temple is situated in the Pacific Ocean near La Paz, Bolivia, and the Temples of Golden Light in Lima and Machu Picchu in Peru. It is surrounded by a city of light. This is a large temple nearly the same size as Pacific Ocean One. It is a beautiful temple filled with the energy of Atlantis and of dolphins, many of whom connect with this temple, along with beautiful seahorses, large and small. Love, beauty, and contentment are the energy of this temple. Inside, you feel as if you are floating or levitating.

In the main hall is a fifteen-sided star. Each point has a meaning that can help you with your inner child. Inside the star is a spherical, clear quartz crystal that enhances the energy of the temple. Your inner child helps you learn to play, as life is not always meant to be serious.

There is a wall of light, pulsating energy around the temple connected to the meridian lines of Mother Earth deep inside the ocean. This then connects to a web of light that forms a further connection to the surrounding Temples of Golden Light. It acts as a monitor, sensing everything that happens and goes on around it.

The temple also has a hall of learning, a place where you can learn about the oceans and sea life. Outside are large pearls that look like pearls of light. If you fancy drifting off to a faraway holiday place, then this is the temple to connect with. You can dream of swimming in an underwater spa, in a coral reef, or inside rainbow tunnel water slides. It is an amazing temple and one well worth visiting during meditation or your sleep-state.

## 87. Pacific Oceanic Three

The third oceanic temple in the Pacific Ocean is near Tokyo, Japan. The nearest earth temple is in the etheric above that city. Pacific Ocean Three is a smaller temple with an unusual shape, and it is dedicated to aquatic life. At the head of the temple are koi carp, which are considered to be higher up on the aquatic scale and have control of other fish. The highest are considered to be the golden koi carp, who have their own intelligence.

Within the temple is a deafening silence, as if you could hear a pin drop. It is quite male in energy and connects to the ancient mermen. There are waterfalls inside that display rainbow colours. The temple holds sacred symbols and key codes of water. When you connect to this temple, these will be downloaded for you to receive. The sacred symbols and key codes will help raise your vibration more quickly and accelerate the ascension process.

This temple represents structure, order, strength, and support within the oceans, and this leads to transformation. It is about authority, hierarchy, and responsibility. We need to understand, acknowledge, and honour the oceans and all ocean life forms.


## 88. Atlantic Ocean One

This oceanic temple is near Bermuda but outside of the Bermuda Triangle in the North Atlantic Ocean. The nearest earth Temple of Golden Light is over Havana, Cuba. Dolphins play a major part within Atlantic Ocean One, as they hold the keys of Atlantis. This is a temple for relaxation and contemplation, and inside, when you visit the main hall for meditation, you will feel a oneness with everything: oceans, earth, mountains, valleys, and sky.

The temple is a gateway to ascension and will bring you into a state of being, a oneness. The actual temple looks rather like a monolith (like a pillar or a monument); it is another unusually shaped Temple of Golden Light, and the main doorway is in the shape of a heart. It is immensely powerful—a very light, bright, and high-vibrational temple. Council meetings with both male and female masters are held here, and decisions are made.

The God Poseidon is able to control the waters around the planet, and this temple is at the epicentre of Poseidon's control. The temple reaches up very high, from the depths of the ocean, up and out into our universe; from there, it connects to the seven universes that surround our own. We really need to know and believe that we are not alone in this universe, let alone other galaxies and universes. The key to this understanding is love.

In the past, there have been negative energies, such as the Greys that abducted people, but they are no longer in our universe. Dark energies are leaving the planet as we lift our vibration. We cannot enter the fifth dimension still holding onto dark energies; they must go.

The temple connects also to the energy of the mer-angels and mermaids, an energy that was here on the planet a long time ago. I believe this planet is much, much older than people realise. We go back way before ancient Egypt, Atlantis, and Lemuria. It is just that our history books are not that old.

## 89. Atlantic Ocean Two

This oceanic temple is situated off the island of Cape Verde near the Gambia, Africa. The nearest temple in the etheric is over Timbuktu in Mali. The Atlantic Ocean Two temple stands out from other oceanic temples because it has a star above it. It reaches far out into our universe, linking to our sun and, via a portal, to many distant galaxies.

The temple is just under the water, not down in the depths of the ocean, and balances the waters around. It is on many levels, primarily working with the energy of whales. There are about eighty different species of whale, part of a group called cetaceans, and they all connect energetically to this temple. The whales' energy feels quite different from any energy we know or even understand. Whales work on a sonic-sound-system energy, linking with each other to convey messages throughout the different oceans. They carry an energetic signature that is important to our oceans.

The temple also holds the energy of what I call humanoid fish beings. They would look strange to us and appear to look like upright beings with fishlike heads who do not speak but are telepathic. As you move through the temple, you can go higher, and at the top is a spaceship platform that lifts up and down when needed. This is certainly a very powerful Temple of Golden Light which can help you deal with issues of relationships, trust, and forgiveness. Connecting to this temple will help you better yourself.

## 90. Atlantic Ocean Three Temple

This very large Temple of Golden Light is in the South Atlantic Ocean, in the middle of the ocean, in line with Rio de Janeiro, Brazil. It is filled with the lovely high-vibrational energy of the dolphins, who are the doorkeepers of the energy from Atlantis. There are eight golden domes on the roof of the temple, and in the middle lies an enormous ice-like sculpture of a dolphin. You can connect with this temple to help you recover from trauma and emotional upheaval and upset, as the calm, soothing, healing energy of the temple will help to heal you.

Reflecting the presence of dolphins, this oceanic temple holds the energy of fun and playfulness and discovering the enjoyment of life. The dolphins would like to communicate with you, as they have much knowledge to give. This is also a place of peace and oneness; the temple is simplistic, exuding a calm and balanced energy filled with the love of God/Goddess for all to connect with. God/Goddess perceives you as an innocent and perfect child of this universe. So take time to connect with this beautiful Temple of Golden Light and to the dolphin energy of peace, calm, balance, fun, playfulness, and knowledge.

## 91. Indian Ocean One
*Listed in Healing*

This is a smaller Temple of Golden Light situated in the Indian Ocean off the coast of Rockingham, Perth, Australia. It is a healing temple connecting to the energy of dolphins and the ancient energy of mermaids and coral reefs. The healing is given on an emotional level, allowing you to de-stress and let go of all energy you no longer need or want, giving you peace, calm, and balance. The temple will transmute all energies that are negative, transforming them into positive qualities.

The Indian Ocean One temple will help you filter and cut through anger and grief quickly, teaching you to deal with the shadows in order to reach the light. Water is an amazing healer and works very well to help heal those with emotional imbalance. The healing from this Temple of Golden Light is vibrational, relaxing, and transformational.

## 92. Indian Ocean Two

This temple is situated in the Indian Ocean off the coast near Colombo, Sri Lanka, east of Singapore and not far from the Maldives. The Temple of Golden Light is huge; it connects not only with the ocean and this universe but with a rainbow bridge to all surrounding universes and multi-universes. An amazing temple of light beneath the ocean, this temple twins with Indian Ocean One. They are strategically placed within a grid to link to the rest of the temples.

There is a slightly different energy in Indian Ocean Two, however, compared to Indian Ocean One. It connects to the dolphins, doorkeepers to Atlantis energy. However, there is also a feeling of Egyptian energy here. The temple has many levels. As you enter, you can feel a multifaceted crystalline energy—the energy of sapphires and diamonds. The temple is connected to the crystalline grid, and these crystals are used to cleanse you. Ceremonies take place here for purification of your mind, body, and spirit. This will help you to shift in consciousness.

The energy of this temple is powerful enough to connect with this universe and the universes beyond. The temple has a docking station, and I have been shown clairvoyantly cryogenic pods similar in appearance to cocoons of light. Time capsules go in and out of the cryogenic pods connecting to other universes.

The multidimensional nature of this temple will have different meanings from one person to the next, depending on what vibration you connect on. It is essentially an ascension temple and will help you evolve and progress spiritually. This will help you rebirth and take you to the next level in your life, enhancing your creativity and imagination. When you connect with this Temple of Golden Light, you will realise that there are infinite, endless possibilities in life.

## 93. Caspian Sea

This is a smaller, simplistic temple which looks quite unusual and connects purely to the waters within the Caspian Sea. The Caspian Sea oceanic temple is situated in the middle of the surrounding countries of Azerbaijan, Turkmenistan, Kazakhstan, and Russia. It is a very calm, serene, silent, yet uplifting Temple of Golden Light.

The Caspian Sea on its own is not able to flow with the rest of the world's oceans, so it has a different energy about it. The temple here aligns to the planet Saturn, which is known as a spiritual academic school in the centre of our solar system and as a rainbow bridge to conscious reawakening. Outside the temple, you are aware of waves of pulsating energy, which you cannot hear but are able to feel. The energy is feminine, as it connects to the mother-of-pearl sea energy. Inside, there is a hushed silence, a knowing that source light energy is here within the temple.

You will find yourself sitting in one of three circular halls for meditation and healing. Here you have no past or future. You are sitting in the *now* moment and not going anywhere. You will simply just be. Divine clarity will be yours as you see the light of all that there is and all that there will be. You will feel very relaxed, as if you are floating in water, and this temple will release stress from you immediately when you connect to it. If needed, the temple will heal you and repair any damage to your aura.

All of the Temples of Golden Light aid relaxation, and some do so more than others. I believe that this temple is particularly good at helping to encourage contemplation and restfulness. When you connect to this temple, it will give you the peace and clarity you require to solve any problem or concern. Other Temples of Golden Light specialise in healing emotions, heart issues, and physical body healing.

## 94. Arctic Ocean

The Artic Ocean Temple of Golden Light is situated north of Spitsbergen, and the nearest temples are Mo i Rana, Norway, and Reykjavik, Iceland. It is a temple of happiness and humour that is all about having fun. The energy here is of whales, particularly that of orca whales, as well as sea lions, seals, penguins. and Arctic birds. Obviously, being near the North Pole, it also holds the energy of the wonderful polar bears.

The temple looks like a snow castle, but it has actually been created with crystalline energy. It has a dual purpose above and beneath the Arctic Ocean: it acts to balance the ocean in this particular part of the planet, yet because it has been placed in the etheric near the earth, you can feel the energy of frozen ice and snow. This enhances the feeling of pure peace when connecting with this Temple of Golden Light, with the sense of peace and silence that exists after it has been snowing.

This is a temple of pivotal importance. It acts as a conduit to help balance the waters and temples in this area. If you wish to have clarity on a subject or a decision in your life, please do connect with this temple. Answers to prayers will be given to you. If you wish to have fun and happiness in your life, it is worth connecting with this light-hearted Temple of Golden Light.

## 95. Mediterranean Sea
*Surrounded by a city of light*

The Mediterranean Sea Temple of Golden Light is between the coast of Valencia and Palma, Majorca, in Spain. An enormous and busy temple surrounded by an amazing city of light, it looks like New York but in another dimension. Like all Temples of Golden Light, it is filled with source light, and this one is full of the energy of dolphins, Atlantis, and mermaids. It connects to all the tectonic plates that lie beneath the oceans, helping them to move when necessary, gently and naturally, without causing imbalance.

The galactic council sits here, makes very important planetary decisions, and connects to the universe. Decisions are made on a universal level benefiting all planets and star systems. Inside are two very large pyramids that give power to the temple. Rainbow light from source filters through the pyramids, shining on all those below. It is a temple that is more for the ascended masters of this world, known and unknown. When important masters are here, the temple is cloaked. You will not know it is there. Access is restricted; you must hold a higher quotient of light, be an ascended master, and hold the sacred key codes and symbols.

The temple will give solutions to many questions and is a sanctuary for those who regularly come to visit. It is a wonderful place for gaining clarity and a clear vision of what you would like to create and hold a vision for, as well as to heal any residual negative energy from issues garnered in this life or any past life before ascension. If this is the right Temple of Golden Light for you, you will know. This temple in the Mediterranean Sea is very important and plays a crucial role within the Temples of Golden Light.

## 96. English Channel

The English Channel Temple of Golden Light is a very small golden nugget of a temple situated off Dover in England. The nearest Temple of Golden Light is Amsterdam, Holland. It is quite different-looking from some of the other Temples of Golden Light.

This temple is a little gem—a passport-style border-control temple which gives you tourist information on all the oceanic Temples of Golden Light. It works like a compass. It is very orderly and has twenty-one docking stations, as various energies are constantly being downloaded from other oceanic temples. Put simply, this temple holds a computer with all the information on the other oceanic temples. If you do not know which to visit through meditation or your sleep-state, please connect to this Temple of Golden Light first. You will then be directed to whichever oceanic temple your vibration is best suited to for healing of your mind, emotions or physical body, or simply for meditation, relaxation, and mindfulness.

The English Channel temple will specifically direct you to oceanic temples, unlike the Istanbul Temple of Golden Light, which directs you to any of the other 143 temples if you are unsure which to visit. Also within this temple in the English Channel is a small teaching centre in which you will learn about the seven universal laws. You will learn how to create abundance and the law of potentiality; how to manifest what you desire by intention; the law of giving and receiving; the law of karma, or cause and effect; the law of least effort; and the law of detachment and the purpose of your life.

# Chapter 6

## *Asia*

I was lucky enough to travel to Agra and Bangalore in India and Beijing in China, where some of the temples have been placed in the etheric of earth. During the trip, I visited the Taj Mahal, built by Prince Jahaan for his wife, Mumtaz, whom I believe was a past-life reincarnation of Princess Diana. This is why I believe Princess Diana visited the Taj Mahal when she was feeling alone and lonely. To me, this building is such a tribute and embodiment of love, and I believe Diana went there simply because she wanted to be loved. I was touched by the photograph of her sitting on the seat in front of the Taj Mahal which is now known as the 'Diana seat', and when I visited, my husband and I had a similar photograph of us taken.

I believe another past life of Diana's was as Florence Nightingale, but that is a whole other story. Princess Diana is connected to all the Temples of Golden Light, especially the children's temples.

Another important location is in a village called Puttiparthi, a two-hour drive from Bangalore. Here is the ashram of Bhagavan Sri Sathya Sai Baba, a very important spiritual teacher. Sai Baba has now left his physical body, but I had the good fortune to meet him three times in the years before he passed over. On one visit, I watched as he actually manifested *vibuti* on the arm of a lady who was sitting in a wheelchair near me. *Vibuti* is sacred ash, and if it is placed on you, it is known to heal the part of the physical body that needs healing. As I watched, *vibuti* just poured out of his hand, which was such an intense experience—I've never forgotten what I saw him do. Sai Baba is coming back for his third incarnation as Prema Baba, and apparently, he will look like Jesus. His first incarnation was as Shirdi Baba.

My visit to Beijing, however, was not so pleasant. After safely arriving and finding our hotel, we signed in and went up to our room. On the first night, I saw dark images of what seemed to be earthbound souls in our room, which reminded me of an old film called *Ghost*. I spent all night clearing the room and sending these stuck souls over to the light. At first, they did not want to pass over, but I created a bridge of light with the help of my angels and earth guides and slowly, they passed over. This is something I have been able to do for many years.

When I was in Agra, Bangalore, and Beijing, I connected with their Temples of Golden Light through meditation. Each time, I felt a surge of energy pass through me, which I knew instinctively meant that these temples were now activated. I saw light from source entering into the temples from above. It was amazing to see, with the whole of each temple lit up and shining with golden light.

## India, Pakistan, and the Himalayas

The following are the ten Temples of Golden Light in India, Pakistan, and the Himalayas:

97.  Agra, India
98.  Amritsar, India
99.  Kolkata, India
100. Bangalore, India
101. Sri Lanka
102. Lahore, Pakistan
103. Hyderabad, Pakistan
104. Kathmandu, Nepal
105. Lhasa, Tibet
106. Thimphu, Bhutan

## 97. Agra, India: Temple of Golden Radiance
*Listed in Main Temples and in Healing | Surrounded by a city of light*

Agra's is a very large Temple of Golden Light, surrounded by a city of light, situated in the etheric close to the Taj Mahal. It is a splendid, ornate, decorative, and palatial temple. Inside are many diamond-coloured crystals. The temple connects to the Indian gods/goddesses Brahma, Shiva, Vishnu, Krishna, Ganesh, Lakshmi, Kali, and many more, making it a beautiful, sacred temple.

It is also a busy temple, with many healing sanctuaries and prayer rooms. Your soul can fragment over many lifetimes as a result of difficult situations, such as dying in shock. This temple has a special sanctuary that specialises in bringing your fragments back together and making you whole again. In the centre is a golden lotus flower that connects to source light. It acts as a vortex of energy, giving out a wonderful golden radiance that covers much of northern India, clearing and cleansing the earth below. Everyone wears white when entering this temple.

## 98. Amritsar, India: Temple of Gold
*Surrounded by a city of light*

This is a beautiful temple in the etheric close to the Golden Temple of Amritsar. Known as the Abode of God or the Temple of God, this is the central place of worship for Sikhism.

The Amritsar Temple of Golden Light is a very welcoming place for families and friends, respecting and valuing all other religions. It is a temple of prayer, forgiveness, and fairness, honouring all life, and the Divine Mother oversees it. The temple is a beacon of light, with a sense of busy cleansing and healing energy, a place of sharing all that one has equally among one's families, friends, and humanity.

As you arrive, there is a waterfall to cleanse your energies. The front door to the temple is in the shape of a heart, as this temple will touch your heart and release any stuck energy in your heart centre. It will also heal emotional issues and may heal physical body disharmonies.

Elephants connect with this temple, removing any obstacles that may be in your way or are blocking you from achieving your goal or dreams. This is a beautiful temple of considerable golden light, so ask and you will receive much, so long as your heart is pure. Surrounded by rainbow angels of love, this is a colourful, vibrant temple of happiness, joy, and compassion.

On earth, the Sikh Golden Temple, located in the city of Amritsar in the state of Punjab, is a place of great beauty and sublime peacefulness. It stands in the centre of a lake of fresh, clear, reflective water. The lake is fed by the River Ravi and is said by some to originate from the Ganges River. Originally a small lake in the midst of a quiet forest, the site has been a meditation retreat for wandering sages and gurus for hundreds of years. The Buddha is known to have spent time at this place in contemplation.

Two thousand years ago, after Buddha's time, another philosopher-saint came to live and meditate by the peaceful lake. This was Guru Nanak (in 1469–1539), the founder of the Sikh religion. After the passing of Guru Nanak, his disciples continued to frequent the site and it became the primary sacred site of the Sikhs. During the leadership of the fifth Guru (Arjan, from 1581-1606), the Temple of God was built of white marble overlaid with genuine gold leaf.

## 99. Kolkata, India: Temple of Love
*Listed in Children and Animals*

Previously known as Calcutta, Kolkata is India's third largest city and a major port. Mother Teresa, who is now a saint, oversees the Kolkata Temple of Golden Light herself with her caring, loving light and Christed energy. Blessed Teresa of Calcutta, commonly known as Mother Teresa, was a Roman Catholic religious sister and missionary who lived most of her life in India, helping the poorest of the poor. Her involvement with this temple makes it particularly special amongst the eighteen children's healing Temples of Golden Light.

This small temple is filled with the energy and love of Jesus Christ and the Divine Mother and with much unconditional love. It is white and gold, with three domed roofs. Inside is a university for young people, a place of learning and caring for others. This temple specialises in the healing of children. All children are innocent and can be healed.

## 100. Bangalore, India: Temple of the Blessed
*Listed in Meditation and Relaxation | Surrounded by a city of light*

Bangalore is officially known as Bengaluru and is the capital of the South Indian state of Karnataka. The Bangalore Temple of Golden Light is a large temple in the etheric towards the north of Bangalore. It aligns to the ashram of Swami Sathya Sai Baba, also known as Shirdi Baba, which is in Puttiparthi, in the area of India called Andhra Pradesh. As well as connecting to Sai Baba, it connects with Babaji and with Mahatma Gandhi, who was a spiritual and political leader. Mahatma Gandhi aligns to all of the Temples of Golden Light, particularly to the Indian temples and the temples surrounded by cities of light, where he teaches non-violence.

The Bangalore temple also links with Shiva, Vishnu, Brahma, Krishna, Rama, Kali, Durga, Shakti, Lakshmi, Lord Ganesh, and many other Indian gods and goddesses. The energy of the temple reverberates outwards, and you can feel this energy in the etheric over the centre of Bangalore, blessing the city.

This golden temple holds immense power and is extremely peaceful and calm. It is filled with the scent of jasmine flowers, and as you enter, you are given a garland of these flowers as a gift. It is an opulent, ornate temple, filled with many gold statues of the Indian gods and goddesses. You will be aware of the energy of the elephants sending you love from within this temple. It is a temple of prayer/ bhajans sharing and of healing, specialising in healing babies, children of all ages, and adults. The healing takes place in the inner temple's healing sanctuary.

The temple is filled with the love of the Divine Mother and is surrounded by seraphim and rainbow angels. Outside is a soothing lake. When you connect, you will feel the energy of the lake's calming waters.

## 101. Sri Lanka: Temple of Spiritual Nourishment
*Listed in Meditation and Relaxation | Surrounded by a city of light*

The Sri Lanka Temple of Golden Light is in the etheric over water above the harbour of Colombo, which is the largest city in Sri Lanka. The harbour is well known for being on a trade route. It is an earthy temple that touches Mother Earth's heart centre, yet at the same time it is a star temple that connects high into the etheric, reaching up and out to the stars, touching the Milky Way within Orion's Belt and up to Pleiades, Sirius, and Andromeda.

This is another very ornate, colourful temple with interesting Sri Lankan architecture and flooring in soft subtle Indian designs. Beautiful elephants of all different sizes surround it, even baby elephants playing together. The temple holds the energy of the tiger, of qualities of strength and courage combined with fire of spirit. In the centre of the temple is an enormous ruby crystal that gives out a radiant energy, healing all those within.

This is a community heart temple of medium size. It welcomes families and friends and is about friendship, caring, and sharing, with hands outstretched across the waters. It is a wonderful place of stillness and contemplation where you can pray for world peace and connect with the whole of our universe. It is filled with the love of the Divine Mother and surrounded by seraphim and rainbow angels.

## 102. Lahore, Pakistan: Temple of Providence
*Surrounded by a city of light*

Lahore is the capital of Punjab, and its Temple of Golden Light is situated in the etheric over the Muslim mosque. The city is the cultural capital and heart of Pakistan, and many people decorate their houses and light candles to illuminate their streets and houses during public holidays. The people of Lahore celebrate many festivals and events throughout the year.

This is a medium-sized, sacred, and ornate temple. It is male in energy and mostly filled with the ability for everyone to be able to speak freely, which seems particularly important here. This is a place where you can see and understand another person's point of view and where one must face the truth about how one treats other people. It is a case of facing your own behaviour and realising how you can affect others with your actions and words. You can transcend all that is not of the light by listening and understanding.

The Lahore Temple of Golden Light is a place of prayer, peace, and relaxation, where one can meditate and feel oneself unwinding from the day's work. Inside is a special inner temple where there is an enormous waterfall filled with bright, floating candles dedicated to God. In the main hall is a golden pyramid for those who wish to access their multidimensional selves, clear them, and bring all aspects of themselves into the light.

## 103. Hyderabad, Pakistan: Temple of Upliftment

Hyderabad is in Sindh in Pakistan and is a city built on three hillocks cascading over each other. The city has a history of Sufism and is a place of worship for Muslims. The Temple of Golden Light is situated in the etheric towards the back of Hyderabad. It is a temple of change and transformation combined with peace, calm, and relaxation.

This is a large and very uplifting Temple of Golden Light. Connecting to the stars and our universe, it is a temple of hope and change. It is connected to golden dragon energy and is surrounded by rainbow angels of love and light. Lord Kuthumi lends his energy to this temple, and it pulsates with light continuously, sending messages of love out into the universe. Messages are received back by way of geometric shapes and symbols.

There are two parts to the temple, the earthy and the heavenly, so it works both up and down. As you move up the stairs, the energy within the temple becomes lighter. In the centre of the temple is a Merkaba, known as the flower of life, changing all those who connect with this temple from the third to the fifth dimension over a period of time. You will need to meditate or connect with this temple in your sleep time regularly, and then you will start to shift and raise your vibration. No other effort is needed—only meditation, or you set the intention before you go to sleep to visit the temple.

To shift from the third dimension, you need to shift first to the fourth and then the fifth. The shift can be as slow or as quick as you like. We all need to shift now, as we have no choice. Our planet Gaia is shifting, so we automatically need to shift too. Some countries are shifting and changing quicker than others, but all countries will shift eventually. Working with the heart and hand of God, all those who connect with this temple will go through a process of transformation. This temple will bring you gifts and, spiritually speaking, take you back to God.

## 104. Kathmandu, Nepal: Temple of Global Peace
*Listed in Meditation and Relaxation*

Kathmandu is the capital and largest city in Nepal, and the city is in the bowl-shaped Kathmandu Valley of central Nepal, surrounded by four major mountains. Kathmandu was devastated by a 7.8 magnitude earthquake in April 2015 in which around nine thousand people died. The Temple of Golden Light is over the heart of the city centre.

The Kathmandu Temple of Golden Light is a large temple filled with the love and energy of Quan Yin and Lord Buddha, providing a place of equal balance of male and female energy, yin and yang. It is a peaceful and happy temple with smiling people all around, where people continually pray for peace in the world. It is a powerful ascension Temple of Golden Light which holds all the keys of the universe.

You feel as if you are on top of the world in this temple, viewing the world from above, looking down on humanity. This temple connects to Middle Earth and to Mother Earth's crystal, sacred, cosmic heart centre through a vortex of energy connecting Middle and Upper Earth. Tibetan monks use firepits here as part of sacred ceremonies. Some of the ascended masters meet here, as they have a room of their own, led by the ascended master El Morya.

The temple is surrounded by elephants and ascended sacred horses—the unicorns—together with beautiful rainbow angels who also work inside the temple. They fill one of the healing sanctuaries with rainbow colours around a large waterfall which emits many colours that heal all your chakras.

This temple is on many levels, and there is a vortex of energy within the temple grounds for those interested in time travel around this universe. Obviously, this can only occur when you are ready to undertake this kind of exploration to further your knowledge of our universe. The vortex is similar to that which is portrayed on the *Stargate* television series.

## 105. Lhasa, Tibet: Temple of Divine Truth
*Listed in Meditation and Relaxation*

*Lhasa* means 'Land of the Gods', and the city is over 1,300 years old. It is the capital of the autonomous region of Tibet in China and lies in south-central Tibet on the northern slopes of the Himalayas. Lhasa is one of the highest cities of the world at 3,490 metres (11,450 feet) and has been the centre of the Tibetan Buddhist world for over a thousand years. The magnificent red and white Potala Palace is a towering place with fortress-like walls and can be seen throughout the city. It was previously the residence of the Dalai Lama. The Lhasa Temple of Golden Light sits in the etheric above the Potala Palace.

This is a small Temple of Golden Light filled with the energy of the Dalai Lama, whom I believe to be the representative here on Mother Earth of Middle Earth. This is a completely earthy temple without a higher aspect. It is a loving temple that connects to gentle dragon energy and works with your heart centre to help you shift to the next level of your spirituality. Everything in life is important: flowers, trees, all of life, including all animals. What you eat is important. Life is special, unique, and sacred.

Inside the temple is a large golden statue of Buddha sitting cross-legged. The Buddha statue is asking you to 'smell the flowers', an expression I am sure you are familiar with. It means to see everything in life through positivity. Smile at everyone, as this is a positive way of showing your love. Always be grateful in life, as the more grateful you are, the better will be the things that come your way.

This is a relaxed temple where you get the feeling that everything is easy and laid back. This temple is sowing seeds for the New Earth. You can connect to this temple to learn what it is like to live in the seventh dimension, where all is total love and peace. There is a healing centre within the temple filled with emerald-green and sapphire-blue crystals to soothe and heal your physical, emotional, and mental bodies. You can hear Tibetan Buddhist monks chanting. This sounds wonderful and aids the vibration of the energy within the temple.

This is a temple of divine truth where you can get rid of your old self and reprogramme yourself by realising the real truth and shedding the veneer that is your outer self. It is a cleansing temple, giving you a new, loving, grateful, peaceful you.

## 106. Thimphu, Bhutan: Temple of Pure Knowledge
*Listed in Meditation and Relaxation*

Bhutan is an ancient kingdom secluded high up in the Himalayas, with unique customs and people with deeply held beliefs. The Bhutan Temple of Golden Light has a very ethereal feel to it. It is located high over the capital city of Thimphu and connects to Middle Earth with a lush green energy. Around it is a pale green mist; below it is a forest of tall trees.

The King of Bhutan is Jigme Khesar Namgyel Wangchuck, who is the fifth and current reigning Druk Gyalpo or Dragon King. Bhutan is known as the Land of the Thunder Dragon, and dragon energy can be felt in the Temple of Golden Light. Twinned with the Lhasa temple, this small golden temple has more feminine energy, planting seeds of new thoughts and ideas for the New Earth. It is filled with love for families and friends and an awareness of the fact that we are one consciousness. The trees and plants here come to life, and if you hurt them, they feel it. This is similar to what is shown in the film *Avatar.*

This is a very light temple energetically. It has a connection to the star systems of this universe. Here you can find out how to utilise your skills and how to change, shake up, or wake up. If you want to learn about the Tree of Life (the Kabbalah), connect with this temple. The qualities you can gain here are peace, truth, knowledge, wisdom, love, honour, and power.

Goddess Jacinta oversees this temple herself with her divine feminine qualities of love, compassion, and understanding. She gives talks inside, seated by a waterfall, and as she speaks, you are cleansed of any negativity. This temple also connects to Lord Buddha and Quan Yin.

Here you can give time to yourself. When you meditate, simply connect with this temple and state how you would like this Temple of Golden Light to help you. Then close your eyes and feel the energy of the temple, and you are there.

## China and Other Parts of Asia

The following are the fifteen Temples of Golden Light in China and other parts of Asia:

107. Hong Kong
108. Shanghai, China
109. Beijing, China
110. Changsha Hunan Province, China
111. Yangtze River, Zhengzhou, China
112. Xianyang, China
113. Dandong, China
114. Gobi Desert, Mongolia
115. Atyrau, Kazakhstan
116. Tokyo, Japan
117. Padang, Singapore
118. Samar, Philippines
119. Hanoi, Vietnam
120. Ipoh, Malaysia
121. Bali, Indonesia

## 107. Hong Kong: Temple of Inspiration

Hong Kong, officially known as a special administrative region of the People's Republic of China, is off the coast of China at the Pearl River Estuary and the South China Sea. This is in the physical of Mother Earth. The temple lies in the etheric of earth over water, above the harbour of Hong Kong, protected by a huge golden angel.

This is a very large, powerful Temple of Golden Light. It is filled with golden dragon energy, which is very peaceful, honourable, protective, and brave, and is mostly known about in the eastern part of the world. The energy of Quan Yin is powerful here, along with the energy of Lord

Buddha. There are huge halls dedicated to each of them where you can sit, pray, meditate, and ask to be connected to your loved ones in spirit and to your ancestors. To connect with your loved ones, you will need to move up the golden stairs to the top floor of the temple.

The temple is filled with vibrant colours of red and green. In the Quan Yin hall is a lovely waterfall that gently fills a large pond full of floating water lilies of all different colours. Different-sized waterfalls seem to be a feature of many temples, as they are extremely relaxing. Quan Yin is known in the East as a goddess equivalent to Mother Mary in the West. She listens to everyone who calls upon her and will bless you with her love.

Sound healing is a good way of healing for some people and takes place here. Within the temple is much peace; it is a place where you can forgive all those who have hurt you and ask for forgiveness for those you have hurt too. This Temple of Golden Light will heal old wounds and hurts, thus healing your heart. Chinese astrology is also taught here, for those interested.

The temple is surrounded by rainbow angels and overseen by the Divine Mother. A council of Chinese masters sits here, including the master called Confucius. The temple has the ability of galactic alignment, meaning it connects to many star systems and holds a special place in helping our planet to shift.

## 108. Shanghai, China: Temple of Abundance

Shanghai is one of the largest cities by population in the world. It is one of the four directly controlled municipalities of the People's Republic of China, with a population of around 24 million. Located on the Yangtze River Delta in East China, Shanghai sits on the south edge of the mouth of the Yangtze in the middle portion of the Chinese coast. The Temple of Golden Light is in the etheric over the district of Pudong near the Pacific Ocean.

The Shanghai Temple of Golden Light is a smaller learning temple where Confucius teaches philosophy and wisdom through questions and answers. The temple is overseen by Ascended Master Lord Lanto, who is lord of the second esoteric ray of love and wisdom. When you walk into the great hall in this temple and sit down, you are sitting in his presence. Lord Lanto took over from Lord Kuthumi, and Confucius has now taken over from Lord Lanto at the Royal Teton Retreat China, which is a retreat of the Great White Brotherhood in China.

Lord Lanto teaches thousands of souls training at inner levels to accelerate their consciousness for the new Golden Age. He is dedicated to the perfection of the evolution of this planet through cosmic Christ illumination. Lord Lanto volunteered with Sanat Kumara to come to earth long ago for the rescue of the planet and her evolution. He was a high priest in the Temple of the Divine Mother on the continent that sank beneath the Pacific, known as Lemuria.

The temple also holds the energy of Quan Yin and dragon energy—indeed, there is a statue of a huge golden dragon in the main hall. Sometimes Quan Yin is seen riding on the back of a dragon, and she comes here in person, in her goddess energy, as part of the Divine Mother. This is called the Temple of Abundance because you may ask Quan Yin for abundance, peace, healing, and grace. Ask Quan Yin for whatever you feel you need in the way of abundance. Hold a vision of your dreams, and abundance will be granted.

Inside the temple is a small university about Taoism, a Chinese philosophy founded by the ancient writer Lao-tzu. How to be a Taoist is taught here, with introspection being the keyword. You will learn human kindness, how to behave, and how to be humble. There are masters of kung fu, judo, and tai chi—in fact, all the ancient oriental practices of self-protection. You can also learn about yin and yang, as there should be balance in everything.

In the healing room are rainbow crystals placed in small pools of rainbow-coloured waters connected by rainbow bridges. In another part of the temple is an entertainment theatre with dancing and singing, as laughter is good for the soul and is very healing. Simply connect and meditate upon this beautiful temple, and you will be cleansed and cleared of all disharmonies and feel peaceful and calm.

## 109. Beijing, China: Temple of Great Peace
*Surrounded by a city of light*

The Beijing Temple of Golden Light is on a ley line and is surrounded by a large city of light. It particularly specialises in healing adults, children, and animals. Some temples are surrounded by cities of light that are near to sacred sites or ley lines. This means the energies become more powerful. I believe that Mother Earth also has meridian lines as human beings do physically, and some temples are on meridian lines as well as ley lines.

Like the Hong Kong temple, this is filled with the energy of Quan Yin and Lord Buddha, with two main halls to connect to each of them. When you connect to this temple, you will sort out in your mind what to do and how to go about things. It is a temple to help you make decisions and choices about which path to take in life. The temple will help you connect to your soul, and this will help you make the right decision. Life is all about choices, but it is up to us to make the right one.

Within the temple is a council of Chinese masters, including Confucius, who is well known in Eastern philosophy. Miracles may happen when you are ready—maybe when you connect to this temple through meditation or your sleep time. Outside is a beautiful large lake of peace for cleansing and clearing, surrounded by even bigger lakes for clearing more emotions. From here, you will learn to rise above any situation.

This Temple of Golden Light is in the etheric at the start of the Great Wall of China on the outskirts of Beijing. The Great Wall of China is a series of fortifications made of stone, brick, tamped earth, wood, and other materials, generally built along an east-to-west line across the historical northern borders of China. It was built to protect the Chinese states and empires against the raids and invasions of various nomadic groups of the Eurasian Steppe. The majority of the existing wall is from the Ming Dynasty. Meditate by connecting to this temple or by thinking of it before you go to sleep at night, and you will gain much clarity in your life.

## 110. Changsha, Hunan Province, China: Temple of Tradition

Changsha is the capital of the Hunan Province in south-central China, located on the lower reaches of the Xiang River, a branch of the Yangtze. Its municipality covers an area of around 7 million inhabitants. The city is surrounded by major rivers, including the

Xiangjiang, the Liuyanghe, and the Laodaohe. Changsha is one of China's twenty most economically advanced cities.

The Changsha temple is small and cosy, and it relates to all aspects of the family. It is traditional and simplistic, filled with joy and laughter. There are many people wearing Chinese hats, as if they have just finished work in the paddy fields. There are traditional teachings of the Tao, Quan Yin, and Buddha, as well as energy of dragons. Similar to the Hong Kong temple, the colours inside are red, green, and gold. The walls are inlaid with images of golden dragons, and there is a beautiful statue of Quan Yin.

It is an earthy, grounding temple, surrounded by lush greenery and small buildings that are all part of the temple grounds—an oasis of sublime peace. It is filled with restorative, healing energy that will help to revitalise you and give you a new zest for life, a new enthusiasm. When you enter, the old energy is removed from you, and you are given new energy, like new clothes, so to speak. As human beings, we need to be able to recharge our batteries and rest, and meditating upon this temple will help you to do just that. You will feel like you are having a holiday or have been on a retreat. It is a respite temple, helping you to evolve. You can find yourself getting off the cycle of life when you meditate upon this temple. It helps you to create your own abundance and be happier and more fulfilled in life.

To connect to this temple, simply close your eyes and imagine a bright golden light, and then see yourself being transported to inside Changsha, Hunan Province, Temple of Golden Light, in traditional China. This temple is in the etheric at the start of the Great Wall of China on the outskirts of Beijing. The Great Wall of China is a series of fortifications made of stone, brick, tamped earth, wood, and other materials, generally built along an east-to-west line across the historical northern borders of China. It was built to protect the Chinese states and empires against the raids and invasions of various nomadic groups of the Eurasian Steppe. The majority of the existing wall is from the Ming Dynasty. Meditate by connecting to this temple or by thinking of it before you go to sleep at night, and you will gain much clarity in your life.

## 111. Yangtze River, Zhengzhou, China: Temple of Communication

Higher up in the etheric is this huge Temple of Golden Light, connecting to all the star constellations, known and as yet unknown, and to all the planets within our universe, known and unknown. The Yangtze River Delta or the Golden Triangle of the Yangtze generally comprises the triangle-shaped territory of Wu-speaking Shanghai. Zhengzhou is the capital of Henan Province, located in east-central China. It is one of eight great ancient capitals of China, south of the Yellow River. Zhengzhou was the capital of China during the Shang Dynasty.

The Yangtze River Temple of Golden Light is a crystal temple filled with jade. Inside is an enormous crystal tree. The beings in the temple are of pure light. They have no form as such; they are light beings. On top of the temple is a huge star that shines continuously. There is a science museum where you can be given an understanding of science and the history of our planet. You can learn about the Kabbalah, the Tree of Life, and the many levels that we have to pass through from the bottom to the top and all that it entails. There is much to know as we move through each individual lifetime.

This is a temple of technology and information, and it is connected to the World Wide Web of communication—a hub communication centre. Information is here for everything there is to know. It is a temple to help us observe the world and take notes as information pours in. It is a powerful temple, and you will experience that when you connect with it. The temple has a very high vibration that extends to the outer limits of our universe. We still have much to learn as a human race, and we know very little at the moment. Information is given to those who are ready to receive, but your ego has to have left you. There is no room for ego as you raise your vibration.

## 112. Xianyang, China: Temple of Tao Tradition

The Xianyang Temple of Golden Light is small, with a lovely, homely feel to it. It is quite old-fashioned in a way, but comfortable and very calm and peaceful. This is a very grounded temple, close to earth and on a special ley line. Ley lines are key in bringing forward powerful energy. This is a teaching temple, and like other smaller temples, it is about the size of St Paul's Cathedral in London.

Like the temple in Shanghai, this temple holds the energy of Taoism, which was founded by Lao Tzu, a philosopher and poet of ancient China. He is best known as the reputed author of the *Tao Te Ching*, but he is also revered as a deity in religious Taoism and traditional Chinese religions. Although a legendary figure, he is usually dated to around the sixth century BC and is believed to have been a contemporary of Confucius. Lao Tzu was and still is a central Chinese figure in culture. These are some of his famous quotes:

- 'The usefulness of a pot comes from its emptiness.'
- 'The best people are like water, which benefits all things and does not compete with them. It stays in lowly places that others reject. This is why it is so similar to the Way.'
- 'When people see some things as beautiful, other things become ugly. When people see some things as good, other things become bad.'
- 'Try to change it and you will ruin it. Try to hold it and you will lose it.'
- 'Those who know do not say. Those who say do not know.'
- 'A journey of a thousand miles starts under one's feet.'
- 'The more that laws and regulations are given prominence, the more thieves and robbers there will be.'

This temple will allow you to contemplate and think deeply as to why you are here and what you are doing with your life. When you connect to the temple through meditation or your sleep time, it will help you to change and move on spiritually, to change your life for good.

## 113. Dandong, China: Temple of Opportunity

This is a small Temple of Golden Light placed in the etheric of Dandong, China. It is the largest Chinese border city facing Sinuiju, North Korea, across the Yalu River, which demarcates the Sino-North

Korean border. This is the location of the Hushan Great Wall at the far eastern end of the Great Wall of China.

Dandong Temple of Golden Light has been placed in the etheric of Mother Earth floating over water so that you can feel the ebbing and flowing of life. It is a calm, soothing, cosy, and homely temple with a large golden angel holding the light over the top of the temple filled with the energy of the Divine Mother. Like all the Temples of Golden Light, this is surrounded by rainbow angels which heal all chakras together over a period of time.

This temple will help you to let go of material possessions and raise your vibration by losing materialism. A cleansing healing temple, balanced by its connection with other Chinese Temples of Golden Light, it will help you to release suppressed, old, stagnant energy and welcome in new, positive, vibrant, happy energy linking with the New Earth. I believe this area has been suppressed for a long time, and now people are starting to emerge from this suppression into the light and love of God/Goddess.

This Temple will bring much light to this area, where it is greatly needed. Once a place of great sadness, now joy is coming through, helping people to laugh and feel love again. This temple will give you peace, calm, relaxation, and joy.

## 114. Gobi Desert, Mongolia: Temple of the Masters

The Gobi is a large desert region in Asia. It covers parts of northern and north-western China and southern Mongolia. The Altai Mountains and the grasslands and steppes of Mongolia bound the desert basins of the Gobi on the north, the Taklamakan Desert to the west, the Hexi Corridor and Tibetan Plateau to the southwest, and the North China Plain to the southeast. The Gobi is the location of several important cities along the Silk Road.

The Gobi Desert Temple of Golden Light is a large temple where very powerful male ascended masters secretly meet in private. When they meet, the temple is cloaked, but when the ascended masters are not there, it becomes a temple of meditation and contemplation. This temple connects to the universal Galactic Federation of Light for this universe and the Great White Brotherhood. Decisions are made here, and then the information is filtered down to millions of light workers on earth. These are usually the souls who are doing their service work helping humanity and Mother Earth.

All the masters meet here, from Jesus Christ and the Apostles, Paul the Venetian, Hilarion, Serapis Bay, and El Morya to Mohammad and Zoroaster, Confucius, St Germaine, Lord Lanto, Commander Ashtar, Lord Maitreya, Lord Kuthumi, Sanat Kumara, Melchizidec, Metatron, Babaji, Sai Baba, and many more, both known and unknown. Many of these ascended masters lived here on Planet Earth at the time of Atlantis and the fall of Atlantis. Sometimes they will channel through willing higher-vibrational souls in order to spread the light.

This Temple of Golden Light is a centre for wisdom and a forum for discussion and debate. Ceremonial robes are worn, and inside there is total silence.

## 115. Atyrau, Kazakhstan: Temple of Changing

Atyrau is at the mouth of the Ural River and is Kazakhstan's main harbour city on the Caspian Sea. The Temple of Golden Light is small and is situated in the etheric over the city of Atyrau. Due to the sensitivity of this country and its religion, the Temple of Golden Light is a Moslem religion-based temple which is linked to a mosque, although this temple is in the etheric of earth.

This is a peaceful temple filled with thousands of lit candles. It is a place of prayer and open discussion. As important issues and topics arise here, they will be discussed. It is a very earthy temple about finding solutions, where prominent male figures speak. Men and women are separated, and females have their own part of the temple, which is outside the main area within the grounds of the temple buildings.

This is a cleansing Temple of Golden Light—cleansing emotions, hurts, and sadness. Hearts need to be opened, but having said that, the old ways of being dogmatic, blinkered, and kept in the dark are going. Times are changing, and prayers have been heard by God. The Atyrau temple of prayer and changes, of letting go of the old ways and bringing forward new ways, is much-needed in this part of the world, and it is supported by all the other temples.

## 116. Tokyo, Japan: Temple of the Dawning of Light

Tokyo is in the Kanto region on the south-eastern side of the main island, Honshu, and includes the Izu Islands and Ogasawara Islands. Tokyo is Japan's capital and largest city. The Greater Tokyo area has a staggering 33 million inhabitants, making it the most populous metropolis in the world.

This is a large Temple of Golden Light with many layers to it. It is surrounded by rainbow angels and situated in the etheric near a mountain close to the city of Tokyo. As you walk up the steps to the entrance, in front of you are large golden dragon statues. This temple permanently pulses white light every second all around the outside of the temple, rescuing stuck souls and guiding them to the light.

I channelled this temple just before the tsunami struck in 2011 over Tohuku. The earthquake and effect of the tsunami devastated much of the north-eastern coast of Honshu and was felt in Tokyo. When the disaster happened, I saw clairvoyantly thousands of souls floating upwards to the light. This amazing Temple of Golden Light freed so many souls. The light of the temple shines for thousands of miles around, allowing all souls to move forward in the light to meet their families and friends.

This Temple of Golden Light is coloured in typically Japanese colours of red and gold and is in the shape of a pentagon, similar in appearance to a five-sided pyramid, which is a sacred geometric shape. Inside there is beautiful thick material on the walls in an oriental design in red and gold, and a golden flame is the centrepiece in one of the large rooms. The main room has a tear-shaped crystal hanging from the ceiling. This crystal connects heaven to earth.

There are various sanctuaries within the temple connected to different religions and philosophies, and there are healing sanctuaries where people can be healed and cleansed of all negativity. This temple can help you clear any negative feelings from past lives and then bring your fragmented selves back to you.

The Temple is filled with the energy of Lord Buddha and Quan Yin, the female Buddha, as well as the energy of Chinese dragons. Quan Yin enjoys a strong connection with Mother Mary, the mother of Jesus, and with the Tibetan Goddess Tara. Quan Yin is a truly Enlightened One or *Bodhisattva* who vowed to remain in the earthly realms and not enter the heavenly worlds until all other living beings have completed their own enlightenment and become free of suffering. She is also known as Maha Karuna, the compassionate Goddess of Mercy.

Quan Yin was considered to be the Bodhisattva Avalokiteshvara and was sometimes shown with eleven heads, a thousand arms, and eyes on the palms of each hand. This portrays her as an omnipresent mother looking in all directions simultaneously, sensing the afflictions of humanity and extending her many arms to them with infinite expressions of her mercy and love. She is often considered to be the most widely beloved Buddhist divinity, with miraculous powers to assist all those who pray to her. She is worshipped around the world, especially in Japan, China, Taiwan, Korea, and Thailand.

## 117. Padang, Singapore: Temple of Learning

The Padang is an open playing field located within the central downtown area of Singapore. In 1819, the founder of Singapore set aside the space for public use, and it has remained of significant importance. It is still used for many events, including National Day parades. The temple is in the etheric of earth above this area and is a wonderful place of peace and calm in our modern world.

This is a large Temple of Golden Light overseen by the Divine Mother and connecting to the universal light of love. A transformational temple where one can learn the basics of humility, morals, and integrity, it is a school of wisdom. The first level feels very earthy. As you move upwards within the temple, you realise that it reaches up and out, with connections to this universe and some of the outer universes. It is a mix of heaven and earth, as above and down below.

The temple is a sacred place of peace and stillness and can connect to many different energies of Buddhism, Christianity, Islam, Taoism, and Hinduism. Within the temple is a shrine to each deity. All the Temples of Golden Light are multifaith, acknowledging different deities, religions, and creeds.

## 118. Samar, Philippines: Temple of Celestial Light

Samar is an island in the Visayas within the central Philippines and is the third largest island in the country. In the etheric high above is a very large Temple of Golden Light. After walking across lush grass, you step inside and realise the enormity of this temple. It is filled with celestial beings, star people, and star beings connecting to another galaxy of pure love, which is more advanced than we are here on Planet Earth.

You can access and align with this energy on the top floor of the temple, where you will experience beings flying in and out. Please connect with this temple to find out for yourself and receive enlightenment. This temple teaches you how to just be and holds pure light and love. When you ask for divine guidance and protection, love is converted into more love, compassion, and mercy.

## 119. Hanoi, Vietnam: Temple of Floating Water

Hanoi is the capital of Vietnam and the country's second largest city. The city lies on the right bank of the Red River. Hanoi is north of Ho Chi Minh City and west of Hai Phong City. It is a city between rivers, built from lowlands, and is sometimes called the 'city of lakes', which provides a scenic and tranquil respite from the traffic and noise of other parts of the city. This is why the Temple of Golden Light has been placed here, over water which is pure and still.

As a floating water temple, the Hanoi temple has a strong energy of water. Holding a soothing, calming vibration moving with the ebb and flow of life, it is a particularly small temple, a baby temple amongst the other Temples of Golden Light. The temple is a warm, vibrant, family place, welcoming everyone. It is filled with the energy of the Divine Mother and surrounded by rainbow angels.

This temple has been placed in the etheric aside the Long Bien Bridge near Perfume Pagoda, Hanoi. It is a temple of divine guidance and healing, as this country is still healing from the past, but it is moving forward at a fast rate. Goddess Jacinta shines her love through this temple, as she is part of the energy of the Divine Mother. Much healing is needed in this part of the world, and the babies born here are of a high vibration deliberately to lift the energy of the families who live here already and to lift the energy of the whole area.

It is also a temple of meditation and contemplation. Here you can learn how to meditate and bring mindfulness into your life. If you meditate, this will open doorways for you.

## 120. Ipoh, Malaysia: Temple of Meditation

This is a large Temple of Golden Light which has many levels and is placed in the etheric over the centre of Ipoh, Malaysia. Ipoh is the capital city of the state of Perak and one of the largest cities in the country. It is north of Kuala Lumpur and south of Penang. On top of the temple is a bright shining star that pulsates outwards, shining for hundreds of miles around. The temple is overseen by the Divine Mother and surrounded by rainbow angels of love and golden light.

It is a very active temple with many people coming here to practice meditation and ask for guidance. Those who enter are humble, curious, and polite. This temple is all about spreading your wings, gaining enlightenment, and realising that there is more to life than money.

The gardens behind this temple are filled with lush greenery and are very well cultivated. Inside the main garden is a large walled garden filled with many beautiful flowers. It is a temple of meditation and contemplation and seeking divine guidance in one's life. If you meditate in this temple, imagine sitting within the wonderful gardens, breathing in the fresh air, and feeling the energy of the flowers and the perfect peace of nature.

## 121. Bali, Indonesia: Temple of Beautiful Light
*Listed in Children and Animals | Surrounded by a city of light*

Bali is an island which lies east of Java and is a province of Indonesia. The religions are mainly Balinese Hinduism, Islam, and Christianity. Bali is an ancient city and part of the Coral Triangle. Its temple twins with the one in Samar, Philippines. It is high up in the etheric over

Singaraja in Bali and is surrounded by a city of enormous light, which connects to the seventh dimension.

A beautiful temple surrounded by rainbow angels and filled with celestial beings of love and light, it is a happy, joyful place and provides a sense of fulfilment and contentment. A large star sits on top of the temple, illuminating brightly and sending a message of love around the world. This is a children's healing temple, healing crystal, rainbow, indigo, and angelic children as well as many others. All God/Goddess children may be healed here. There are three children's healing sanctuaries and one sanctuary for healing adults inside the temple.

Also inside are spinning pyramids, base to base. Imagine a pyramid pointed upwards and then imagine another pyramid pointed downwards. This allows the energy from the universe to flow through the temple, as well as the energy of our universe and all the others that surround us. This makes the Bali temple extremely powerful.

# Chapter 7

## *Rest of the World*

A few years ago, I travelled to Egypt with my husband, and we booked a Nile cruise. This was something we'd done before, but this time it was very different. While we were in Egypt, the Arab Spring broke out. We spent four days having a wonderful time aboard our cruise boat, unable to watch any television and unaware of what was happening around us.

At the end of our four days, we were met by a tour guide and taxi driver who drove us and another couple to Luxor. Everything was fine until we arrived at the outskirts of the city, where we were stopped by Egyptian soldiers waving big rifles, wanting to know where we were going. We were directed off the motorway, and very soon, our driver and tour guide were lost. Another tour guide was sent to help direct us to our hotel. As we waited, I noticed that the streets were deserted, and I had an uneasy feeling. The other lady in the taxi felt the same way. It was late at night now. Everywhere was dark, and all the shops were closed. It was becoming quite spooky, to say the least.

After an anxious hour, the new tour guide arrived, to our great relief. We moved through the dark, dusty, deserted back streets of Luxor sensing that something was very wrong. All we wanted was to be inside the hotel asleep, as it was getting very late. As we drove past the Karnak temple, we saw an army tank parked in front and about a hundred armed police officers wearing masks and body armour. Apparently the city was now under curfew, and I felt like I was heading into a war zone. We found out later there had been riots in Luxor, Aswan, and Cairo while we had been cruising. As you can imagine, this was not something I expected to experience on holiday.

We woke up in the morning to find plain-clothes police officers everywhere in the hotel and grounds. There was a curfew every day starting at two in the afternoon. Our tour guide, a lovely young man, explained that the government had been taking so much money in taxes from ordinary people that they had decided to rebel. So there we were in the middle of unrest, riots, and violence.

We did walk outside and joined a sightseeing tour to visit the Karnak temple, but we could not relax. We decided it would be best just to stay in the hotel for the rest of our stay until it was time to fly home. Our hotel was lovely, and we made the most of the swimming pool. But I remember that as we ate dinner one evening in the restaurant on the hotel grounds, we looked out over the River Nile and saw a large boat going by with *Police* in large letters on the side, which we found quite disturbing.

We heard many stories from other hotel guests complaining of how the unrest was spoiling their holiday plans. Amidst all of this, I had time to tune into the temple there, and I realised when I had time to think that the activation of the Egyptian temple was partly responsible for the unrest that had clearly been bubbling under the surface for some time.

Now, thankfully, things are much better in Egypt, and the temple is fully activated and able to shine its light. I travel to countries when I feel guided to, and the reason is always linked to the Temples of Golden Light. When I first channelled the temples, I did not fully understand my role in all of this, but in time I began to realise that I act as a catalyst for the activation of the temples. I can link with any temple at any time, it seems, but sometimes there is a need for me to be physically present in the country.

Egypt was the first country that I visited doing this temple work. I intended to link with the temple in the etheric near the Sphinx, by the Pyramids at Giza, when we were on the Nile; my idea had been to combine work with a pleasant holiday. I did not anticipate this level of reaction, but clearly, we were looked after by the temples and the rainbow angels.

As light exposes negativity, so all situations under the surface need to be dealt with. Please understand, however, that it is the temples that do the work. I am their ambassador, their representative here on earth. Our planet needs healing, and with love and the help of the Temples of Golden Light, humanity and Mother Earth will be helped to heal.

The 144 Temples of Golden Light link together to form a powerful network able to shine a light around the world, clearing away negativity and old energy. Their vibration is the force that will help us shift into the Golden Age and deliver healing for us and our planet, bringing qualities of love, compassion, grace, understanding, mercy, freedom, joy, and happiness. In this chapter, I will describe the temples that have been placed in the northern and southern polar regions as well as in Russia, Africa, and the Middle East.

## Antarctica, Arctic, Iceland, and Greenland

The following are the Temples of Golden Light in Antarctica, Arctic, Iceland, and Greenland:

122. Antarctica
123. Arctic
124. Reykjavik, Iceland
125. Ammassalik, Greenland

## 122. Antarctica Temple of Golden Light
*Listed in Main Temples and in Meditation and Relaxation |
Surrounded by a city of light*

The Antarctica temple is the fourth largest Temple of Golden Light after Istanbul, New York, and Athens. The silence within this temple sounds like the muffled silence when it has snowed. It is a teaching and healing temple which energetically connects to the whole of this universe, including the star systems Pleiades, Sirius, Andromeda, and all of the planets.

This temple is surrounded by rainbow angels and holds crystalline energy, bringing forward a new healing vibration. Also connected here are universal golden-winged angels of ascension and many other

129

celestial beings of light and love. This temple is all about balance and alignment and will help to regulate the waters of our planet, bringing about new beginnings, new birth, and rebirth.

## 123. Arctic Temple of Golden Light

The Arctic is a polar region located at the northernmost part of the earth, comprising the Arctic Ocean and parts of Alaska (United States), Canada, Finland, Greenland, Denmark, Iceland, Norway, Russia, and Sweden. This region has seasonally varying ice cover and is surrounded by treeless permafrost. The cultures in the region are the Arctic indigenous peoples, and they have adapted to its cold and extreme conditions. These include the Inuit, Buryat, Chukchi, Evenks, Inupiat, Khanty, Koryaks, Nenets, Sami, Yukaghir, and Yupik, who still refer to themselves as Eskimos.

The Artic Temple of Golden Light is a very peaceful, still temple that is of medium size. It holds the energy of polar bears, penguins, seals, walruses, baleen whales, narwhals, beluga whales, Arctic hares, lemmings, musk ox, snowy owls, Arctic foxes and wolves, wolverines, ermines, and Arctic ground squirrels, to name but a few. As a temple of observation, it looks at the world on a global scale and sends the following message:

> What have we done to our lovely world? Humanity needs to put right what it has done wrong—the harm that it has caused the sea creatures and humanity. The creatures here only send you love, no matter what is done to them.

This is a teaching temple for humanity to learn how to treat God's creatures, as we are all one. There should be no separation, but unfortunately, man has harmed many of God's creatures, and this needs to be addressed.

The temple looks etherically like a golden-white palace and seems to continually change its shape slightly, as the temple is a crystalline structure. It is a place of learning, of teaching people about love and not money, and of teaching people to change their views through eyes that can see what has gone wrong and how to put it right. This temple has a strong connection to Middle Earth, and from Middle Earth comes a loving balance. It is an interesting temple for those who feel drawn to connecting to it. You will learn to see the world through a much broader spectrum of truth. The Arctic temple twins with the Antarctica temple.

## 124. Reykjavik, Iceland: Temple of Being

Reykjavik is the capital and largest city of Iceland, and the temple is in the etheric of the city above Hallgrimskirkja church. This is a small Temple of Golden Light which twins with Ammassalik, Greenland's temple. The energy of this temple is crystalline and churchlike. Filled with the energy of Jesus Christ, it is grounding and healing, allowing the release of old deep-rooted emotional issues, the letting go of the old, and the bringing in of the new. It is a place where you can receive grace, forgiveness, guidance, clarity, and counselling, and feel refreshed when you leave. This temple will take you back to basics and help you make choices, allowing you the knowledge that you have the power to change.

The homely, cosy, warm, and vibrant energy will give you building blocks and grounding skills to enable you to make any changes within your life. You can aspire to be the very best that you can be. You can also work with abundance and manifestation issues if you have them, as these can be healed.

This temple holds a high vibration on its higher levels, connecting to Pleiades, Sirius, and Andromeda in Orion's belt. It is overseen entirely by Archangel Metaziel and the rainbow angels and connects to the many golden ascension angels who work directly for Archangel Metatron, so it is a very light temple. The temple connects to Thor, the Icelandic god who defends all souls of the light—those that stand for goodness and purity. He travels on a chariot of fire, fighting any darkness. He resides in another universe but comes to this universe when he is needed, simply by crossing a bridge of light from his universe to ours.

Healing takes place with colours, as colours are aspects of vibration. God speaks in terms of colour and tone, allowing all bodily organs, bones, muscles, tendons, ligaments, discs, vertebrae, and tissues to be healed. The body regenerates itself every twelve months, so it is truly possible for it to heal itself, given the right tools of light, colours, sound, herbal medicine, natural oils, flower therapies, nutritionally healthy food, and plenty of water to flush out the toxins, also combined with a good healing practice. When healing takes place, it regenerates the stimulation of energy in the cell memory or DNA structure. Almost every disease can be healed by colour, sound, or healing. Diseases affecting bones can take a little longer—about a year.

## 125. Ammassalik, Greenland: Temple of Quiet

Ammassalik is an island off Greenland separated by the Sermilik Fjord in the west and by the Ikaasartivaq Strait in the northeast. The southern coast of the island is washed by the waters of the open North Atlantic. The highest point of the island is a glaciated peak in the northern part at 1,352 metres (4,436 feet). The Temple of Golden Light is situated in the etheric of this mountain and is surrounded by rainbow angels.

This is a very earthy, smaller Temple of Golden Light with a strong connection to Middle Earth. It is as if the temple has long golden roots to Mother Earth's sacred, crystalline, cosmic heart centre. There is a churchlike feel, basic and simple, but peaceful and quiet with a stillness, like when it has snowed. The temple is a place of prayer and worship, a place for a gathering of people. It specialises in helping people who are lost or feel alone in life. Seek and ye shall find. In other words, from this temple, you will receive help when you are lost.

The Ammassalik Temple of Golden Light is also for clearing, cleansing, and learning. It is a bright light that has been placed over a dimly lit area of the planet, so it requires the other temples, part of a huge grid of brilliant light, to hold it up with their light. In time, all the temples will be balanced, each holding a high quotient of light radiating outwards, healing humanity and the earth.

## Russia

The following are the Temples of Golden Light in Russia:

126. Moscow
127. St. Petersburg
128. Siberia
129. Omsk
130. Ayan Stanovoy Mountain Range

## 126. Moscow: Temple of Contemplation
*Surrounded by a city of light*

Moscow is the largest city in Russia. It is situated on the Moskva River. Christianity is the predominant religion in the city; the Russian Orthodox Church is the most popular. The temple is situated in the etheric above the Cathedral of Christ the Saviour on the northern bank of the Moskva River. It is a very large white-and-gold Temple of Golden Light, Russian in style and decor. There are opulent balconies on many levels of this tall temple. Inside it is very ornate and filled with colourful Russian furniture.

The temple connects to Archangel Honoriel, the twin flame of Archangel Metaziel; both oversee the rainbow angels. Consequently, this is a very angelic temple, busy but peaceful. There is a special section for children, with children in spirit looked after by St Margaret and St Phillip. Healing takes place for children, and from this temple, the souls of crystal children are prepared for their incarnations on earth. There is also a school for learning, with many classrooms. The school connects to this universe. Love is the message of this temple, and the fact that we are all one consciousness.

Deeper inside the temple, there is a vibrational sound and tones healing chamber for those who wish to have sound healing therapy and a school of learning to show how to use this relatively new healing modality. All people on the planet hold their own musical tone for healing themselves. Once you have found yours, you can be healed of all disharmonies. It is a temple of learning, listening, and hearing through vibrational sound healing. Miracles can happen here for children and adults alike, as all is pure and positive energy.

## 127. St Petersburg: Temple of Golden Energy
*Listed in Children and Animals*

The city of St Petersburg was founded by Tsar Peter the Great and named after him. For most of the following two hundred years, it was the imperial capital of Russia. Its name was changed to Petrograd and then to Leningrad before being changed back to its original name in 1918. St Petersburg is Russia's second largest city and is an important port on the Baltic Sea.

The St Petersburg temple is large, covering two thirds of the city. It is situated in the etheric over the golden-domed St Isaac's Cathedral. The Temple of Golden Light has been created in typical Russian style, and everything inside is white and gold. It is a very light, bright temple of enormous light connecting to source. Inside are several healing sanctuaries for children and adults. This temple specialises in healing children from all walks of life. There are large prayer and meditation rooms, and rooms for talks and learning.

Anastasia was one of the tsar's daughters, and her energy is felt within this temple. She is a gentle, sweet soul who is the embodiment of love, light, and beauty, and she helps others when she can. She loves children and babies, and she wishes only to heal and help all those who ask for the Divine Mother's help.

The St Petersburg Temple of Golden Light connects to Archangel Gabriel and his twin flame, Archangel Hope, and is filled with loving angels. Many saints also connect with this temple, as it is a high-vibrational sacred place of healing and prayer. It is a temple of releasing fear and gaining hope.

## 128. Siberia: Temple of the Universe

The Siberia Temple of Golden Light is very high in the etheric above a desolate area of northern Siberia where time has been forgotten. Interestingly, this is one of the first temples that I channelled, and

I learnt that it lies on a very important ley line. The nearest town would be Nordvik, but even this is a very long way from the Temple of Golden Light. What appears to be a small entrance leads up and into an enormous temple spanning a very large area and appearing to be in the middle of nowhere. It is a beacon of light for thousands and thousands of miles.

The roof of the Temple of Golden Light is domed-shaped, with multifaceted crystals that shine and sparkle. This changes to a flat roof when needed. The roof seems to spin as a signal to outer space. Indeed, this temple connects to our entire universe, connecting with star systems and galaxies and planets that physically we know little about but spiritually are well known. It also connects to spaceships that travel through this universe under the guidance of Commander Ashtar. All celestial beings must connect to the Galactic Federation of the Light; otherwise, they cannot enter our universe. It is a really good temple to connect to and then link with star systems, galaxies, and other planets within our universe.

This temple is a waiting place for crystal children, indigo essence children, and rainbow children, all waiting to be born to parents who wish to have higher vibrational children. These children are the souls of the future.

## 129. Omsk: Temple of Caring

Omsk is a city in Russia located in southwestern Siberia. The temple is very simplistic and traditional, with wooden carvings. It is situated in the etheric over the centre of the city and has the motto 'we are one'.

At this earthy temple, you can learn about growing foods organically, dancing, being happy, and seeing the positive side to life in Russia. It is a community temple of love and peace, of coming together with caring and sharing qualities, and of helping you to regain self-worth by taking back your power from others.

Generally, when people meet in this part of the world, they stay together and can become childhood sweethearts. Life is basic and simple but never dull. There will be more indigo essence children born here in this part of the world to help raise vibration and energy. Surrounded by rainbow angels, this lovely temple of divine energy is perfect to connect and meditate with when you wish to feel relaxed and rejuvenated—when you wish to live in the moment.

## 130. Ayan, Stanovoy Mountain Range: Temple of Vibrational Quickening

This is a small but powerful Temple of Golden Light which is very still and silent, having been placed in the etheric above the town of Ayan near the Stanovoy mountain range. It is particularly ornate and looks and feels like a Russian tsar's palace, very regal and filled with beautiful, elaborate Russian furniture.

It is an amazing temple for ascension and for raising your awareness. Holding the space for people who want to ascend quite quickly, you are shown how to let go of old stuff, accelerate your spiritual growth, and remain grounded and calm. The Divine Mother guides you with grace, ease, and dignity.

The temple is a river of light—a silver stream of consciousness and of pure thought. It is also a sound healing temple, transferring sound from one source to another. It sends sound to be heard by those who are receptive. It also changes sound and receives sound. You will receive information telepathically through thought transference. You will learn how beautiful you are and heal any negative issues.

You can connect to this peaceful, meditative temple by thought intention, by meditation, and by prayer. The rainbow angels of love and rainbow light surround the temple.

## Africa

The following are the Temples of Golden Light in Africa:

131. Cape Town, South Africa
132. Nairobi, Kenya
133. Lilongwe, Malawi
134. Huambo, Angola
135. Mogadishu, Somalia
136. Timbuktu, Mali

137. Casablanca, Morocco
138. Tunis, Tunisia
139. Cairo, Egypt

## 131. Cape Town, South Africa: Temple of Stillness

Table Mountain is a flat-topped mountain forming a prominent landmark overlooking the city of Cape Town in South Africa. Table Mountain is at the northern end of a sandstone mountain range that forms the spine of the Cape Peninsula. To the south of the main plateau is a lower part of the range called the Back Table. On the Atlantic coast of the peninsula, the range is known as the Twelve Apostles. The range continues southwards to Cape Point.

The Cape Town Temple of Golden Light lies in the etheric on top of Table Mountain. Archangel Gabriel and his divine twin flame, Archangel Hope, are connected to this light, bright temple along with their legions of angels. Archangel Gabriel is the messenger archangel, well known for when he visited Mother Mary to tell her of the arrival of Jesus. A peaceful, serene, earthy temple, it has been placed in an area of the planet that has less light, so it needs the light of the other temples to hold the space of the light to shine brightly below it.

The energy of this temple is Christed energy—that of Jesus Christ and of the Holy Spirit. Prayer meetings are held here regularly, helping to bring the wisdom of resolving conflict, clothing the poor, and feeding the homeless. At the moment, the temple is fairly quiet, but it will become busier in time, and the energy will strengthen the more we connect to it. It is a large temple with many coloured, domed roofs. Inside is a beautiful healing sanctuary with a crystalline rainbow-coloured floor that connects to source and feels very powerful. Outside is a lake populated with pink flamingos.

This is also a soul rescue temple. A pulsating light can be seen at all times, signalling to stuck souls to come to the temple and be rescued. It is a wonderful healing Temple of Golden Light, working with the violet flame of transmutation. An enormous rainbow angel of a very high vibration oversees the temple, bringing through it every vibration of healing light imaginable.

## 132. Nairobi, Kenya: Temple of Ascension

Nairobi is the capital and largest city in Kenya. The place name *Nairobi* comes from the Maasai phrase *Enkore Nairobi*, which translates to 'cool water'. The phrase is also the Maasai name for the Nairobi River, which in turn lends its name to the city.

Interestingly, the Nairobi temple was one of the last temples to be activated. It is now fully active. Because it is in an area of less light, love and light are sent from the other Temples of Golden Light to support this new, large temple. It is situated on the edge of Nairobi and is strategically placed on an important ley line. Like all temples, it is filled with the love and light of the Divine Mother and surrounded by the beautiful rainbow angels. As the energy lifts within and around this temple, more angels will come. At the moment, the temple is quiet, but once the temples are known, it will become busier.

Inside the main hall is a golden pyramid reaching energetically up and out to the stars and to galaxies within our universe. In another large room is a pentagon-shaped crystal light chandelier that opens and closes when it needs to and brings source light, rainbow light, and particularly violet light to all those within the temple at that time. This brings through the energy of the flower of life, promoting everyone's ascension path. Ascension means raising your vibration. We need to raise our vibration to help Mother Earth align her energy to this universe and surrounding universes.

## 133. Lilongwe, Malawi: Temple of Transformation

Lilongwe is the largest and capital city of Malawi. It is located in the central region near the borders with Mozambique and Zambia and is named after the Lilongwe River. Like many of the African temples, the Lilongwe Temple of Golden Light is traditional, churchlike, and earthy. Everyone who enters this divine sanctuary of pure bliss wears white clothing.

Inside the temple is a healing pool that you may bathe in to release and cleanse your body of old stored energy. This will be replaced by new, positive, vibrant, abundant energy, giving you vitality and joy.

Adults, children, and animals may be healed by connecting with this temple. Ask for divine guidance and protection.

This medium-sized temple is filled with orange and red wood carvings representing different tribes for the area. In the main hall are three silver crosses placed on three altars representing Jesus Christ and the Christed energy of love, forgiveness, and compassion. Mother Mary is here holding love and light for everyone, showing people the way of truth, clarity, and integrity. Like Cape Town's temple, this also connects to St Germaine of the violet flame for transformation from negative to positive. You can connect to Archangel Zadkiel and his twin flame, Archangel Amethyst, to further clear yourself of old energy.

Like Cape Town's temple, the Malawi Temple of Golden Light performs soul rescue, meaning any stuck souls that have not crossed over to the light will be rescued and taken over through a bridge of light to the heavenly realms. This temple in the etheric of earth is above barren land on the outskirts of Lilongwe and is transforming the energy of the land below, bringing through rainbow light and love.

## 134. Huambo, Angola: Temple of the Lotus Flower

Huambo is the second largest city in Angola in Southern Africa and gets its name from Wambu, one of the fourteen Ovimbundu kingdoms of the central Angola plateau. Placed over the centre of the city is a medium-sized Temple of Golden Light with a large heart that lights it. It is a temple of the Divine Mother overseen by Goddess Jacinta and surrounded by rainbow angels. Goddess Jacinta is a Mayan elder who connects deeply to the earth, trees, plants, flowers, bushes, and rainforests. She greets you with open arms as you enter the temple.

The temple has many levels; the higher up you go, the lighter it gets. There is a spiral staircase to different levels of ascension, and when you are ready to ascend to each level, you move on. You earn your ascension journey; what you put in, you will get out of it. Then you will receive pearls of wisdom. Each person is given a white rose as a sign of purification.

You will learn human values of truth, honesty, integrity, and love, and you will receive clarity. Many angels are helping you here in this

Temple of Golden Light. You can enter the temple heavy-laden and leave totally uplifted. This is a wonderful temple of ascension for everyone to visit during meditation or sleep time. I have called this the Temple of the Lotus Flower because it reflects the unravelling of one's soul just like a lotus flower, which is such a beautiful experience.

## 135. Mogadishu, Somalia: Temple of Compassion

Mogadishu is the capital and largest city of Somalia. Located in the coastal Banaadir region on the Indian Ocean, the city has served as an important port for centuries. Mogadishu is situated on the Indian Ocean coast of the Horn of Africa. Its small Temple of Golden Light has a traditional churchlike feel, with a large chapel room for prayer and church services. Indeed, all the African temples are churchlike, as they are only just beginning as a continent to move from the third dimension towards the fifth. It is a slow shift, so being churchlike is the right energy for Africa.

The Mogadishu temple is filled with the energy of the Divine Mother and Jesus Christ, and it is surrounded by rainbow angels. It is connected to Archangel Gabriel and his divine twin flame, Archangel Hope, and their legions of angels. Inside the temple, the rooms are large and spacious. There is a healing room with a rainbow crystal that emits healing energy. The healing angels, accompanied by golden harp music, perform sound healing.

In another room, there are discussions on human values, mindfulness, consideration for others, and honouring one's brothers and sisters. Tribal ceremonies are also held here, holding the purest and highest intentions. The temple exists on many levels, and as you rise, you move up on a white staircase edged with gold. The higher up you go through the temple, the more the energy becomes angelic. Remember, you do not necessarily need to change; you just need to see things differently now. We and our planet are shifting and raising vibrations. When humanity measures wealth by love, respect, and gratitude, we will all be rich.

## 136. Timbuktu, Mali: Temple of Peace and Calm

Timbuktu is located at the southern edge of the Sahara near the Niger River. The town is surrounded by sand dunes, and the streets are covered in sand. An earthy Temple of Golden Light, quite low in the density of the etheric of Mother Earth, is situated over the centre of Timbuktu. It is churchlike and has the appearance of being built from wooden material.

There are different areas to this temple, and one is filled with the love and happiness of gospel music. Gospel singers wear blue gowns with white frilly collars. It is a place of worship, fun, laughter, happiness, singing, and dancing. The other part of the temple is so peaceful that white doves are regularly seen there. It is a temple of hope, peace, and calm.

This is a major African temple connecting to Jesus Christ, overseen by the Divine Mother, but honouring all tribes, creeds, and faiths, like all Temples of Golden Light. As a large temple, it holds the light for the area and is able to spread that light for thousands of miles around. This Temple of Golden Light clears people's heart chakras, helping them to move forward into yet more light. It also connects to the ascended master Paul the Venetian, who helps with creative expression.

Start talking and thinking that you are blessed. That activates the blessing, and then you will receive even more. Think gratitude, and you will receive more blessings.

## 137. Casablanca, Morocco: Temple of Soothing Calm

The temple is situated in the etheric near the mountains above Casablanca, the largest city of Morocco, in the western part of the country on the Atlantic Ocean. It is the largest city in the Maghreb as well as one of the largest and most important cities in Africa.

This temple connects in particular to the Muslim energy of Mohammed. Created in the shape of a mosque, it shines with whitewashed walls representing the pure and sacred in heart. Here you can clear your heart chakra, learn the way of the pure heart, and rise above any negative occasion, even though you may not agree with those around you, their circumstances, situation, or behaviour. Honesty, integrity, and promoting hard work are strong values of this Temple of Golden Light, surrendering to the divine and trusting God's grace. You may enter stressed but leave peaceful, calm, and serene, knowing that all will be well.

This is a Temple of Golden Light for discussion, talks, debates, speakers, meetings, and learning. Divine light shines on all who enter. It is a wonderful place of peace for brotherhood and sisterhood. Here, the males meet in a separate area from the females. This is the way it is in this temple. All temples are created to suit the needs of the area and country. The Divine Mother knows her people.

## 138. Tunis, Tunisia: Temple of Faith

Tunis is the capital of Tunisia and is situated on a large Mediterranean Sea Gulf of Tunis, behind the Lake of Tunis. The city extends along the coastal plain and the hills that surround it. There are many faiths in Tunisia—Moslem and Christian, to name two—and life can be quite tough. Sometimes when life gets tough, we need faith to get us through each day and provide guidance and protection.

The temple is situated over the centre of Tunis and is overseen directly by Lady Nada. It is a small, very peaceful temple—an escape from reality. Lady Nada is the twin flame of Jesus Christ and an aspect of the Divine Mother. She is the embodiment of love, and all who connect with her will feel her love, light and peace.

Like all the temples, this one has a large, rounded, domed roof and permanently on top is a large golden angel. The temple is ethereal and holds overwhelmingly high energy, connecting to golden cherubs placed over the city. Once you enter through the heart-shaped doorway, you become aware of beautiful rainbow lights shining on the mosaic ceiling, clearing all those inside. There is a muffled, cotton-wool silence. The healing that takes place within the temple is more for physical than emotional healing, such as of old war wounds from past lives and atrocities, disabilities, and disfigurements.

## 139. Cairo, Egypt: Temple of Egyptology
*Listed in Healing | Surrounded by a city of light*

Cairo is the capital of Egypt and the largest city in the Middle East. The area around present-day Cairo has long been a focal point of ancient Egypt. The fortress known as Babylon remains the oldest structure in the city. Cairo is also associated with ancient Egypt, as it is close to the ancient cities of Memphis, Giza, and Fustat, which are near the great Sphinx and the Pyramids of Giza. The entrance to this Temple of Golden Light is under the Sphinx by the front right paw. The appropriate energy will open the doorway. It is not difficult, but you do need to love everything and everyone and really want to be healed and move on.

The Temples of Golden Light are sacred places, but this temple is extra special. Two big black panthers guard it, only allowing those who are invited or have the right energy to enter. This means that if you are drawn to this temple, it is right for you. The energy of Goddess Isis is here, along with energy from the gods Osiris and Thoth; the goddesses Nefertiti, Hathor, Maat, and Sekhmet; and the pharaohs Akhenaten, Tutankhamun, and Rameses, as well as many other Egyptian gods/goddesses and pharaohs. A large star shines continually above the temple, emitting constant light. The temple connects to Sirius, the star constellation in Orion's belt.

The history of ancient Egypt is explained in full for those who wish to learn. You enter and travel down a long golden corridor to an inner chamber where you are first greeted by Tutankhamun. You are then guided towards the pyramid-shaped healing chamber of the goddesses Isis and Nefertiti, where you will receive healing for emotional and physical issues and healing for your mind.

Connecting with this temple will very much accelerate your spiritual journey, as it is possible for you to be given the keys to the universe. This is an important ascension Temple of Golden Light, surrounded by rainbow angels and protected by ascension angels. The ascension angels are here to help you raise your vibration; they have golden wings and hold a high vibration themselves.

## Middle East

The following are the five Temples of Golden Light in the Middle East:

140. Beirut, Lebanon
141. Bethlehem, Israel
142. Jerusalem, Israel
143. Al Basrah, Iraq
144. Abu Dhabi, United Arab Emirates

## 140. Beirut, Lebanon: Temple of Grace

Beirut is the capital and largest city of Lebanon. It is located on a peninsula at the midpoint of Lebanon's Mediterranean coast. Much healing is needed in this country. People's hearts need to be healed, as this country has suffered considerably in past times.

The Beirut Temple of Golden Light is a very large healing temple with a golden domed roof placed in the etheric right over the city centre. Above the temple is a big golden angel of love and golden light, and like other temples, it is surrounded by rainbow angels of rainbow light and filled with the love of the Divine Mother. It is quite grounded and very peaceful. It is a place of learning, contemplation, forgiveness, and healing.

On the grounds of the temple are beautiful gardens, one with a large three-tiered fountain and a moat. As you enter the temple, you will feel the energy of your heart opening and expanding. You will be able to see the bigger picture of life and our world.

The temple connects to the Sirius star system, which is sixth-dimensional and therefore very loving and respectful. In this temple, you will feel the pure love of God/Goddess giving you the qualities of oneness and respect as well as love and light. You may well ask, 'What is it all about?' Here, you will receive the answer.

## 141. Bethlehem, Israel: Temple of Christ Energy

Bethlehem is well known as the birthplace of Jesus Chris, and the city is inhabited by one of the oldest Christian communities in the world. Bethlehem is a Palestinian city located in the central West Bank about six miles south of Jerusalem. The Temple of Golden Light is overseen by Lady Nada, the twin flame of Jesus Christ. This is a smaller but powerful temple. Over the top are golden crosses symbolising Jesus, who died on the cross. This is a beautiful temple filled with Christ energy, angels, and candles. It is light, bright, and very uplifting. A bridge of light connects it to source.

The Bethlehem Temple of Golden Light is a place for manifesting abundance. Please remember that what you ask for, you will receive, so be prepared to have all that you wish for. It is important to think clearly and be discerning before you ask. This is also a temple of prayer, where you can ask for mercy about anything. The energy of the Ark of the Covenant is here. Truth will be revealed, and peace will fall on our planet.

You will learn here that it is not difficult to be nice, unselfish, or helpful. You will learn that indeed, we are all one; we should think of everyone as our own family and not feel that we are separate in any way. You need to be the hands and the heart of God, helping all those around you in their time of need. Helping others is your vocation. God will look after you as you look after others. Unconditional love is your goal from now onwards. Be love, think love, do love.

## 142. Jerusalem, Israel: Temple of Loving Light
*Listed in Healing*

Jerusalem is on a plateau in the Judaean Mountains between the Mediterranean and the Dead Sea. One of the oldest cities in the world, it is considered a holy city in the three major Abrahamic religions of Judaism, Christianity, and Islam. The old city is home to many sites of religious importance—among them the Temple Mount and its Western Wall, the Church of the Holy Sepulchre, the Dome of the Rock, the Garden Tomb, and the Al-Aqsa Mosque.

This temple connects to the whole of the universe. In the centre is a huge pillar of light, a vortex of divine energy that connects to source light. It is one of the larger temples, and its energy can be felt for thousands of miles around. This temple is completely white and is filled with Christed consciousness energy, sending out beams of love from Jesus Christ for all humanity. It is overseen by Lord Maitreya, who overshadowed Jesus Christ for the last three years of his life. The temple is also overseen by a huge master angel with massive golden wings. This is a very high-vibrational Temple of Golden Light.

The message here is to love everyone as if it was your last day here on earth, and to forgive everyone. What is the point of holding on to old thoughts and energy? That does you no good at all. Let go and release. Love, health, and happiness are what you need to achieve, and this temple will help you to heal emotional imbalances.

The Jerusalem Temple of Golden Light is all about truth, beliefs, faith, and being able to express yourself with love, respect, and consideration towards others. Bring peace, calm, balance, and harmony into your life by practicing meditation, prayer, or contemplation. Help others to heal and move on. Be a beacon of light, smile at everyone you meet each day, and brighten up their day with your kind words and smiles.

You are blessed to be living on this planet at this very important time of her ascension. Mother Earth is raising her vibration, and we must raise our vibration too, otherwise we will be left behind. We have been born for a reason. It is time to fulfil your purpose now.

## 143. Al Basrah, Iraq: Temple of Pink Gold

Basrah is located on the Shatt-al-Arab, a river in southern Iraq between Kuwait and Iran. It is Iraq's main port and played an important role in early Islamic history. The city was occupied by British troops during the Iraq War, 2003–2007, and it has often been a place of unrest and security concerns.

The Basrah Temple of Golden Light is overseen by Goddess Lathinda, one of the three goddesses who oversee all the Temples of Golden Light. Like every goddess, Lathinda is an aspect of the Divine Mother. The temple is all about feminine energy, compassion, understanding, self- empowerment, self-worth, self-respect, motherhood, and the inner child. It focuses on learning to cry tears of joy, speaking your truth, clearing emotions, and learning to love yourself, particularly when no one else does.

In this part of the world, women are suppressed, so this temple helps women to honour themselves through patience, gratitude, and love. This temple is all about women and helping them to change through passive co-operation and loving themselves. You are important, you are loved, and you are blessed.

Swords are crossed over the main doors to indicate that no men should enter. Around the doors are many white roses that symbolise purity. Inside the main hall are lotus and lily flowers, all white in colour, which surround a massive sapphire-blue crystal. The temple is a place of prayer and healing emotions, teaching you to have freedom of spirit with your prayers. God hears all prayers, sometimes through your guardian angels, and they are answered and replied to with love. Prayer can change all things. It has a ripple effect, spreading outwards and creating greater awareness.


## 144. Abu Dhabi, United Arab Emirates: Temple of Transmutation

Abu Dhabi is the capital of and the second most populous city in the United Arab Emirates. The 144th temple of Golden Light has been placed in the etheric over desert land on the outskirts of the city. This Temple of Golden Light connects to star constellations, angels, and celestial beings of infinite love and light. It is medium-sized with a golden domed roof and crystalline walls. Because of its connection to the heavens, it has a galactic energy. The temple emits a continuous rich golden-orange flame—the colour of Archangel Metatron's aura.

The temple transmutes all negative energy that may be within you, giving clarity on your life purpose and your reason for living and incarnating on this planet. It will help you get rid of old negative energy and bring through the light from within you. The temple also gives moral guidance, such as letting go of judgment, and asks you to question yourself. It is a place of learning, transmuting the old and bringing in the new.

Archangel Michael, with his legions of angels, holds a key position within this temple, cutting all old cords with his sword of light and clear crystal truth. He tells you that the power is within you. You must do the work yourself, and then he will help you. As you walk through the temple, you will know it is filled with unconditional love and streaming with pure consciousness. When you connect with this temple, you will change for the better. Like other temples, this is overseen by the Divine Mother and surrounded by rainbow angels of love and golden light.

# Chapter 8

## *Healing*

It is time for us all to shift. No more thinking selfishly. It's time to heal our heart, emotions, and physical body. It's time to share, be considerate, show loving kindness, and be friendly. If you do not receive these qualities back from others, tell yourself that you did the very best you could and do not take things personally. Our planet Gaia is shifting and raising her consciousness, so we must join Mother Earth and do the same.

How do we shift? We need to think in ways that are positive rather than negative. We need to love instead of live in fear. We need to think in terms of creating our own reality to manifest all that we need to create and recreate for our future. Let go of hurt, anger, and resentment, as these feelings will only hold you back. Take a giant step forward and forgive. We must take responsibility for our actions and stop blaming others. It is time to grow spiritually—time to up our focus on living a good way of life. It is time to take our power back! Why give your power away when you can have it for yourself?

Love everything that you do, whether it gives you what you want or not. Life is an experience, so love yourself and all that you do. Something may not have worked out, so change it and try again. Work with the universe, not against it, and I guarantee you will be successful. Let go of that ego—the one that gets annoyed when things do not go right, the one that says *I want that designer dress, designer suit, and expensive shoes*. If you do things right, you can have all that you want and wish for, so detach, take a step back, and allow the universe to help you. Do not have any expectations. Leave them outside the door and simply accept with a loving heart.

You can change anything with love and a pure heart. You can manifest, create, and show loving kindness to everyone and everything, and this will come back to you, just like a mirror reflects back. You are beautiful, so let your light shine. Be the being of love you truly are. This will help you heal your heart.

Count your blessings. Be deeply grateful for whatever you have: your family, children, parents, friends, job, health, home, sanity. You may smile, but to have your own stress-free mind is a wonderful thing and a valued attribute. Your gift to the world can be your love, so take time to smile at people you pass walking on the sidewalk. Take time to help an elderly person across the road. Take time to help people and be neighbourly.

Everyone is so busy these days. Try to take the time to stop, sit, relax, be still, and be calm. Your time here on the planet is short compared to the age of our Planet Earth. So what are you doing right now in your life? Are you happy, and if not, why not? Change things. Do not be sad, as there is always hope just around the corner. But you have to act now. Life is for living and not being sad and unhappy. Focus on being the best you can. Realise that everything you have is good and bless all of it.

Even your age is good. Age is an issue of mind over matter: if you don't mind, it doesn't matter. We create our own lives by our thinking, so think big and do good things and the universe will reply with love. Be positive with your thinking, and positive things will definitely happen to you. If you have a problem, meditate, and this will uplift you, as when you meditate, you connect with your soul and spirit. We all have a guardian angel, so when you meditate, ask to connect with your angel for divine guidance.

Celebrate your life as being successful. If things did not work out as you planned, it does not matter. Do not look back. Be grateful for the way your life was and is now. In some strange way, all things happen the way they are meant to, and for the right reasons. We all come through the veil of amnesia to be born here and live on this lovely planet. What we think is going to happen does not necessarily happen. Life can be much better. We can think that we made wrong decisions, but nothing is wrong. We did the best that our awareness at the time would allow. Regret nothing and be happy. Be your own gift of love.

If you can believe in angels and archangels, let them into your life and connect with them. If you have faith and believe in God/Goddess, allow him/her to help you with the Temples of Golden Light. If you connect with an ascended master or masters, permit them to help you, as they are here for you.

The temples are a gift from source to humanity to help us heal on all levels—physically, emotionally, mentally, and spiritually. The temples carry unique attributes, enabling us all to embrace, love, and nurture our inherent spiritual abilities. Connect with these temples, and you will be helped. It is time for the goddess energy to return and rebalance Planet Earth. The temples are surrounded by rainbow angels and are situated all around the globe. They are overseen by three goddesses, all of pure love and light.

## Heart Healing

The following are temples that particularly heal your heart or your emotional and physical body; the number in parentheses after the name of each is its number within the full set of 144 temples:

- Glastonbury, England (3)
- Paris, France (8)
- Lourdes, France (9)
- Venice, Italy (17)
- Omaha, Nebraska, United States (49)
- Havana, Cuba (68)
- Uluru, Australia (78)

## Glastonbury, England: Temple of the Heart One
*Listed in Europe | Surrounded by a city of light*

Glastonbury is the heart chakra of the world and has been since 2012. This temple is as tall as the Tor and in the etheric over the whole of Glastonbury, Chalice Well, and Glastonbury Abbey. What it does is help ground you to Mother Earth, connecting you to her heart chakra, aligning you with pure love and trust for our planet, and helping you to gain family values and traditions.

If you need to focus on anything in your life—whether family, health, relationships, or career—this is the temple to connect with, as this Temple of Golden Light will bring you towards your heart's desire. It will ground you with stability, hope, and fortitude. Simply focus on the Glastonbury Temple of Golden Light for love, balance, and insight. This temple will help you see things more clearly and give clarity to any situation.

## Paris, France: Temple of Golden Light One
*Listed in Main Temples and in Europe | Surrounded by a city of light*

This temple is situated in the etheric behind the Sacré Coeur and connects to Mother Mary and Jesus Christ, along with many angels and archangels, particularly Archangel Raphael and his legions of angels. The temple is surrounded by a city of light and is one of the high-vibrational Temples of Golden Light connecting to the Divine Mother and the angels on high. Inside the temple is a beautiful healing chamber of light with a rose quartz crystal couch to lie on.

## Lourdes, France: Temple of the Golden Heart
*Listed in Europe*

The Lourdes Temple of Golden Light is small but aligns to the absolute heart of God/Goddess. This temple is overseen by a magnificent angel of golden light and by St Bernadette herself. You can ask St Bernadette for a dispensation to heal your heart and to heal anyone you know—adults, children, and animals. She may telepathically give you a message or gift, and you may sense St Bernadette's energy as she blesses you.

There are no words, no thoughts, no speaking; you are simply being, and you will connect with the oneness of the universe and Mother Earth's heart centre. This is a wonderful ethereal Temple of

Golden Light which links to God's heart. This is the nearest you will get to paradise and total bliss.

## Venice, Italy: Temple of Loved Ones
*Listed in Europe | Surrounded by a city of light*

This is a large ethereal temple of golden light over Rialto Bridge extending to St Mark's Basilica, surrounded by a city of light. The temple connects to Jesus Christ, Mother Mary, Archangel Raphael, and legions of their angels. This temple is a gateway to heaven, as it connects people to their loved ones who have passed over. It is the only one of the 144 Temples of Golden Light that enables you to connect with these loved ones.

The temple also helps you to forgive any family member or friend who has ever hurt you and allows them to forgive you too, for forgiveness is the key to happiness and wholeness. Our physical body is a vehicle for our soul, and our soul is a vehicle for our spirit, so we never die. Eternal life goes on. Your memories are many, so take time to be with your loved ones, and if you need to forgive someone, then please do that now, as forgiveness is extremely important—much more important than you may think. Forgive everyone who has ever hurt you, even though it may be difficult—perhaps the hardest thing you have ever done. Please forgive them now so that you can move on in grace and love. Send love to all situations and give gratitude for the experience. If you wish, give any situation to God/Goddess and be grateful for the lesson learnt.

Healing takes place in this temple by sound and vibration. Your heart is healed through tones of music. Each person on the planet has a musical tone, and if you can find your tone, you will be instantly healed of all disharmonies. How amazing would that be? When you listen to music, you may find that a particular tone resonates with your body. That will be your tone; when you hear it, you will know it.

This is a powerful healing temple on all levels of mind, body, and spirit, healing old wounds and old hurts and releasing old energy you no longer need. Your soul only wishes you happiness and love. This is an incredibly peaceful, calm temple—a meeting place for your loved ones, family, and friends—held together by God/Goddess energy of divine love.

## Omaha, Nebraska, United States: Temple of Soul Journey
*Listed in the Americas*

This temple works with the heart chakra—my heart to your heart, we are one. It is in the etheric over the centre or heart of Omaha. It is a medium-size earthy temple of unconditional love. As our heart chakra twins with the solar plexus chakra, this temple helps clear and cleanse any negativity connected to these chakras, removing any old issues and trauma and helping you to open up to unconditional love.

The Omaha temple teaches people how to forgive and about how important forgiveness is for their souls. If one passes over in anger, hate, or resentment, that will impede the journey of one's soul until forgiveness is sought and given on all levels. So you need to forgive everyone everything they may have done or said to hurt you, and other people need to forgive you if you have done something to hurt or harm them. It is very important that this is done before one passes over into the world of spirit. When people are religious, this simple act of forgiveness is made easier, but not everyone these days is religious.

## Havana, Cuba: Temple of Hearts
*Listed in the Americas*

In this Temple of Hearts, your heart will be developed, cleared, and cleansed. We have three heart chakras: the heart chakra, higher heart chakra, and cosmic heart chakra. This temple will help you develop your heart chakra centres as well as raise your vibration. You will be helped to clear your heart centre, and this sometimes takes special work, as forgiveness for your own actions and for others' actions towards you will need to be addressed.

## Uluru, Australia: Temple of the Star People
*Listed in Main Temples and in Australasia and Oceanic | Surrounded by a city of light*

Uluru is a very large temple, the Aboriginal star temple, holding a beautiful energy of bright light surrounded by a city of light. It is filled with beings of light, natural medicinal plants, and nature. On top of the temple is a massive star beaming outwards to other star systems. To find out how to heal naturally, connect with this Temple of Golden Light and learn how the Aborigines healed with natural medicine, the old ways, the old remedies. Natural healing remedies are much better for our bodies, as they have no side effects. You will learn how to respect the earth's energy and respect other people, gaining qualities of peace, virtue, and honour.

## Emotional Healing

How do we understand emotional adulthood? Acceptance keeps us emotionally balanced, and lack of acceptance will create emotional anxiety. When something happens but not in the way you want and you are patient, that means you accept it; but when you do not accept it, you become angry. What you give out, you get back, and sometimes karma can boomerang back to you immediately – but not always in the way you think. If it's negative, you learn quickly from this lesson, but if it is positive, then love will always come back to you. The universe will make sure of that, but it can sometimes come back in unexpected ways. Do love, be love, think love, have no expectations, and then good things will happen to you.

At certain times of the year, like Christmas and Easter, we can think about forgiving others, but we really need to forgive all year round. Let this be a time of forgiving all who have hurt you. You will only begin to heal when you let go of past hurts and anger and forgive anyone you think or feel has hurt you. Trust, surrender, and accept all that has happened to you with a loving heart, in this lifetime and any past lifetimes. You will be amazed at the love you receive on a higher level from others. The small act of forgiveness can be extremely powerful. There is only one thing to do with love, and that is to show it. When we keep our hearts closed and seem aloof, we hold on to all past hurts, anger, and resentment.

The answer is to open your heart and give love, and then move on. It is so simple, and yet it can be so difficult for people. It will open so many doors to self-love, self-respect, self-worth, freedom, creativity, and health. Love-consciousness energy does not judge, criticise, or react to negative energy, because it is a higher consciousness quality. It is all about happiness, joy, love, and the ability to express oneself with honesty and integrity while living in divine truth and the Now moment.

You will definitely know you are there when you can smile at every human being without passing judgment or criticism—when you can look into each person's eyes and truly give love for the sake of love. Try to love in your everyday life. Be grateful for small acts of kindness, whether a few words of comfort or an act of physical kindness. We are in essence all one consciousness. We are all human beings living on this plant at this time, so let us celebrate this unity, this oneness. Let us work together in friendship, in love, and in caring and sharing. Please see the beauty that exists in yourself and others and allow your inner light to shine, as this will release all negative emotions and facilitate a healing for you.

Here are some temples that specialise in healing emotions; the number in parentheses after the name of each is its number within the full set of 144 temples:

- Madrid Spain (13)
- Lisbon Portugal (15)
- Mount Shasta, California, United States (41)
- Indian Ocean One, off Rockingham, Perth, Australia (91)
- Cairo, Egypt (139)
- Jerusalem, Israel (142)

**Cairo, Egypt: Temple of Egyptology**
*Listed in Rest of the World | Surrounded by a city of light*

Cairo is the capital of Egypt and the largest city in the Middle East. Cairo is also associated with ancient Egypt, as it is close to the ancient cities of Memphis, Giza, and Fustat, which are near the great Sphinx and the Pyramids of Giza. The entrance to this Temple of Golden Light is under the Sphinx by the front right paw. The appropriate energy will open the doorway. It is not difficult, but you do need to love everything and everyone and really want to be healed and move on.

The Temples of Golden Light are sacred places, but this temple is extra special. Two big black panthers guard it, only allowing those who are invited or have the right energy to enter. This means if you are drawn to this temple, it is right for you.

You enter and travel down a long golden corridor to an inner chamber where you are first greeted by Tutankhamun. You are then guided towards the pyramid-shaped healing chamber of the goddesses Isis and Nefertiti, where you will receive healing for emotional and physical issues and healing for your mind. Connecting with this temple will very much accelerate your spiritual journey, as it is possible for you to be given the keys to the universe. This is an important ascension Temple of Golden Light, surrounded by rainbow angels and protected by ascension angels. The ascension angels are here to help you raise your vibration; they have golden wings and hold a high vibration themselves.

## Jerusalem, Israel: Temple of Loving Light
*Listed in Rest of the World*

This temple connects to the whole of the universe. In the centre of the temple is a huge pillar of light, a vortex of divine energy that connects to source light. The message here is to love everyone as if it was your last day here on earth and to forgive everyone. What is the point of holding on to old thoughts and energy? That does you no good at all. Let go and release. Love, health, and happiness are what you need to achieve, and this temple will help you to heal emotionally.

The Jerusalem Temple of Golden Light is all about truth, beliefs, faith, and being able to express yourself with love, respect, and consideration towards others. Bring peace, calm, balance, and harmony into your life by practicing meditation, prayer, or contemplation. Help others to heal and move on. Be a beacon of light, smile at everyone you meet each day, and brighten up their day with your kind words and smiles.

You are blessed to be living on this planet at this very important time of her ascension. Mother Earth is raising her vibration, and we must raise our vibration too, otherwise we will be left behind. You have been born for a reason. It is time to fulfil your purpose now.

## Madrid, Spain: Temple of the Divine Flame of Love
*Listed in Europe*

The Madrid Temple of Golden Light is incredibly peaceful and serene, with beautiful artwork inside and a painted ceiling just like the famous Sistine Chapel. The energy of this temple is filled with the love of the angels, including cherubs, Jesus Christ, Mother Mary, and Mary Magdalene. It is also connected to the energy of many Spanish saints, including St Teresa of Avila. They all help you to forgive and heal emotionally. Even old, stored, stuck energy can be released when you connect to this temple.

Archangel Raphael's energy is felt in this beautiful temple of sacred energy, love, and peace. Issues of the heart and solar plexus are helped here. It is very much a family Temple of Golden Light, visited by parents, children, and all family members. The sick, homeless, and lonely are encouraged to receive healing, to heal their lives, and to live in a more positive, abundant way.

## Lisbon, Portugal: Temple of Peace
*Listed in Europe*

The Lisbon Temple of Golden Light is so very calm. Situated in the etheric on the outskirts of the city, this large temple exudes serene peacefulness. It is a cleansing, clearing temple; you enter heavily laden with sadness and come out much lighter, leaving behind heavy energy. The temple helps clear heavy solar plexus and heart issues.

## Mount Shasta, California, United States: Temple of Truth
*Listed in the Americas and in Meditation and Relaxation*

Mount Shasta is a special, sacred place of immense peace and healing. In its Temple of Golden Light, there is a strong Native American energy. It is a temple where people speak their truth with love whilst sitting in a circle. White Buffalo Calf Woman offers words of wisdom in her native tongue. Chief Running Bull and Chief White Eagle are known to come, sit inside, and give interesting talks on peace and love.

Healing is performed, and a new healing modality will come through this temple. Very troubled souls can come to receive healing to remove past life issues, and current life issues can be released when they are ready. It is a place of undoing and unravelling strong feelings that have caused disharmonies and discontent throughout life. You will only begin to heal when you let go of past hurts, forgive those who have wronged you, and learn to forgive yourself for your mistakes. People who need emotional healing should connect with this temple, and enlightenment will also be given.

## Indian Ocean One, off Rockingham, Perth, Australia
*Listed in Australasia and Oceanic*

This is a smaller Temple of Golden Light situated in the Indian Ocean off the coast of Rockingham, Perth, Australia. It is a healing temple connecting to the energy of the dolphins and the ancient energy of mermaids and coral reefs. The healing is given on an emotional level, allowing you to de-stress and let go of all energy you no longer need or want, giving you peace, calm, and balance. The temple will transmute all energies that are negative, transforming them into positive qualities.

The Indian Oceanic One Temple of Golden Light will help you filter and cut through anger and grief quickly, teaching you to deal with the shadows in order to reach the light. Water is an amazing healer and works very well to help heal those with emotional imbalance. The healing from this Temple of Golden Light is vibrational, relaxing, and transformational.

## Physical Healing

We function as human beings with many working chakras, which are also called energy centres. The higher up we go energetically to raise our vibration, the more chakras we activate. Light workers are souls that are here bringing forward a higher quotient of light within their four-body system: mental, emotional, physical, and spiritual. These light workers are now working with more activated chakras to share and spread the light of source.

However, sometimes light workers and others can get lost along the way, and this can cause disharmony within their chakras. When we forget our mission, our purpose for being here on Planet Earth, we can become ill or unwell. Certain chakras no longer work or spin properly, so we then need to find healing to replace our lost energy and repair our chakras and our disharmony due to our misunderstanding of life. We then become healed and see the light, so to speak, realizing our soul's purpose.

Up until now, people have usually needed to visit a healer to be healed, but now they can be healed directly by the temples or by being guided to someone by the temples. It just depends on what is wrong physically with the individual. Please understand that sometimes physical healing may take some time, depending on how long we have had disharmony. Having said that, sometimes miracles can happen overnight.

Here are a few temples that may heal on the physical level; the number in parentheses after the name of each is its number within the full set of 144 temples:

- Rome, Italy (16)
- Budapest, Hungary (24)
- Phoenix, Arizona, United States (44)
- Atlanta, Georgia, United States (53)
- Boston, Massachusetts, United States (58)
- Margaret River, Perth, Australia (79)
- Agra, India (97)

**Rome, Italy: Temple of Light**
*Listed in Europe | Surrounded by a city of light*

This temple is in the etheric over the centre of Rome. It is a large golden temple surrounded by a city of light overseen by a huge golden master angel. It has an earthy churchlike feel to it and is filled with very large, lit candles. Smaller areas are also filled with glowing tea-light candles. It is a temple that heals on a physical body level, healing all adults, children, and animals, including sea creatures. It holds the love and energy of Mother Mary, Jesus Christ, Mary Magdalene, and

St Francis of Assisi, as well as Archangel Raphael and the rainbow angels.

Working with heart issues and disharmonies of the physical body; healing issues of 'poor me' and victimhood consciousness; and forgiving the sins of all who think they have sinned, this temple teaches you to think of not *I*, but *we*. You can ask for grace in your life and for blessings to be bestowed upon you and your family. Ask also for absolution and to be shown your own beauty from within, as God/Goddess will show you your own divine spark of God/Goddess that is within you.

## Budapest, Hungary: Temple of Open Heart
*Listed in Europe*

The Budapest Temple of Golden Light has an earth energy that you feel immediately when you arrive. It is very peaceful, with beautiful gardens. There are many healing rooms, and you are invited to look around the temple and then move into a room for healing of your physical, emotional, mental, or spiritual body. You are directed to lie down on a soft couch as golden seraphim angels surround you and give you healing.

Focus your attention on a part of your body that needs healing and then telepathically link with the golden angels to explain why you wish to be healed. You will feel the love of the angels as they surround you and send you healing light. In the background, you will hear angelic harp music sounding vibrational healing tones. This is so soothing, and as the golden healing light moves through the whole of your body, you feel peacefully blessed with God/Goddess love. You know that all will be well and that soon you will recover from your disharmony and be able to put this all behind you.

## Agra, India: Temple of Golden Radiance
*Listed in Main Temples and in Asia | Surrounded by a city of light*

Agra's is a very large Temple of Golden Light, surrounded by a city of light, situated in the etheric close to the Taj Mahal. The temple connects to the Indian gods/goddesses Brahma, Shiva, Vishnu, Krishna, Ganesh, Lakshmi, Kali, and many more, making this a beautiful, sacred temple. It is also a busy temple, with many healing sanctuaries and prayer rooms. Your soul can fragment over many lifetimes as a result of difficult situations, such as dying in shock. This temple has a special sanctuary that specialises in bringing your fragments back together and making you whole again.

## Boston, Massachusetts, United States: Temple of Golden Rays
*Listed in the Americas | Surrounded by a city of light*

A very powerful temple with high energy, the Boston temple is a holy place of pure light, giving peace, serenity, and calm. Golden rays of divine light shine down and through this temple, as if someone has switched on a bright light. Archangel Metaziel oversees this temple, which is surrounded by rainbow angels, whose presence is very strong. They provide healing to all those who come here to be healed. People are absolved of issues and helped to move on. This temple represents physical healing and balance in your life.

People can reach enlightenment through this temple. Enlightened souls do not ask anyone to believe anything; they simply point the way and leave it to others to realise it for themselves. To become enlightened, you need to have cleared all your karma by 70 per cent.

Love is the doorway to enlightenment. Love humanity as well as your own divinity. Everyone is on the same pathway, so cancel negative thoughts by replacing them with positive thoughts. Love and accept yourself every day, and remember you are total love.

Meditation is a good practice and will help you to keep thinking clearly and positively each and every day. Meditate and connect to this wonderful Temple of Golden Light. Visualise yourself being bathed in light and healed of all disharmonies as you connect to this temple. See your family, friends, and any animals all bathed in light and healed of physical, emotional, mental, or spiritual imbalance. Ask and you will receive enlightenment. Trust and be patient, as all good things come to those who wait.

## Phoenix, Arizona, United States: Temple of the Future
*Listed in Main Temples and the Americas | Surrounded by a city of light*

The Phoenix Temple of Golden Light will bring a new healing modality—a new vibrational healing tool brought through from the higher realms to help us heal. This will facilitate miracles when people are ready to heal.

The temple looks and feels quite futuristic and aligns to many star people of celestial light. It is the eleventh largest temple and has a spaceship-landing docking station. Strongly connected to the Arcturians, who are fifth-dimensional beings and here to help our planet ascend, the temple is filled with many other Christed ETs trying to help us ascend rather than destroy ourselves. The Arcturians work as one, and they do not speak, as they have no need. They are telepathic with each other. They can read people's energy and auras and work on a higher vibration.

## Atlanta, Georgia, United States: Temple of Goodwill
*Listed in the Americas*

The Atlanta temple will help you heal physically of all disharmonies. Connect with this Temple of Golden Light and meditate whenever you wish to, and please feel free to offload your problems here, as you will be helped and healed with divine healing light. Everyone who talks about their problems here is given divine blessings when healing takes place. For example, if you feel guilty about something that you did or did not do, you will receive healing here.

This is a smaller temple, about the same size as St Paul's Cathedral in London. Set in the open air under the stars, it offers comfort, peace, healing, and reassurance. There is an ethereal feel, and it is surrounded by many rainbow angels. It connects to Jesus Christ and the Apostles, Mother Mary, Mary Magdalene, Raphael the Archangel of healing, and Michael the Archangel of truth, strength, and protection. Prayers are said here on a global scale, and people can pray here for family members to be healed and for divine guidance.

## Margaret River, Perth, Australia: Temple of Crystalline Energy
*Listed in Australasia and Oceanic and in Meditation | Surrounded by a city of light*

The Margaret River Temple of Golden Light is a lovely cleansing, clearing, healing temple of great power with an Aboriginal connection. It connects to all of the other Australian temples. It is a healing temple, with a powerful healing sanctuary inside holding the energy of earth crystals. A healing retreat is a welcome relief from everyday life and concerns. Meditate upon this temple when you want to rejuvenate your energy.

In and around Margaret River, there are hundreds of crystal caves, of which six are open to the public. The earth above is extremely special in energy. Walking around the town of Margaret River, you are aware of the crystalline energy moving up through the earth, and this energy is transmitted to the Temple of Golden Light in the etheric above.

# Chapter 9

## *Children and Animals*

On our planet at the moment are many higher souls who have volunteered to be born here to help raise the vibration of humanity and earth as Planet Earth is ascending. Sometimes these children have a tough time of it and become unwell because of the density and strictness of our planet. There are particular Temples of Golden Light which may help them where crystal, indigo, rainbow, and diamond children will help to heal the children who connect to these temples through sleep time or meditation or by a loved one praying for their child or children.

I know that this sounds unusual, but when I channelled the temples, that is what I was told by spirit. To me, this makes sense—children understand each other, and so children can be helped to heal other children. These temples are beautiful, with special sanctuaries for healing children. These sanctuaries connect to rainbow angels, fairies, and unicorns.

There are six specific animal healing temples placed around the globe, so if you have an animal that needs healing, please connect with your chosen temple through meditation or in your sleep time and give your animal's name and the reason why they are poorly. Alternatively, you can pray to the temple for healing for your animal; either practice is fine. Do not limit this to dogs, cats, and horses, as the temples can heal every form of animal.

Recently in Aberaeron, Ceredigion, in Wales, I activated a small animal healing sanctuary in the physical and aligned this sanctuary to the Snowdonia Temple of Golden Light in North Wales, which is purely an animal healing temple. I held a sacred ceremony in the barn on land belonging to a lady called Jude, and I called on St. Francis of Assisi who is connected to all of the animal healing temples. I noticed that the barn began to be filled with bright light, and with my inner vision, I could see that the place was surrounded by rainbow angels giving peace, calm, and healing.

I have highlighted temples that specialise in healing children, babies, and one's inner child and those that specialise in the healing of animals. I also include details of the only unicorn temple which is in the etheric over Geneva. They are listed with their number in the full 144 in parentheses.

## Child Healing Temples

The main Istanbul Temple of Golden Light (1) heals children as well as adults and animals. The other seventeen temples, which focus more exclusively on healing children and one's inner child, are in the etheric over the following:

- Berlin, Germany (10)
- Mo i Rana, Norway (26)
- Warsaw, Poland (30)
- Zagreb, Croatia (34)
- San Francisco, California, United States (42)
- Portland, Oregon, United States (48)
- Little Rock, Arkansas, United States (51)
- Minneapolis, Minnesota, United States (55)
- Kauai, Hawaii, United States (59)
- Callao, Lima, Peru (61)
- La Paz, Bolivia (62)
- Rio de Janeiro, Brazil (63)
- Honduras (70)
- Sydney, Australia (82)
- Kolkata, India (99)
- Bali, Indonesia (121)
- St Petersburg, Russia (127)

## Berlin, Germany: Temple of the Crystal and Rainbow Children
*Listed in Europe*

The Berlin Temple of Golden Light is light and bright. It is filled with fun, laughter, and happiness. One of the children's temples overseen by the Divine Mother, it is filled with the energy of the angels of peace and surrounded by healing rainbow angels. The children in the temple are crystal children, rainbow children, and indigo children.

This temple connects people to their own inner child by promoting singing, dancing, drawing, painting, and all forms of creativity. Here, children teach adults the art of enjoyment and how to play. Many adults have forgotten how to laugh and be happy, focusing only on earning a living and on survival, but there is so much more to living than worrying about monetary matters. The children will teach you how to let go, how to trust and have faith, and how to know that all things beautiful will come to those who act like children. That does not mean being irresponsible; it simply means to go with the flow of life, use your intuition, love your neighbour as yourself, understand everyone (no matter what you think or feel they may have done or not done), and have no judgment or criticism of other people.

By connecting people to their inner child, this temple helps to clear solar plexus and heart chakra issues. To connect with this temple, set your intention and focus upon it. If you are connecting on behalf of a child, please write down the child's name on a piece of paper. Light a candle, and if you have a favourite crystal, put it in your lap or place it by your side to make the connection stronger. Now close your eyes, wait, and listen to what comes from this connection.

As you enter the temple, you will be aware of a coloured rainbow doorway. As you take a step inside, you will notice an enormous coloured fountain. You may feel drawn to laugh, smile, draw, sing, dance, or paint—whatever you feel, just go with the flow of life. You may feel tears of joy and happiness or feel yourself releasing old heartaches and stuck energy. You may see yourself following your heart, appreciating yourself, understanding, and having no expectations of others. You may feel your soul awakening.

## Mo i Rana, Norway: Temple of Divinity
*Listed in Europe*

The Mo i Rana Temple of Golden Light is a lovely children's healing temple. Inside is a beautiful sanctuary with big pink rose quartz crystals and many rainbow angels. The temple is in the etheric in the middle of a huge pine forest. It is tall like a tower reaching up and out into the stars systems of Pleiades and Sirius, linking with the Cat People and the Hathors from Venus called the Golden Ones.

The connection to the earth is strong, as this temple connects to Middle Earth and Agartha, a city that is said to reside in the earth's core. It also links with the tree spirits as well as the elemental kingdom. This temple gives out beams of pink light that look like the aurora of the Northern Lights, attracting celestial beings, star people, star seeds, and angels—all loving, gentle souls. It is an ethereal temple of divine love, peacefulness, quiet stillness, and motionless energy.

## Warsaw, Poland: Temple of Caring
*Listed in Europe*

Poland has accumulated suffering from the First and Second World Wars, so much healing needs to happen here. Old memories need to go; those memories fill the earth with negative energy and hold patterns of suffering. All will be healed by this Temple of Golden Light.

This is a children's healing temple of tremendous light with a children's healing sanctuary inside, healing all disharmonies. Simply pray for your child for healing to take place. It is also a soul rescue temple, rescuing stuck souls from wartime and taking them over to the light using a bridge that is permanently situated within the centre of this temple. Many souls from surrounding countries will be drawn to this temple. Changes for the good are happening in Poland, and this is a large powerful temple holding much light for this area.

The Warsaw temple is very light and angelic. It connects to Archangel Raphael, Mother Mary, and Jesus Christ. It is a beautiful temple with huge ceilings and paintings of angels, cherubs, and saints of Poland.

## Zagreb, Croatia: Temple of Healing Children and Your Heart
*Listed in Europe*

The Zagreb Temple of Golden Light is in the etheric over the centre of the city, which lies in front of the Medvednica mountain range near the river Sava. Its primary function is the healing of children and your soul. It will help those with heavy heart issues, removing past life issues and old programming. This temple is filled with the pure love of the Divine Mother and is surrounded inside and out by rainbow angels. A temple with many healing sanctuaries—healing all pain, suffering, sadness, and emotional upset—this temple also heals ancestral karma and is a place where people can talk and offload all their problems whilst being counselled.

This is a large temple connected to star beings of light and many angels and fairies. It is filled with twinkling starlight and connects directly to Pleiades. The energy shines out like small silver stars, healing all those within. Archangel Chamuel and his divine twin flame, Archangel Charity, bless all those who come here.

## San Francisco, California, United States: Temple of Compassion
*Listed in the Americas | Surrounded by a city of light*

The San Francisco temple is in the etheric over water alongside the Golden Gate Bridge. It is a beautiful compassionate temple understanding every aspect of human life. Deep inside the temple is a large healing room with a very large pale pink rose-shaped crystal emitting loving energy from its centre.

This very angelic Temple of Golden Light, surrounded by a city of light, that works to heal your heart and to heal children of all ages, no matter how big or small their problem. Archangel Chamuel's and Archangel Charity's legions of angels will visit you and your children when you have healing here. Lady Nada, the twin flame of Jesus, works personally within this Temple of Golden Light, offering words of comfort, love, and compassion to help those in need.

## Portland, Oregon, United States: Temple of Universal Light Two
*Listed in the Americas*

The Portland Temple of Golden Light is situated in the etheric of Mother Earth over the centre of the city near the river. Portland is the largest city in the US state of Oregon near the confluence of the Willamette and Columbia rivers, and it was once inhabited by two bands of the Upper Chinook Indians. From the city, you can sometimes see the mountains of Mount Hood, Mount St Helens, Mount Adams, and Mount Rainer.

This is a beautiful healing sanctuary for children, surrounded and filled with rainbow angels. It is also a major healing temple for the physical body. All physical disease can be healed by this temple for adults, children, and animals. A very large Temple of Golden Light up high in the etheric of Mother Earth, it connects to the whole of this universe and the star constellations of Pleiades, Sirius, and Andromeda. From here, you can communicate with this universe and all of the planets: Venus, Mercury, Mars, Jupiter, Saturn, Neptune, Uranus, and Pluto.

## Little Rock, Arkansas, United States: Temple of Blessings
*Listed in the Americas*

This is a children's healing temple which also heals adults. It is a lovely, small, cosy, warm, comfortable temple with a churchlike community feel, and it is on four levels. There are separate levels for healing of children and of adults, for prayer and counselling, and for meditation. A beautiful temple filled with angelic energy, it connects to Jesus Christ and the Apostles, Mother Mary, and Mary Magdalene. It is surrounded by golden seraphim angels as well as rainbow angels. It is called the Temple of Blessings because it is a temple of prayer and healing.

The temple provides a bright and light sanctuary, somewhere you can go to be cleared and cleansed while you meditate. You will look at what you have in life and learn to appreciate the simple things. You will learn and understand that people care about you no matter what you did or did not do. You will learn about and be given unconditional love. God loves you and gives you whatever you pray for, so think well before you pray and ask for divine dispensations. The Lord loves those whose hearts are filled with purest divine love, so work with the creator and all will be well.

Every cell of your being is made up of love. This love is now being activated to its full potential. What you think you create; what you feel, you attract; and what you imagine, you become. Your dreams are precious diamonds of the soul. Bring them into the light and allow your inner light to shine.

## Minneapolis, Minnesota, United States: Temple of White Buffalo Calf Woman
*Listed in the Americas*

This Temple of Golden Light has many healing modalities, including a lovely healing sanctuary that is filled with rainbow angels, helping all children who need healing. The temple is overseen by a Native American named White Buffalo Calf Woman who represents the Divine Mother in her many aspects as well as Mother's Earth's love. The temple connects to Jesus Christ and the rainbow angels that heal all energy centres at once.

The creator sent the sacred White Buffalo Calf Woman to teach people how to pray. These prayers can come through many different ceremonies, including the sweat lodge for purification; the naming ceremony for children; the healing ceremony to restore health to mind, body, and spirit; the marriage ceremony for uniting male and female; the vision quest for communing with the creator for direction and answers to one's life; and the sun dance to pray for the well-being of all the people.

## Kauai, Hawaii, United States: Temple of Beauty
*Listed in the Americas*

This Temple of Golden Light lies in the etheric over Mount Wai'ale'ale near the centre of the island. A special healing temple for children, it is filled with beautiful Lemurian energy (from a time before Atlantis), which holds a very high, pure vibration of celestial light. The temple has many qualities of beauty, sunshine, happiness, healing, honesty, truth, and simplicity. Think of palm trees and soft music, and you are there.

## Callao, Lima, Peru: Temple of Silence
*Listed in the Americas*

This is a smaller temple in the etheric over Callao, on the edge of the ocean not far from Lima and near the rainforests of South America. The energy is strongly grounding because of the rainforests and is enhanced by the energy of Jesus Christ and Mother Mary. There is a churchlike feel to this loving, peaceful children's temple, where the focus is on healing children. There are many healing rooms for children, and all children here will be healed by rainbow angels. Be prepared to see miracles happen.

## La Paz, Bolivia: Temple of Change
*Listed in the Americas*

An earthy, very grounded Temple of Golden Light surrounded by a lovely green mist, it is filled with the energy of Christ consciousness and the Divine Mother. This is a temple for healing the mind, body, and spirit of children and adults alike. Prayer is an important part of the connection with this Temple of Golden Light, so pray for your child or anyone else who needs healing and wait and see what happens. Inside the temple are many healing sanctuaries, which give peace and calm. This temple is where earth meets heaven, as indicated by the vortex of light in the centre of the main hall—a huge pillar of light which connects to source.

## Rio de Janeiro, Brazil: Temple of Purity
*Listed in the Americas*

This is a temple dedicated to children's healing and to helping all crystal children, indigo children, and rainbow children understand their purpose of being able to lift the energy of others all around them and change situations. Many special Christed angels that can heal children oversee this temple. It is a high-energy temple aligning with Jesus Christ and the Apostles, Mother Mary, and many blessed saints of the pure in heart, together with healing angels of peace, love, happiness, and spiritual harmony. This temple connects to God's heart.

Children and babies can be healed when one connects to this temple through sleep-state and meditation. Inside the temple are many children all holding hands, teaching about friendship and unity. This is their temple—a temple of innocence and purity. Archangel Metaziel and the rainbow angels surround the temple.

## Honduras: Temple of Solace
*Listed in the Americas*

This is another earthy, grounding Temple of Golden Light. It is situated in the etheric of Puerto Castilla on the northern coast of Honduras. I believe that the children of Honduras will change this country, as many crystal children have decided to be born here. A large number of high-vibrational children work within this temple, healing other children as well as adults who visit in their sleep time for healing and cellular renewal.

In the centre of the temple is an enormous clear quartz crystal used for healing the sick, tired, and weary. As you enter, you will sense a feeling of love and peace and be dazzled by the bright light. You will be accompanied by Christed energy and surrounded by rainbow angels who heal all chakras.

## Sydney, Australia: Temple of Golden Peace
*Listed in Australasia and Oceanic | Surrounded by a city of light*

The Sydney Temple of Golden Light is in the etheric in front of the Blue Mountains, which are known for their Aboriginal connection. It is a very large temple and has the power to radiate its light for thousands of miles. It is a temple for the healing of children, as well as adults and animals.

This golden temple has a large star on the top and six domed minaret roofs. Inside the main hall is a giant golden pyramid used to harness the energy of the universe, all held inside this huge temple. There is a large pink rose quartz crystal healing all those within and a healing sanctuary with the energy of Quan Yin, the female Buddha, to help anyone heal and move on after cleansing and clearing any negative energy. Sound healing sessions are also held here regularly.

## Kolkata, India: Temple of Love
*Listed in Asia*

Mother Teresa oversees the Kolkata Temple of Golden Light with her caring, loving light and Christed energy. This small temple is filled with the energy and love of Jesus Christ and the Divine Mother and with much unconditional love. It is white and gold, with three domed roofs. Inside is a university for young people—a place of learning and caring for others. This temple specialises in the healing of children. All children are innocent and can be healed.

If you have a child who needs healing, please connect with Kolkata's sacred, healing Temple of Golden Light. Connect by meditation or in your sleep time. Visualise yourself inside this temple, name your child and what the disharmony is, and ask what you can do to help to heal your child.

## Bali, Indonesia: Temple of Beautiful Light
*Listed in Asia | Surrounded by a city of light*

The Bali Temple of Golden Light is high up in the etheric over Singaraja and is surrounded by a city of enormous light, which connects to the seventh dimension. A beautiful temple surrounded by rainbow angels and filled with celestial beings of love and light, it is a happy, joyful place and provides a feeling of fulfilment and contentment.

This temple heals crystal, rainbow, indigo and angelic children as well as many others. All God/Goddess children may be healed here. There are three children's healing sanctuaries inside the temple. Focus on the temple and through meditation or prayer ask that your child be healed. Ask for God's grace to be given, and a dispensation may be granted.

**St Petersburg, Russia: Temple of Golden Energy**
*Listed in Rest of the World*

The St Petersburg Temple of Golden Light has been created in typical Russian style, and everything inside is white and gold. It is a very bright temple of enormous light connecting to source, and it specialises in healing children from all walks of life. Anastasia was one of the tsar's daughters, and her energy is felt within this temple. She is a gentle, sweet soul who is the embodiment of love, light, and beauty, and she helps others when she can. She loves children and babies, and she wishes only to heal and help all those who ask for the Divine Mother's help.

Connect with this Temple of Golden Light if you have a child or children who are unwell, and please pray for them. Simply focus in meditation or prayer upon this temple and mention the name of your child or children. Blessings and miracles will happen.

**Animal Healing Temples**

The animal healing temples are in the etheric over the following:

- Snowdonia, Wales (5)
- Sicily, Italy (18)
- Denver, Colorado, United States (45)
- Buenos Aires, Argentina (67)
- Vancouver, Canada (75)
- Cairns, Australia (81)

**Sicily, Italy: Temple of Healing All God's Creatures**
*Listed in Europe*

This is the main animal healing Temple of Golden Light and is exclusively for the healing of animals. It is a small temple overseen by St Francis of Assisi and St Clare of Assisi, assisted by St Anthony of Padua, Italy, the patron saint of all animals and children. This temple is filled with the energy of Jesus Christ and Mother Mary, and it is surrounded by four large king unicorns and protected by the winged horse Pegasus.

In front of the temple are statues of lions and unicorns, and behind it is an enchanted forest. This temple is filled with love from the elemental spirits, fairies, and tree spirits. The large waiting room is itself a healing sanctuary. It is filled with golden statues of cats, dogs, horses and other animals, and there is a strong connection to Sirius. Here animals talk to each other, which is not dissimilar to what happens on earth, where animals are usually telepathic with each other.

All animals are God's innocent creatures and as such need to be treated with love and respect. Simply close your eyes and connect to this temple by thought, prayer, or meditation and ask for your animal to be healed. Love heals all disharmonies. Your prayers will be answered, and you will know what to do.

## Snowdonia, Wales: Temple of Healing All Animals
*Listed in Europe*

The Snowdonia Temple of Golden Light is a small but very powerful temple of healing light. It is purely for the healing of animals and is surrounded by four large king unicorns who guard the temple, as well as by the winged horse Pegasus. Franciscan monks help out here. It holds an earthy energy with a castle-like feel to it, and there are many carvings on the walls of doves, eagles, hawks, and owls. In the courtyard, there is a splendid fountain enhanced by the light of the unicorns. This temple is a healing sanctuary for all animals, including goats, sheep, horses, donkeys, deer, cows and so on.

If you have an animal that needs healing, then as you connect to this temple, please pray and see your animal being completely healthy again. Miracles will happen once you have connected to this beautiful temple. All animals can and may be healed.

The temple is totally peaceful, and you will feel the powerful, absolute love and total peace it holds within the Christed energy. Just imagine this Temple of Golden Light in the etheric over Snowdonia in Wales and take three deep breaths, each time breathing in gold and breathing out love, and then you will be there.

## Denver, Colorado, United States: Temple of the Eagle
*Listed in the Americas*

This Temple of Golden Light in the etheric over Denver is filled with Native American energy and overseen by a Native American chief called White Eagle and by White Buffalo Calf Woman. The temple has a lovely pure earthy energy. It is a place where you can feel the peace of the trees and nature from within. This is an animal healing temple of great power, compassion, and humility. At the back of this beautiful temple is a large lake, and there are many harmless eagles that will communicate with you.

## Buenos Aires, Argentina: Temple of Sound Healing
*Listed in the Americas*

Buenos Aires is the largest city in Argentina, and its Temple of Golden Light is over the river called Rio de la Plata. Mother Mary, St Francis of Assisi, and Archangel Raphael with his legions of angels oversee this temple. It is an animal healing temple with an animal healing sanctuary. You can ask in prayer for healing for your own or someone else's animal.

## Vancouver, Canada: Temple of Rainbow Angels
*Listed in the Americas*

This is a smaller Temple of Golden Light in the etheric near the Rocky Mountains over a quiet area of Vancouver. It is a churchlike temple with a beautiful stained-glass window in the main hall and is more of a place of worship than other temples. This is a lovely animal healing temple of happiness and calm. It is also a place of prayer, forgiveness, and compassion, as well as peace.

All animals have chakras, and they also have souls. They are looked after by a deva in charge of that particular animal group of souls. Animals are born here and come from their own planets to experience life. They are here to give love, help, and comfort to adults, children, and other animals.

## Cairns, Australia: Temple of Golden Light Two
*Listed in Australasia and Oceanic*

This is a very Aboriginal Temple of Golden Light with the pure energy of Australia. It is a small, but powerful animal healing temple of love connecting to St Francis of Assisi. Inside is a spiralling staircase around which animals are treated with gentleness, respect, and compassion, helping them to recover from disharmony, whether that is from ill health or unkind treatment by humans. There is a crystal healing sanctuary for animals that need more specific healing. Animals have as much right as we do to live without fear, in good health.

If you know of an animal that needs healing, please focus on this temple with the name of the animal and mention what the matter is. Close your eyes and ask for the animal to be healed.

## Unicorn Temple

## Geneva, Switzerland: Temple of Groundedness
*Listed in Europe*

Geneva has a very grounding, earthy Temple of Golden Light connecting to Middle Earth and Camelot. Four large unicorns and the winged horse Pegasus guard this unicorn temple. Many other unicorns surround the temple.

A happy temple, it connects to the fairies and elementals, which gives it a woodland feel and brings through the tree spirits of the nature kingdom. The air is filled with butterflies and dragonflies. This temple heals animals as well as adults and children.

Unicorns are ascended horses. They are wondrous beings of tremendous light filled with so much love for humanity. You can call on them, and they will help you immediately.

I have included this temple in the chapter with animal healing temples because this is a special temple filled with the love and light of many unicorns that can heal you and all animals. Within the unicorn kingdom, there are many king and queen unicorns. I believe there is a planet of unicorns in this universe, as well as in other universes. Meditate on or visit this temple in your sleep time, and you will definitely feel, sense or see unicorns, and they will send you healing from their healing horn.

### Unicorn Poem

Deep inside of everyone is the power of pure love,
The essence of the universe—it's gifted from above.
The magic and the mystery, just waiting to be born.
Just like the air of wonderment that is your unicorn.
Believe it is within you. Trust that it is there.
Free your soul of heartache; release it to the air.
The wonder and fulfilment of living life in love
Is the magic of your unicorn that is gifted from above.
Seek out the love inside you. Find peace deep in your soul.
Your unicorn stands with you; it is that which makes you whole.
The mystery and the magic in the power of the horn
Is the unconditional love in your soul—the love of your unicorn.

— Julie Griffiths

# Chapter 10

## *Meditation and Relaxation*

Meditation has been proven to reduce stress and anxiety levels. It can remove negative emotions like anger and resentment, changing these to positive feelings. It allows you to feel happier and more relaxed, allowing your mind to be more positive and focused. Meditation can help you to live in the present moment and, with regular practice, can give you more restful sleep. How we think, feel, and react to what goes on around us depends on how we see things. Being more relaxed as a result of meditation will help you to cope better with life's challenges.

Meditation can bring about change in very positive ways because it requires the meditator to use both sides of the brain together. Practicing meditation can help you to be calm, focused, inspirational, understanding, and self-confident, as meditation alters your brain waves. It can help to heal the physical body as well. When we meditate, endorphins are released from the brain and sent to any area of the body that is in disharmony so healing can take place.

We are seeing meditation being introduced more and more in schools and workplaces. As a meditation teacher, I have been running meditation groups and spiritual workshops for many years. It is always so lovely to see people change for the better.

Everyone can connect with the many Temples of Golden Light through meditation. Your connection with the temples can help to heal you emotionally, mentally, and physically. I personally meditate and know that meditation can change your DNA in positive ways if practiced regularly. Try to practice for ten minutes a day at first and then gradually increase to thirty minutes. It is good to have an area in your home where you feel comfortable to sit and meditate.

## Temples to Connect With in Meditation

In this chapter, I'll recommend a few temples for you to connect with when you are meditating. These temples all have amazing energy of peace and contemplation, making them ideal for meditation. I have written some meditations to help you link to these temples and to bring about peace, calm, and relaxation, helping you to live in the moment. Dare to breathe in the goodness of who you really are by meditation and awaken to your own brilliance. The number in parentheses after the name of each temple is its number within the full set of 144 temples:

- Margaret River, Perth, Australia (79)
- Bangalore, India (100)
- Sri Lanka (101)
- Kathmandu, Nepal (104)
- Lhasa, Tibet (105)
- Thimphu, Bhutan (106)
- Antarctica (122)

## Kathmandu, Nepal: Temple of Global Peace
*Listed in Asia*

The Kathmandu Temple of Golden Light is a large temple filled with the love and energy of Quan Yin and Lord Buddha, providing a place of equal balance of male and female energy, yin and yang. It is a peaceful and happy temple with smiling people all around, where people continually pray for peace for the world. This temple connects to Middle Earth and to Mother Earth's crystal, sacred, cosmic heart centre through a vortex of energy connecting Middle and Upper Earth. The temple is surrounded by elephants and ascended, sacred horses—the unicorns—together with beautiful rainbow angels who also work inside the temple.

## Thimphu, Bhutan: Temple of Pure Knowledge
*Listed in Asia*

Bhutan is an ancient kingdom secluded high up in the Himalayas, with unique customs and people with deeply held beliefs. The Bhutan Temple of Golden Light has a very ethereal feel to it. Located high over the capital city of Thimphu, it connects to Middle Earth with a lush green energy, as well as dragon energy.

This small golden temple has more of a feminine energy, planting seeds of new thoughts and ideas for the New Earth. Goddess Jacinta oversees this temple herself with her divine feminine qualities of love, compassion, and understanding. This temple also connects to Lord Buddha and Quan Yin.

This is a very light temple energetically. It has a connection to the star systems of this universe. Here you can find out how to utilise your skills and how to change. If you want to learn about the Tree of Life (the Kabbalah), then connect with this temple. The qualities you can gain from this temple are of peace, truth, knowledge, wisdom, love, honour, and power.

## Lhasa, Tibet: Temple of Divine Truth
*Listed in Asia*

This is a small Temple of Golden Light filled with the energy of the Dalai Lama. It is a loving temple that connects to the gentle dragon energy and works with your heart centre to help you shift to the next level of your spirituality. Inside is a large golden statue of Buddha sitting cross-legged and asking you to 'smell the flowers', meaning to see everything in life through positivity and to be grateful and smile at everyone.

This temple is sowing seeds for the New Earth. You can connect to this temple to learn what it is like to live in the seventh dimension, where all is total love and peace. It is a cleansing temple, giving you a new, loving, grateful, peaceful you.

## Bangalore, India: Temple of Blessed
*Listed in Asia | Surrounded by a city of light*

Bangalore Temple is a large Temple of Golden Light connecting to Babaji, Sai Baba, and Mahatma Gandhi, as well as the well-known gods/goddesses of the whole of India. This golden temple holds immense power and is extremely peaceful and calm. It is filled with the scent of jasmine flowers. It is an opulent, ornate temple, filled with many gold statues of the Indian gods and goddesses. You will be aware of the energy of the elephants sending you love from within this temple. Outside is a soothing lake. When you connect, you will feel the energy of the lake's calming waters.

## Sri Lanka: Temple of Spiritual Nourishment
*Listed in Asia | Surrounded by a city of light*

The Sri Lanka Temple of Golden Light is in the etheric over water above the harbour of Columbo. It is an earthy temple that touches Mother Earth's heart centre, yet at the same time it is a star temple that connects high into the etheric, reaching up and out to the stars, touching the Milky Way within Orion's Belt and up to Pleiades, Sirius, and Andromeda.

This is a very ornate, colourful temple which is surrounded by elephants. It holds the energy of the tiger, of qualities of strength and courage combined with fire of spirit. It is a community heart temple of medium size. It welcomes families and friends and is about friendship, caring, and sharing, with hands outstretched across the waters. The Sri Lanka temple is a wonderful place of stillness and contemplation where you can pray for world peace and connect with the whole of our universe.

## Margaret River, Perth, Australia: Temple of Crystalline Energy
*Listed in Australasia and Oceanic | Surrounded by a city of light*

The Margaret River Temple is an ethereal, smaller Temple of Golden Light in the etheric over the centre of Margaret River, WA, Australia.

Linda Jarrett

This is a lovely, cleansing, clearing, healing temple of great power which has an Aboriginal connection. It links to all of the other Australian temples. It has many levels, starting with crystalline energy, an Aboriginal energy, and then moving up higher to a very pure angelic energy. Goddess Lathinda oversees this temple personally. It is a healing temple with a powerful healing sanctuary holding the energy of earth crystals.

## Antarctica Temple of Golden Light
*Listed in Main Temples and in Rest of the World | Surrounded by a city of light*

The Antarctica temple is the fourth largest Temple of Golden Light after Istanbul, New York, and Athens. It has many levels from the bottom to the top. The first level is the energy of penguins, whales, dolphins, polar bears, sea lions, seals, and Antarctic birds. Higher up, it connects to the whole of this universe, including the star system Pleiades, Sirius, Andromeda, and all of the planets. It gives out a beacon of light that is so powerful that it resonates out into this universe.

Inside the temple in the main hall is a huge crystalline lotus-flower-shaped crystal that at times opens and slightly closes. In another hall within an inner room is a multifaceted diamond held within a pyramid. You can imagine how powerful this must be. The crystals give out signals—special encodings—and talk to each other. They download DNA that will help humanity to change; people will become more loving and kind. The DNA codes are released into humanity when the crystals open and close. This is a slow and gentle process, as the crystals are powerful. It is important to trust the love of the universe to guide us through this next step of the Golden Age.

## Guided Meditations to Connect with Temples of Golden Light

At the beginning of each meditation, you will need to ground yourself to Mother Earth. Some of the meditations will take you through those first steps, but for those that don't, you will need to do the following:

- Imagine yourself in a sacred space, a place you can create and fill with anything you like, anything that makes you feel good. It is a special place to sit back and relax.
- Ground yourself by visualising long, thick, golden roots flowing from the bottoms of your feet through all the layers of soil and rock and through the crystalline grid into Mother Earth's sacred cosmic crystal heart centre. Visualise an area of water deep within the planetary core and see two crystals of your choice, or you can visualise a pink crystal representing unconditional love and a hematite crystal representing grounding.
- Place your roots around the two crystals in the water and begin to feel Mother Earth's energy flowing back up your golden roots into your feet. Allow the whole of your body to be filled with Mother Earth's subtle healing energy.

Through the meditations, you will feel as though you have been on a journey to one of the Temples of Golden Light, but as with any journey, you must return. So at the end of each meditation, take your time to feel that you are back where you started, in your sacred space. Stretch your hands and feet and your arms and legs if you wish to and smile.

## Meditation to Connect with the Temple of Golden Light in Kathmandu, Nepal

Now is the time to journey to meet the ascended masters of light, love, and wisdom. Take a nice deep breath—take it all the way down the back of your spine. Relax and be in touch with the rhythm of your breathing. Do not try to alter or force it. You are feeling centred, calm, and peaceful. Visualise your heart chakra gently opening up like a rose in perfect bloom. Travel on the heart and wisdom energy into your inner landscape and find yourself in peaceful surroundings. Activate all your senses so that you can see objects and colours. Smell the fragrances and hear the sounds.

From where you are, look out at the surrounding landscape. Nearby there is a pathway leading high up onto a mountain. This mountain is in Nepal. Make your way up the mountain, taking note of the scenery as you go.

As you come near to the top, you will see a thin veil that looks like a cloud that hides the peak. Go through this thin veil, and as you do, you will find yourself in the Temple of Golden Light above Kathmandu. Breathe in the wonderful fresh clean air. You can hear the angels and the birds singing and water gently flowing. You see a three-tiered fountain flowing with fresh water and birds merrily singing and bathing in it.

You go over to the fountain and join these pretty creatures and drink from the water, which is fresh and cooling to you. You hear a gentle voice behind you saying, 'Welcome. To what do I owe this pleasure?' You are seeing an ascended master. This could be Quan Yin, White Tara, Green Tara the Buddhist Goddess, Lord Buddha, Dwyul Kwul, Dalai Lama, El Morya, Mother Mary, Jesus Christ, Lady Nada, or any ascended master of your choice.

You ask if you can look around the Temple of Golden Light, and you are given a guide who takes you along a corridor. You see many doors to the left and right. These doors lead to meditation rooms for all who wish to come to the temple to meditate. You look into one of the meditation rooms and feel the sunlight hit you as it filters through the windows in cascading colours of a rainbow.

There is a feeling of pure peace, and you feel a wave of love as you stand in the presence of God and the angels. You feel them bless you as you look around. They want you to know that you can come here anytime. You turn and step out of the room, and your ascended master takes you out into a courtyard. At the far end of the courtyard is a gate. You walk towards the gate and see a waterfall on the other side. You are invited to step into the waterfall. The water is like holy water in which you may bathe. It will cleanse and clear away anything negative, making you feel well and whole again.

As you sink into the water, you feel and sense the power of the rainbow angels assisting you. You feel their gentle hands stroking and cleansing your body from top to toe. Enjoy and relax. As you relax, you hear the rainbow angels speaking to you, giving you messages of love and light. Open your hands to receive a gift from your ascended master.

Now you feel a rush of love and warmth run through your body as the cleansing is completed. It is time to step out of the water. You say goodbye to the rainbow angels and head back with your ascended master. Your ascended master gives you a message that will personally help you in this lifetime. You thank your ascended master and walk away, back to where you started. When you feel ready, gently stretch your hands and feet and smile.

## Meditation to Connect with the Temple of Golden Light in Thimphu, Bhutan

We will connect with the Temple of Golden Light situated over the centre of Thimphu, the capital of Bhutan. Goddess Jacinta oversees this small golden temple with a feminine energy. Goddess Jacinta is one of the three goddesses who oversee all 144 Temples of Golden Light. This temple connects to Lord Buddha and Quan Yin.

Visited by families, the temple represents gentleness, peace, truth, wisdom, and knowledge. This is a very light temple energetically, having a connection to the star systems of this universe. Here you can learn to utilise your skills and learn how to change—to shake up or wake up. The Bhutan Temple of Golden Light twins with the temple in Lhasa, Tibet. It is a small but very powerful temple, about the size of St Paul's Cathedral in London.

I would like you to ground yourself by visualising yourself sitting in front of a very large old beautiful tree of your choice. Think of large trees such as oak, willow, pine, chestnut, or cherry blossom. Choose any tree. Start to evenly breathe slowly in and out. Please do this three times, breathing in and out slowly, then again breathing in and out, and one last time, breathing in and out. As you do this, feel your body start to slow down into a relaxed state. Once again, focus on your breathing. Breathe in the fresh air as you sit down in front of your favourite old large tree. Visualise yourself connecting to Mother Earth's sacred crystalline heart centre.

You find yourself travelling to the Himalayas. See yourself inside the Bhutan Temple of Golden Light, being led by Goddess Jacinta down a long, wide, golden hallway with thick, soft, red carpet beneath your feet. She is guiding you to the beautiful large garden behind this peaceful, calm temple. You find yourself at the entrance to the garden.

Peace, calm, and happiness are yours. You simply need to know how to achieve this. Gardens are perfect places to relax and dream, leaving the stresses of the outside world behind you. You will experience a dazzling array of rainbow colours and fragrances. You will be inspired by this garden, which is filled with many varieties of flowers perfuming the air with their sweet scent, giving you peace and calm and relaxing you.

Imagine a long, pretty wooden tunnelled archway surrounded by Himalayan climbing flowers. As you walk through the archway, you feel that this is a special day; you feel that good-to-be-alive feeling. When you reach the end of the flower archway, you notice that it opens out onto a very large, beautiful garden. Stop awhile and take time to absorb the beauty and peace of this garden sanctuary. You may like to sit on a bench in the garden or continue walking. As you walk, you may like to touch the leaves of the bushes and trees and flowers. Feel the energy of nature calming you down, relaxing you, soothing you. Take time for you—time to heal.

You are feeling more peaceful, calm, and balanced. Everything will fall into place and become clear when it is meant to, so switch off and take it easy for awhile. By relaxing and letting go of desired outcomes, you create the space for the universe to help you and give you just what you want or need. If you trust, the universe will open up infinite possibilities for you. You begin to feel a new sense of clarity, purpose, and direction. The world around you is simply a mirror reflection of your inner world to give you what you want. So trust.

You feel all the cells of your body gently vibrating as old negative energy leaves you. This is replaced by positive energy—by joy and happiness. It is time to be joyful, to celebrate, to appreciate all that you have achieved to date, and to appreciate all your blessings. You smile to yourself, knowing that everything happens at the right time and in the right place. Your time of waiting and confusion will soon be over.

You become aware of the energy around your body being cleared, and this enables your pathway to become apparent, giving you renewed clarity, focus, and purpose. Visualise yourself as being abundant in all ways. Whether it's a new job, help with your education, a new home, a new relationship, good health, or healing for your family, ask the universe now for your abundance. Hold your vision in your heart. We are here to be happy, so you will be given whatever you ask for. Think well and discriminate clearly before you ask. Feel yourself being supported by the universal life force of love and golden light.

Feeling grateful for the peace and calm that you have experienced in the temple and its gardens, listen to your breathing and return to where you started. Stretch out your hands and your feet and smile.

## Meditation to Connect with the Temple of Golden Light in Lhasa, Tibet

Please make sure you are grounded and anchored to Mother Earth as you begin this meditation. Visualise your own golden roots flowing through the rock and soil all the way down to Mother Earth's sacred crystal heart centre. This temple in the Himalayas has an ethereal feel to it; it is a temple of divine truth and gratitude. Visualise a small golden temple that aligns to the energy of peace, gratitude, nature, and happiness.

As you enter the temple, you instantly feel peace and calm, as if you are going for a walk in nature. Imagine the flowers, trees, and bushes. Absorb yourself in this wonderful energy. The energy within the temple is so calming. Count your blessings and be deeply grateful for whatever you have: family, children, parents, friends, job, health, home, and sanity. You can smile, but to have your own stress-free mind is a wonderful gift and a valued attribute. Take time to smile at other people; take time to stop, relax, be still, and be calm.

You find yourself in a restful, peaceful, large room being one with all that there is: universe, earth, stars, sun, and moon. You know how to take each day as it comes, to live in the moment. What you cannot do today, you will do another day. Breathe deeply, breathing in love and breathing out gold. Do this three times, finding peace within yourself. Still your mind. Do not allow thoughts to enter that are not positive. Be grateful, be humble, be still in this quiet time. You may reflect, you may gain inspiration, you may even think of something quite funny, as laughter clears away any negativity. Focus on all you have and bless everything and everyone.

Forgive all those who may have upset or hurt you. Open your heart and give love. We are all one consciousness. We have all at some time sat under the moon, the stars, and the sun on the earth. See the beauty in others and yourself. Try to love in your everyday life. Be grateful for any small acts of kindness, whether a few words of comfort or a physical act. Allow yourself to work together with others in friendship, love, caring, and sharing. Love those around you. Do love, be love, think love, and shine your inner light always.

Feeling at peace and full of gratitude for all that you are and all that you have, bring yourself back to where you started from, stretch, and smile.

## Meditation to Connect with the Temple of Golden Light in Bangalore, India

Please ground yourself by visualising long, thick, golden roots flowing through all the layers of soil and rock and through the crystalline grid into Mother Earth's sacred cosmic crystal heart centre. Visualise an area of water deep within the planetary core and see two crystals of your choice. Place your roots around the two crystals in the water and begin to feel Mother Earth's energy flowing back up your golden roots into your feet. Allow the whole of your body to be filled with Mother Earth's subtle healing energy.

The Bangalore Temple of Golden Light is a large temple in the etheric towards the north of the city of Bangalore. It aligns to the ashram of Swami Sathya Sai Baba, also known as Shirdi Baba, an ashram in Puttiparthi, in the area of India called Andhra Pradesh. This temple of immense power and healing emits golden light continuously around the healing grid of the 144 temples. It is a beautiful, opulent, typical Indian temple, very sumptuous and ornate, decorated as in the time of the Raj, and filled with the smell of jasmine flowers and statues of the great Indian gods/goddesses. It is guarded by etheric elephants and surrounded by a city of light.

You find yourself entering this splendid Temple of Golden Light and making your way into the inner healing temple to meditate, perhaps to ask for enlightenment or simply for peace. This Temple of Golden Light connects to the many Indian gods/goddesses, including Shiva, Vishnu, Brahma, Krishna, Rama, Kali, Durga, Shakti, Lakshmi, Mahatma Gandhi, and Ganesh. It is surrounded by rainbow angels.

As we connect, for many of us, it is a time of reflection. Some of us have been through rough times and have gained much wisdom. Change is inevitable for all of us; we are forever growing, changing, and learning. The key is to embrace change and give it a chance to show you the next steps in your life. As you sit in the Temple of Golden Light, I ask that you release all old energy that you no longer need. Each moment is a new opportunity to release that which no longer serves you and embrace your spirituality from within.

Live from your heart and listen to your guidance. Each new moment is an opportunity to be grateful for each and every blessing that we have received, past and present. Each new moment is a chance to discover and remember something beautiful about ourselves that we had let fall by the wayside. Do not be afraid to sit and reflect. While parts of it may be painful, the enlightenment brings release and will lift your vibration to new heights. For you are spirit first; you always have been and always will be. Embrace this, and you will open incredible doorways of light that reflect from within you and join you. Now you can share all that is in creation.

The process of transitioning, shifting, and raising your vibration comes in phases and often seems slower than we would like it to be. This is because when we go through shifts, our vibrational energies rise, and it takes our physical bodies more time to come into alignment. If we shift too quickly, we could be ill or depressed. The most important gift for people in the world is truth based on pure thoughts. True thoughts constitute real wealth. Your good or bad fortune is related directly to your thoughts. Sowing the seeds of thought, you will achieve good karma and grace.

You are receiving golden light energy to honour and embrace your new pathway. This energy flows through your crown chakra all the way down and through your other chakras, settling in your earth star chakra approximately ten inches below your feet. Feel this golden light energy as it flows through you. You are receiving enlightenment. Feeling grateful for the golden light energy and the enlightenment you have received, gently and slowly bring yourself back to where you started. When you are ready, stretch your hands and your feet and smile.

## Meditation to Connect with the Temple of Golden Light in Sri Lanka

Ground yourself and connect with Mother Earth's heart centre by visualising golden roots flowing from the soles of your feet all the way down through the rock and soil and crystalline grid. When you repeatedly do this, you are lengthening your earth star and Gaia earth chakras. Please now chant twenty-one *oms* to clear your body of any negativity, purify your chakras, and connect yourself to the earth and our universe.

This Temple of Golden Light is in the etheric of Mother Earth over the water of Colombo harbour. It is very close to the earth but at the same time reaches very high up and out into our universe, aligning with the star systems Pleiades and Sirius. A temple of prayer that connects to the whole of this universe as well as the whole of Mother Earth, this Temple of Golden Light is seen as extending hands across the water, offering friendship.

You travel on your heart wisdom to the Temple of Golden Light over Colombo. You see this temple surrounded by beautiful elephants all different in size—even baby elephants playing together. You feel the energy change as you enter the temple. As the door opens and you enter this wonderful Temple of Golden Light, you notice just inside the door an enormous statue of Lord Buddha together with many golden statues of Indian gods/goddesses and statues connected to many different religions, as well as a statue of the Muslim leader Mohammad and a golden statue of Jesus Christ and Mother Mary.

You join many people in the main hall who are praying for world peace. You find yourself a spot and sit down to join them, knowing that you are part of something big and beautiful, and knowing how important it is for you to be here at this time of great changes on our planet. Visualise Planet Earth; see the countries, oceans, clouds, skies, and the sun. Your focus is placed on an ascended master who has just entered the hall. It is the ascended master El Morya, master of ray one of the esoteric rays, the ray of divine will or 'will to do good'. If you are on ray one for your personality ray, that means you are very spiritual and know that you are here for a reason and that you have a job to do. El Morya now links with you and may give you a message or gift, so listen for your message and sense or feel your gift.

The Sri Lanka Temple of Golden Light is a temple of friendship, of understanding, of brothers and sisters sharing and standing side by side with nothing getting in the way—not religion, money, or any other negative impediment. It is a place of plain and simple friendship, caring, and sharing. Now you find yourself moving up high through the temple. You feel yourself being lifted up higher and higher. You feel as if you can touch the stars—Pleiades, Sirius, Andromeda, and the Milky Way galaxy, all within Orion's Belt. You feel you are out in space looking down on our planet. Take time to connect to Pleiades, Sirius, Andromeda, and the Milky Way. Choose where you would like to journey to. What do you see, feel, or sense? Look around you. Where are you? Feel yourself exploring the universe and travelling through space. As you reflect on the wonderful journey you have been on, gradually bring yourself back to where you started. Stretch your hands, wiggle your feet, and smile.

### Meditation to Connect with the Temple of Golden Light in Margaret River, Perth, Australia

We will visit the Temple of Golden light in the etheric over Margaret River, Perth, Australia. In and around Margaret River, there are hundreds of crystal caves, which means that the earth above is extremely special in energy. The temple is very light and holds the energy of these earth crystals. There is also Aboriginal energy, as Aborigines are the custodians of Australia, together with angelic energy from the rainbow angels. It is a powerful healing temple connecting all the way up to source, to the divine, the heart of God/ Goddess. Goddess Lathinda oversees this temple with her bright light energy.

You find yourself entering this small Temple of Golden Light. Feel the powerful ethereal energy as you walk to the entrance. You are greeted by rainbow angels with arms outstretched to meet you. You find yourself floating through the temple with your rainbow angel. Notice the colours of the angels' wings. They are very high-vibrational angels, and they can balance all your chakras at the same time—not just one chakra but all chakras. When you are ready to be healed, they can heal you.

You are invited to enter into the amethyst healing chamber. You step inside and see before you a healing couch made of amethyst. Make yourself comfortable with pillows and cushions on this special couch. Your rainbow angel will hold your hand while you receive healing, helping you to remove all old unwanted energy no longer needed by you to heal and move forward. As you rest awhile in this healing chamber you feel the powerful healing energy flowing through the whole of your body, starting at your feet and flowing all the way through your body chakra by chakra, one by one, starting with your earth star chakra. This chakra is approximately eight inches below your feet.

Feel your connection to Mother Earth's heart centre, her loving subtle energy flowing back up to you, then feel your base chakra clearing and being cleansed, allowing you to feel fully grounded and in your body, living in the present moment. Now feel your sacral chakra of creativity and expression. As you focus on each chakra, feel the healing energy clearing any negativity. Connect now with your navel chakra, just above your sacral centre. This is a new chakra that needs to be activated as we enter into the fifth dimension. As we move through the chakras, feel all the chakras releasing old energy, as all old stuff needs to go, Allow the amethyst crystalline energy to clear and cleanse your solar plexus.

At this point, if anyone has taken your power, you will get a picture in your mind or a feeling, so please place this person in a circle of light and ask for your energy back. You will see golden spheres returning to you and entering your solar plexus, enabling you to feel empowered with your own energy. You may also want to give back energy that you may have taken yourself or loaned to anyone, so allow them to receive this energy back from you if it is the right time to do so. Moving up to your heart chakra, soothe away any hurts or anger and unhappiness and allowing this chakra to be cleared; this will allow you to work with the threefold flame of love, power, and will. Feel your body being cleared, cleansed, and freed of old energy.

Now move to your throat chakra, the centre of your divine expression, your voice. You may feel a sensation in your throat as it is being cleared. Connect with your third eye. This chakra will open, helping you to help yourself and others. Then move to your crown chakra, the thousand-petalled lotus flower, your connection to the divine and to source. This chakra will now be cleared and cleansed.

Take a moment to ask for healing for your family, friends, and acquaintances. Also, ask for healing for the animals and sea creatures, and ask for healing for Mother Earth, as she has suffered much over time from negative energy. See Mother Earth surrounded by a bright golden light of healing and ask all your angels, earth guides, rainbow angels, and archangels and their divine feminine counterparts to join us now. Ask for whoever you wish to join you in your sacred space. Please ask for healing and peace for Mother Earth. Hold out your hands in front of you and visualise yourself holding Mother Earth in the palms of your hands. See her being healed and being blessed with peace as she aligns to other solar systems, galaxies, and the seven universes that surround this universe. We are the co-creators of this planet. We are the universe. We are part of everything, and everything is part of us. We are all that there is—and all that there is, is us.

It is now time to gently climb down from the amethyst crystal couch, leave the healing chamber, and slowly leave the Temple of Golden Light over Perth. Gradually make you way back to where you started, wiggle your hands and feet, and smile.

## Meditation to Connect with the Temple of Golden Light in Mount Shasta, California

Gently close your eyes and ground yourself. Visualise light coming down from source into the crown chakra that is just above your head. We now journey to Mount Shasta, California, in the United States, over trees, hills, farms, valleys, and the countryside, seeing animals, sheep, goats, cows, bulls, and horses below us.

You are travelling across the ocean. Feel the warmth of the sun on your face. Feel a warm, soft breeze. You are relaxing; you hear the soft chirping of birds around you. You become aware of a very bright white light. The light is getting brighter and brighter, like a star. The nearer you get, the brighter the light becomes. You begin to feel your connection to this sacred mountain. The connection to Mount Shasta becomes stronger until you can sense, know, or see it in the distance. You can feel the energy as you get closer.

You arrive at Mount Shasta. Its aura is a beautiful lilac colour that surrounds the whole of the mountain. You now see the temple on top of Mount Shasta emitting golden light. You arrive outside the temple and are greeted by your rainbow angel and legion upon legion of Archangel Gabriel's angels who are waiting with outstretched arms to welcome you.

Archangel Gabriel represents clarity and purity, and he is a messenger of God. Archangel Gabriel works closely with this temple, helping to ground you, and he will also help you create your own reality and manifest whatever you need. There is a special hall in the temple where Archangel Gabriel will greet you himself, and you now find yourself in this grand hall. Archangel Gabriel welcomes you. As you step inside the hall, the light is immensely bright. It completely dazzles you. Focus on what you would like to clear and ask him to clear and cleanse you. Feel yourself releasing old unwanted energy, old negativity, old programming, and old mindsets—everything that no longer serves you. You will then receive clarity on a question or questions that you may ask Archangel Gabriel.

Now Archangel Hope appears in the grand hall, bringing with her a softer energy of hope and enlightenment. She gives you a gift, and Archangel Gabriel gives you a message. Know that all is well and as it should be. Your vibration is lifting even further.

You then leave the grand hall and are guided by your rainbow angel into another large room. This time, you meet the ascended master St Germaine of the Violet Flame, who asks you to always make sure that you clear and cleanse your aura when you connect to someone who is negative, as that person's negativity can contaminate your own aura and bring you down. Visualise the flame of St Germaine all over you, then step to one side. Again, step into the violet flame, and feel the negativity being transmuted. Again, step out of the flame. Step inside the flame one more time and step out of it. Do this three times, as the number three is a very powerful universal number. Now you will be cleared, and you may ask Mother Earth to transmute all negative energy for you.

You now visit the Native Indians within the temple. The Cheyenne tribe surrounds you. You feel as if you are in a Native American camp. Everyone is happy, and the air is filled with laughter where the earth is honoured and respected and the Great White Spirit of God is honoured and respected. You may be aware of a great Native American, Chief Sitting Bull, or Chief White Eagle, or White Buffalo Calf Woman.

Listen to any messages and feel the peace. Allow yourself to simply let go of all that does not resonate with you anymore; release and relax. See yourself as strong of mind and kind of heart, helping all those around you to find peace and happiness. You yourself are receiving peace, and you are given a gift by the Native Americans.

Now send healing around the world. Focus on beautiful Mother Earth. See yourself emitting golden healing light to humanity, the animals, and Mother Earth herself. You are joined by the rainbow angels and all the archangels and their divine feminine counterparts and legions of angels, together with the ascended masters and the celestial beings from on high, the gods/goddesses of love and peace, and of course your very own earth/spirit guides and master earth/ spirit guides.

Feeling relieved after shedding so much negative energy, bid farewell to all those who have helped you and slowly make your way back to where you started. Feeling blessed, wiggle your fingers and toes, stretch your feet and hands, and smile.

# Chapter 11

## *Meditations to Connect with the Twelve Main Temples and the Main Animal Healing Temple*

Writing this book has been challenging at times, because there have been so many temples to write about. Even now, I have to stop and think where they all are, but when I think of the temples in groups as continents, I can remember exactly where each is situated. I know that writing this book has helped me to grow spiritually, and I have become more patient with myself. I feel that I have evolved as a spiritual human being for the better.

I have also learnt so much about Planet Earth and this universe, and it has been fun putting the book together. It has taken some time to channel this work and write about it. I hope that by doing so, I will have helped humanity and Mother Earth. The temples are here for you to connect with and to help you heal yourself. The goddess energy is coming through on a galactic wave from source, as our planet needs to be balanced with the feminine energy.

I have written some meditations for you to connect with the twelve main Temples of Golden Light and the main animal healing temple. You can connect with the temples through meditation or in your sleep-state. The more you practice this, the quicker the connection. Some amazing results of healing have taken place already on all levels: physical, emotional, mental, and spiritual. Once you have the connection, you can ask for divine guidance, healing, protection, and abundance. Remember, nothing is impossible. We have endless, infinite possibilities available to us. So create the best life possible for yourself and your family, friends, and acquaintances. Do love, be love, and think love.

## Meditation to Connect with the Temple of Golden Light in Istanbul, Turkey

Ground yourself into Mother Earth by visualising long, thick, golden roots flowing from the soles of your feet all the way down through the rock and soil, deep, deep, down into Mother Earth's sacred crystal cosmic heart centre. You are about to journey to the amazing and beautiful Temple of Golden Light in the etheric of Istanbul, Turkey. This temple is enormous, covering nearly the whole of the city of Istanbul.

Archangel Metaziel and Archangel Honoriel work under the direction of Lord Metatron. They both oversee the rainbow angels who surround all of the Temples of Golden Light. This temple is within a city of golden light, pulsating, vibrating, and emitting golden light radiance for thousands of miles around. It is a place of enlightenment and an educational learning temple, holding the wisdom of all healing modalities, ancient and new.

You are amazed at the size of the temple. You find yourself outside a very large ornate golden front door. El Morya, the ascended master, welcomes you inside, and you are guided through the main part of the temple to the enormous inner hall. Coming down from the ceiling there is a huge clear quartz crystal gently emitting a strobe-like crystalline energy. It is a large tower of crystal light. Gradually this large crystal starts to unfold like a lotus flower, and as this happens, it gets bigger and brighter. An even brighter crystal shimmers and sparkles beneath it, sending light outwards. You can see facets of light, orbs of light, and the whole of the room ignites into bright light as source light is now entering the temple. It is expanding and covering a huge area, becoming a satellite, a beacon of light directing light energy all around the city of light.

You realise that light from source ignites all 144 Temples of Golden Light around the world, which act as a grid of very powerful healing light. You feel this energy flowing through you, given to you as a blessing, and you start to release old programming, old mindsets, and old energy no longer needed by you. Breathe into this new energy as you feel re-energised, revitalised, and refreshed. See any pain being released. All sadness and hurts are leaving you; they are replaced by hope, happiness, and positivity. You are feeling very peaceful.

Into the main hall slowly walk the three goddesses who oversee the many Temples of Golden Light: Lady Nada, twin flame of Jesus Christ who represents the divine feminine Christ energy; Jacinta, the Mayan elder who works with the rainforests and Mother Nature; and Lathinda of the golden light, who comes from another universe bringing her own divine energy. All three are goddesses in their own right, working to bring heaven to earth. They stand before you smiling radiantly, welcoming you to this amazingly beautiful Temple of Golden Light. They would like you to know that these new temples replace some of the older retreats, ashrams, and temples in the etheric. The Temples of Golden Light are the new temples for the next two thousand years—for the Golden Age.

Lady Nada previously served as a high priestess in the Temple of Love on Atlantis. She now steps forward to welcome you. In her final incarnation on Atlantis, she was the youngest of a large family, opting to support all her brothers and sisters instead of choosing a life for herself. She knew that helping others was more important than her own life. Lady Nada is the master of the seventh ray and sits on the karmic board. She sends you a blessing.

Jacinta steps forward to welcome you to the Temple of Golden Light. She is here to help raise your awareness of Mother Earth. No longer will Mother Earth suffer in silence; her vibration is lifting once more to be in a higher place, so she can take her rightful place in the universe. Jacinta is a Mayan elder of long ago, when we lived in peace and happiness and when we understood the earth and honoured the seasons, our planet, and the universe. Mother Earth can heal all of you quietly herself, so look inward to yourself, live in peace, and do no harm to others, and no harm can come to you. Live with God/Goddess in your heart, and the universe will look after you. Jacinta sends you a blessing.

Lathinda now steps forward to welcome you. She is a wonderful golden-light goddess with long golden hair. She understands life's uncertainties, obstacles, challenges, and heartaches, and she most of all understands you. She has incarnated on earth many times. She was

Tutankhamun's older stepsister in ancient Egypt. She was in service to Mary Magdalene in biblical times as a servant. She knows your pain and suffering, as she has lived here many times. Lathinda will connect you to your own divine light. Feel yourself imbued by the radiance of your divine light. Experience now your own magnificence as you ground into the crystal cosmic heart of Mother Earth. Lathinda sends you a blessing.

Explore this majestic Temple of Golden Light. Wander through the magnificent rooms. Let go of all worries and concerns. Trust and surrender to God/Goddess and the universe. Everything will fall into place. Have no expectations, only trust, as you become peaceful within the stillness. You may like to find yourself sitting on a magic carpet flying around the city of light, taking note of what you sense or feel. Breathe in love, and breathe out gold three times. You have been blessed by the Temples of Golden Light. Start to make your way back to your sacred space. Gently wiggle your feet and hands and smile.

## Meditation to Connect with the Temple of Golden Light in New York, New York, United States

Sitting comfortably in your sacred space, take in three deep breaths. Breathe in love and breathe out gold. Again, breathe in love and breathe out gold. Lastly, breathe in love and breathe out gold.

Visualise yourself on a ferryboat sailing around the Statue of Liberty in New York City. The sun is shining, the air is warm, and you can hear the waves of the sea splashing gently. You look up to the left of the Statue of Liberty and begin to see a golden light shining brightly. The light is getting bigger and brighter. You begin to see a magnificent huge golden temple with golden domed roofs and a beacon of light on the top in the shape of a star. This temple is tall, large, and rounded in shape. It is one of the more elaborately decorated temples.

The Illumined Ones reside here—ones who are not usually seen or spoken about. The temple has many levels. Ascended masters and Lord Maitreya meet here. They have their own offices within this temple on a higher level, where decisions and changes for the highest good of our planet take place. The three goddesses—Lady Nada,

Jacinta, and Lathinda—have their own offices. They have the gift of being able to sit on karmic boards. Dispensations can be given to those who ask. Changes may be put in place for some people. The temple also holds the energy of Archangel Michael and his twin flame, Archangel Faith, as well as Archangel Metaziel and his twin flame, Archangel Honoriel, who are both new to our planet.

You first connect with the ascended masters. You will find your own master as you walk along the golden corridors. You will see doors to the left and the right, each opening to a room with an ascended master inside. You will be drawn to a particular master. This could be Jesus Christ, Lord Kuthumi, Dwhal Kwul, Hilarion, Paul the Venetian, El Morya, Lord Lanto, Lord Maitreya, Commander Ashtar, Lord Rakoczy, Serapis Bay, St Germain, Mother Mary, Mary Magdalene, Quan Yin, Pallas Athena, Lady Portia, Goddess Isis, or any other master who you personally resonate with. All is well, and all will be. You are in the right place at the right time. Now it is time to see your own particular master—the one you are drawn to. You sit before your own ascended master and talk as if you are old friends. You ask for guidance, abundance, and protection. You receive peace and calm.

You begin to feel lighter and brighter. You see things more clearly. You are given a vision of your future, so hold this vision in your mind and pause awhile as you do so. Ask for what you need to be able to support this vision. Ask the master and the universe to be able to help you all the time, 24/7, until your vision is fulfilled. As you speak to your master, the room fills with more golden light. You are receiving enlightenment. You turn around and leave this room and make your way along the corridor to the main hall. You are now going to meet the three goddesses who oversee the 144 Temples of Golden Light.

Lady Nada, Jacinta, and Lathinda are waiting to greet you. In the main hall, they grace you with their energy. Choose a goddess you wish to connect with and follow her. Feel the energy of your chosen goddess; feel her softness and gentle power. She is interested in you and your life and how you are doing. Perhaps things are not happening the way you would like them to. Speak your truth to the goddess in question so that she may help you to gain further insight into your life and help you with any questions.

Your chosen goddess now gives you a gift and a message. Again, you are being filled with golden light and love of source light. She asks you to look after your body, as this is your temple. Take plenty of exercise, eat healthily, and do work that helps you to be fulfilled. Ask for your abundance. Be clear about what you want it for and why, and you will receive it, maybe in unexpected ways. Live in peace and calm, knowing that the universe will look after you and your family, and then you will receive many blessings.

It is time to leave her room, and you find yourself walking back to the main hall where you sit awhile and contemplate your future by meditating in the great hall of this special temple. You are receiving new key codes of golden light. Your future is bright and positive. See yourself floating back into the ferry below. Gradually bring yourself back to your sacred space. When you are ready, stretch your hands and feet and smile.

### Meditation to Connect with the Temple of Golden Light in Athens, Greece

This temple in the etheric over Athens is the third largest of the Temples of Golden Light and a leading force in moving forward into the new Golden Age. Pallas Athena, Apollo, Zeus, Aphrodite, Artemis, Hermes, and Poseidon oversee this pivotal temple where council meetings are held. The temple is situated above the Acropolis, the sacred temple to the Goddess Pallas Athena. Her own temples are frequently found at elevated positions in cities, the most famous being the Parthenon, which dominates Athens. For the ancient Greeks, she was one of the most important Olympian deities. The goddess of wisdom and skill, she was also a warrior goddess. She taught mankind how to tame horses and works with Pegasus the winged horse.

Apollo, another Greek deity, is a God of diverse function and was the most influential and revered of the Greek gods. He is the god of healing and the element sunshine, so ask Apollo if you wish the sun to shine on your special day. Artemis is the twin of Apollo; she was connected to the moonlight.

Zeus was regarded as the controller of the elements—sender of thunder, lightning, rain, and wind. As supreme god, he would rule over the earth and sky. His brother Poseidon would rule over the seas, and his brother Hades would rule over the underworld. Zeus was seen as the protector of cities.

Aphrodite was the goddess of love and romance. She came from Venus and was also worshipped as a sea goddess. Hermes, the son of Zeus, was associated with the protection of cattle and sheep and was often closely connected to deities of vegetation, such as Pan, who was a messenger of Zeus.

This Temple of Golden Light has been created in true Grecian style: gold and white with beautiful marble pillars. You arrive at a huge doorway, and Pallas Athena, the Grecian goddess of wisdom and skill, greets you. Behind the large Temple of Golden Light is a large healing pool. You are invited to step inside the pool of calm water, and a Grecian maiden wearing a long white flowing gown hands you a towel. You gently step into the healing waters, feeling your body being healed. Focus on where you feel unwell and any disharmony and allow the water to soothe your discomfort away.

You become aware that a dolphin has joined you in the healing pool. (The dolphins are the keepers of the records of Atlantis). You have a telepathic link with each other, and as you link, you are encoded with ancient knowledge from Atlantis. The dolphin is passing on wisdom and healing to you. Relax into this healing energy, releasing all stuck energy. You are creating a new rhythm, a new you, releasing the past, and welcoming your future in light. You clear more to allow your original divine blueprint to shine. Trust, surrender, and flow with the heart of the universe.

Your dolphin makes his clicking sound and nudges you in a playful way. You realise that it is time to leave and make your way out of the healing pool, saying goodbye to your dolphin. You dry yourself with your towel and start to walk through the courtyard into the main part of the temple. Once you are outside looking at the temple, you reflect on your experience and slowly start to make your way back to your sacred space. Gently wiggle your hands and feet, open your eyes, and smile.

**Meditation to Connect with the Temple of Golden Light in Antarctica**

Make sure you are fully grounded by visualising long, thick, golden roots flowing through all the layers of soil and rock and through the crystalline grid. Feel yourself firmly anchored to Mother Earth. Take three deep breaths all the way down to the bottom of your spine.

You connect to the Antarctica Temple of Golden Light at the South Pole. This is the fourth largest of the Temples of Golden Light and is a high-energy temple, having many levels from the bottom to the top. On the first level, you will notice the energies of the penguins and the whales, dolphins, polar bears, sea lions, seals, and Antarctic birds. On another level higher up, you can connect with all the known star systems of Pleiades, Sirius, Andromeda, and Orion's Belt. This Temple of Golden Light gives out a beacon of light that shines all around our universe. The light is passed from star system to star system and planet to planet and then onto the seven universes that surround us.

It is a huge crystalline temple with a multifaceted diamond light coming through a large crystal lotus flower that opens and then slightly closes inside a pyramid in the centre of the temple. Please be aware of the four huge, beautiful, golden universal archangels that represent north, south, east, and west of our beautiful planet. They oversee the Temples of Golden Light, and each has a twin flame. I act as a conduit for them to anchor their energy onto our planet to help our vibration shift. Surrounding this Temple of Golden Light are rainbow angels, so feel them blessing you with their love and support. Different groups of rainbow angels work with each Temple of Golden Light to balance your chakras and help people and animals to heal in order to move forward into yet more light and understanding.

The Arctic Temple and the Antarctica Temple are twin temples of the southern and northern hemispheres of our planet. You connect to the universe here and are given blessings. There is an absolute silence and stillness. This temple is all about balance and alignment and will help to regulate the waters of our planet, bringing about new beginnings, new birth, and rebirth. Be assured that when doing spiritual planetary work, you will always be in the right place at the right time, and you will receive blessings for your good works.

Feel the oneness as you connect to this temple. It connects to many celestial beings of the light from our universe and many angels, planetary earth angels, and universal angels, as well as all of the known archangels and ascended masters, all bringing their light here to help raise the vibration of humanity and Mother Earth. Indeed, it is a very important temple.

All of the Temples of Golden Light are goddess temples and as such are filled with beauty, compassion, purity, and understanding. You are now feeling balanced, peaceful, and ready to slowly return to your sacred space.

### Meditation to Connect with the Temple of Golden Light in Sedona, Arizona, United States

You will journey to the sacred Temple of Golden Light in the etheric over Sedona. You are travelling along what appears to be a golden corridor of light and pure golden energy. You see in the distance an enormous bright, golden light. This is the Temple of Golden Light. Above the temple is a large golden angel. Rainbow angels surround this temple with their beautiful healing energy. Feel their love all around you, blessing you. Now feel their rainbow angel wings of love around you, allowing you to feel safe.

You arrive at the entrance to the Temple of Golden Light and either see, sense, or feel a very large golden door as it opens automatically for you to enter. The temple is filled with powerful energy—so powerful it may overwhelm you at first. This temple is a maze of corridors and has many levels. Your rainbow angel accompanies you inside and takes you to meet some Native Americans who work on the first level. The Native Americans know how to heal naturally with herbs. They may impart some information to you, and you can ask them questions about your health and diet or your lifestyle.

You are now shown around another part of the temple—a very large healing sanctuary connected to Archangel Raphael and Mother Mary. You find yourself in a healing room, and above you is a huge emerald-green crystal chandelier that emits healing energy. This chandelier spins gently over you, healing your etheric body as well as your physical body. This energy is changing your DNA to a higher vibration.

This is a busy temple with so much going on, but it is run in a very orderly way. Every level is organised with love, patience, and understanding. All the energies within our universe work here, and there are two portals to other universes. This is known as a trans-dimensional portal to multi-universes. As you can imagine, this is a very powerful temple. On the highest level, there are celestial beings of immense light. We are not alone; we are protected by the commonwealth peacekeepers who are part of the Galactic Federation Council that operates to keep the peace between galaxies, star systems, planets, universes, and multi-universes.

You are now being shown different parts of our universe—maybe a part of this universe that you come from or are dimensionally working in. What can you see, feel, sense, or experience? Feel peaceful and know that you are part of something much bigger than yourself. You are given information about our universe, and you may feel quite small by comparison. Pause for a couple of minutes while you breathe in this new energy. You now feel a oneness with the earth, the oceans, the mountains, the sky, and our universe. You are a part of everything and everyone. Many lifetimes we have all sat under the sun, the moon, and the stars, and upon the earth. We are one with our universe. Trust and surrender to the divine will of God/Goddess.

As the time comes for you to leave, you receive a blessing from the Sedona Temple of Golden Light. You slowly make your way back to where you started, rub your hands together, stretch your fingers, and smile.

**Meditation to Connect with the Oceanic Temple in Pacific Ocean One**

Of the twelve Oceanic Temples of Golden Light, this is the largest. It is also the seventh largest temple overall and holds considerable amounts of light. It is placed in the ocean between the Hawaiian Islands and the west coast of the United States, directly aligning with the Temple of Golden Light in the etheric over San Francisco, California. It is filled with the energy of Lemuria, and this is combined with Atlantis energy so that the two merge as one, giving a lovely soothing energy. This Temple of Golden Light is in a city of light beneath the ocean and looks like an Atlantis temple with pillars under the water.

Here you will connect to the energy of the dolphins, whales, sea turtles, sea lions, seals, porpoises, elephant seals, penguins, and all the sea creatures, particularly the koi carp who hold a high place in the sea world, as well as seahorses, shellfish, and starfish. We will connect to the mermaids, mer-angels, and mer-people, and to the God Poseidon, also known as Neptune.

You find yourself surrounded by etherical dolphins that are connected to this temple. Feel the love from the dolphins to you. They are the keepers of the keys of Atlantis. The dolphins will take you on a journey to this temple deep in the ocean, surrounded by a city of light. You see yourself riding through the water on the back of a dolphin and noticing all of the sea creatures.

You arrive at the temple with your dolphin, who explains that it will be there waiting to take you back. The doorway to the temple is in the shape of a golden heart. You enter the temple and feel this wonderful light, soothing, healing energy. Important decisions are made here, and council meetings are held. This temple plays an important role in controlling the waters of our planet, as all of the tectonic plates have not moved yet, and when they do this has to be monitored. The energy of this temple rises up from the depth of the waters within the etheric of our ocean, right out into the universe.

The temple (as with all the Temples of Golden Light) has healing areas. You are invited into a healing pool. You find yourself floating in a beautiful, aqua-blue, large bathing pool within the temple, so just relax and allow any concerns and worries to float away. All is well. You are looked after by your angels, who are stroking your forehead; your earth guides, who love you very much; and whoever else in spirit you trust to help you within your life.

Be aware now that a mer-angel has joined your guardian angel, so you will feel a slightly different energy as you allow yourself to relax and be healed. All is well. Do not fear anything. You are strong. You can stand in your own power and deal with any problems that may occur.

Hand over any concerns or worries to those who look after you. Trust, accept, and surrender. God/Goddess will look after you. Release any emotional issues that you may be holding on to still. Let go and let God/Goddess in. Trust that you are in the right place at the right time. We are all eternal beings of light and love, experiencing life and maybe paying back karma. Maybe you have finished your karma and have chosen to stay to help humanity and our lovely planet. Life is but an experience. Feel the peace and stillness of this wonderful temple.

It is time to step out of the healing pool and make your way back to the dolphins. Before you leave, look around the temple beneath the ocean and move from area to area. Try to remember what you see, feel, and sense, and anything else that stands out as being important to you. Feel the golden web of light. Be conscious of the fact that the temples form a network of golden light around the globe.

Your dolphin is waiting for you, and as you hold on to his fin, he brings you back to where you started. With a sense of gratitude for your magical experience, stretch your hands, wiggle your toes, and smile.

## Meditation to Connect with the Temple of Golden Light in Machu Picchu, Peru

Ground yourself by visualising long, thick, golden roots flowing through all the levels of rock and soil through the crystalline grid into Mothers Earth's cosmic, sacred, crystal heart centre.

You are journeying to the Machu Picchu Temple of Golden Light, high up in the etheric of Mother Earth and surrounded by a city of light. It is a very large temple with many levels which work with high energy, emitting golden rays of light constantly. Every vibration on this planet and within this universe is connected to this Temple of Golden Light.

The temple aligns to the star people, celestial beings, angelic realm, masters, and Christed ETs overseen by Commander Ashtar. Higher up, this temple has a landing station for spaceships, as it is connected to the A lines that are above the ley lines. New technology will come through this temple. Decisions are made here connected to the Galactic Federation of Light. Twelve great beings sit on the galactic federation board, and there are nine universal beings of great light, including Goddess Lathinda, Lady Nada, and Goddess Jacinta, along with the Divine Mother.

You find yourself in the main hall of the temple. There is a large golden pyramid the size of the Eiffel Tower in France. This leads to a multidimensional portal of light which, in turn, leads to otherworldly realms. As you can imagine, this is a huge, magnificent Temple of Golden Light. As you connect, your crown chakra is cleared of all negativity and opens up to the universe. Your causal, cosmic, and stellar gateway chakras are all activated so that you may feel at one with this universe of great light and Mother Earth.

Trust God/Goddess to guide you in all that you do and expand your thinking, as it may be time for you to move on to the next level. There is no need for anxiety or fear. You are simply being encouraged to think a little bigger. This will happen with ease and only in ways that make you feel comfortable. Trust the universe and let the universe guide you in all that you do.

You must follow the seven spiritual laws of this universe to manifest what you want in life:

1. The Law of Pure Potential
2. The Law of Giving and Receiving
3. The Law of Karma or Cause and Effect
4. The Law of Least Effort
5. The Law of Intention and Outcome
6. The Law of Detachment
7. The Law of Divine Purpose in Life

It is time to see yourself leaving this temple. Slowly make your way back to where you started, wiggle your feet and hands, and smile.

### Meditation to Connect with the Temple of Golden Light in Stonehenge, England

Stonehenge is one of the most famous sites in the world. It is the remains of a ring of standing stones set in earthworks. The Temple of Golden Light is in the etheric of Mother Earth directly above Stonehenge, and it emits a golden radiance for thousands of miles around the temple. It is a multidimensional vortex of energy connecting to many different energies and star systems, and this temple aligns to the whole of this universe.

Now, sitting comfortably, visualise Stonehenge in your mind's eye. It is a cool, slightly windy day; the sun is just peeping through the sky. It has been raining, and you are fortunate enough to clearly see a rainbow in the sky. Your rainbow angel surrounds you with love and golden light and takes you on a journey to the Stonehenge Temple of Golden Light in the etheric.

You notice in the distance a very bright light, and you realise as you draw closer that this Temple of Golden Light is surrounded by a wonderful city of golden light. You are amazed at what you see, sense, and feel—a seventh-dimensional city of immense light. You are shown around the city of light before arriving at the large temple in the centre.

You become aware of silence. Even though the temple is quite busy, the energy here is calming and will give you balance, peace, and harmony. You realise that the temple is on many levels, and you find yourself moving up energetically in a glass lift. You marvel at what you see. Take a moment to look, sense, feel, or simply know what is around you.

Within the temple, there is an inter-dimensional doorway—a Stargate to other worlds and universes—but only when you are ready are you allowed to use this. You may find yourself transported to different planets and star systems. Try to remember what you sense, feel, or see. The temple is a meeting place for like-minded people and connects to star beings, celestial beings, and very high-vibrational angels. It is surrounded by rainbow angels who are overseen by Archangel Metaziel and his twin flame, Archangel Honoriel.

You find yourself in the centre of this enormous Temple of Golden Light, and you notice a golden pyramid that is a dimensional doorway leading to other realms of existence. You enter through the doorway of the golden pyramid with your rainbow angel, who shows you how to inter-dimensionally travel through time and space. You feel quite small and insignificant as you realise the enormity of our universe, but how amazing is the feeling of having the opportunity to travel around it? You visit star systems and planets. You feel peaceful and energised, allowing yourself to receive healing if you need it. The universe is made up of energy and allows us to move with synchronicity, flow, and ease when we allow ourselves to connect with this vast energy life force.

When you are ready, start making your way back to where

you started. Feel yourself back in your body after this wonderful experience. Stretching your hands and toes, now smile.

## Meditation to Connect with the Temple of Golden Light in Uluru, Australia

We will journey to the temple over Uluru, Ayers Rock, Australia. This temple represents the spirit of the Aborigines. There is an enormous star above the centre of the temple connecting to Pleiades, Sirius, Andromeda, and Venus. Ayers Rock is known by its Aboriginal name of Uluru. It is a sacred part in the Aboriginal creation mythology or dreamtime—reality being a dream. Uluru is a large magnetic mound and is located on a major planetary grid point much like the great pyramid in Egypt.

Visualise Uluru at Ayers Rock. See it as a beautiful, deep red, enormous mountain rock. Make your way up the mountain and find yourself sitting comfortably on the top of Uluru, looking out at the surrounding area. The sun is setting, and you look at the beautiful sunset. It is awesome.

Now it is night-time, and you look at the amazing stars in the night sky. You can understand how the Aborigines lived. They lived naturally; they knew where to find food and water. Aboriginal people knew which plants healed which ailment. They lived with Mother Earth. They honoured Mother Earth and respected her.

Above, you see the centre of our Milky Way galaxy rising over this part of the planet in the sky. Feel yourself floating upwards towards the temple. Directly above Uluru, the island mountain, you find yourself in a beautiful temple with lush vegetation inside representing leaves, plants, and bushes that were sacred to the Aboriginal people. Every plant has a purpose in Aboriginal custom. Medicine men sometimes employed plants and herbs in their rites. They healed non-spiritual complaints using herbs and other remedies. This was practiced by all Aborigines, although older women were usually the experts. To the Aboriginal people, home was their land. They had no possessions, no clothes—only each other.

You are being led now by an Aborigine who guides you around the temple. You wander slowly from room to room, marvelling at the Aboriginal culture and the energy of the sacred tribes. You find yourself in a large room where there is an image of a large beautiful Australian tree. This is where you enter into dreamtime. Dreamtime allows you to place yourself onto your spiritual pathway. It is an energy source called *Tjukurpa.*

Everything in the Aboriginal world contains an essence or spirit that had its beginnings in dreamtime. You sense the Australian animals, the koala bears, the kangaroos, and the beautiful Australian birds. You feel a oneness with all things—the earth, the sky, the stars in the heavens, the mountains. You are at peace. You feel tranquillity; an air of gracefulness has descended upon you. All is well in your world.

You now find yourself feeling, sensing, and knowing what you want to achieve in this life. Take a moment to think about what you want to be doing with your life, what you would like to achieve, and what you would like to see happen. You are recreating and reshaping your future reality. You are a co-creator of your own reality. You see yourself living your creation. See it, feel, it, and know you will achieve what you want.

Feeling grateful for the experience, find yourself leaving the temple and floating back down to earth. When you are ready, wiggle your feet, stretch your hands, and smile.

## Meditation to Connect with the Temple of Golden Light in Agra, India

This Temple of Golden Light is in northern India, in the etheric over the city of Agra. This is where the Taj Mahal, the wonderful palace that Prince Jahan built in honour of his wife, is located. Prince Jahan was an incarnation of Lord Kuthumi. This Temple of Golden Light is surrounded by rainbow angels and by seraphim angels of the highest order. It connects to the Indian gods and goddesses:

- God Shiva, the destroyer and restorer, is God the Power, God the omnipotent. In the Christian tradition, he is known as God the Father.
- God Vishnu, the Preserver, is God the Love, God the omni-provident. In the Christian tradition, he is known as God the Son.

- God Brahma is God the Creator, God the omniscient. In the Christian tradition, he is known as God the Holy Spirit.
- God Krishna is an avatar of God Vishnu, Avatar Rama, Guru, and divine instrument from the God Vishnu.
- Lord Ganesh is the God with an elephant head and human body. He is the God of Good Luck and will help you remove all obstacles.
- From the Supreme God or Parabrahman comes Shiva, Vishnu, and Brahma.

From the heart of God come the different avatars, prophets, messiahs, buddhas, and bodhisattvas.

You now find yourself entering the Temple of Golden Light in the etheric over the centre of Agra. You walk into a courtyard at the back of the temple, sit down in the courtyard in silence, and become aware of the stillness and peace. You notice a large three-tiered fountain flowing with fresh water, where birds are merrily singing and bathing. You go over to the fountain and join these pretty creatures and drink from the waters, which are fresh and cooling. You see a kindly looking person seated under a tree on a stone bench and hear a voice saying, 'Welcome. To what do I owe this pleasure?' You turn around and on your right-hand side, you see the Maha Chohan, Ascended Master Lord Kuthumi, who incarnated as Prince Jahan, St Francis of Assisi, and Balthazar, one of the three wise kings when Jesus was born.

You take a walk with Lord Kuthumi through this large Temple of Golden Light and walk through the main hall. The doors lead to meditation rooms for all those who wish to come to the temple and meditate. Mind-calm gives you a new relationship with yourself, giving conscious awareness that is present within you, so that you may be free of any stressful situation and truly enjoy a successful life free from fear, problems, and limitations. Meditation gives you peace of mind and a clarity of focus. Feel your mind being still. Feel a peace-filled presence within you. You look into one of the rooms and feel the sunlight touch you as it filters through in the cascading colours of a rainbow.

There is a feeling of pure peace. You feel a wave of love as you stand in the presence of God/Goddess and the angels. You feel them bless you as you look around. They want you to know that you can come here anytime you wish to meditate.

You turn and step out of the room, and Lord Kuthumi takes you back to the courtyard. At the far end are huge wooden gates. You walk through the gates, and not so far in the distance is a large waterfall. You make your way over to the waterfall, and you are invited to step into the water. This is like holy water in which you may bathe. It will cleanse away any negativity, making you feel well again.

As you lower yourself into the water, you feel and sense the power of the rainbow angels assisting you. You feel their gentle hands stroking and cleansing your body from top to toe. Enjoy and relax. Rainbow angels are singing to you, giving you messages of love and light. You feel a rush of love and warmth run through the whole of your body as the cleansing is completed.

It is time to step out of the water, say goodbye to the rainbow angels, and head back with Lord Kuthumi to the temple. As you thank Lord Kuthumi, he gives you a message that will personally help you in this lifetime. You slowly come back into the awareness of your sacred space. Gently wiggle your fingers and toes and smile.

## Meditation to Connect with the Temple of Golden Light in Phoenix, Arizona, United States

This is a very large Temple of Golden Light placed in the etheric directly over Phoenix, aligning to many star people of celestial light and connecting to Commander Ashtar. It is a vibrational healing temple that can and will facilitate miracles and healing on all levels, but mostly the cellular memory level. This will help you remove all emotional blocks that can cause disharmony within our bodies. This is a very important temple because of its healing powers and ability to connect with this universe and the seven universes that surround it.

You find yourself entering this very large temple. If you have a physical or emotional problem that needs healing, all will be well. Whatever your reason for connecting to this temple, you will find yourself being given the answer. As you enter the temple along with your rainbow angel, you immediately feel the change in energy. This is a high-energetic Temple of Golden Light with a wonderful healing and balancing energy, connecting to the most advanced beings of bright light within our universe.

You find yourself moving towards the centre of the temple where there is a crystal flower of light with an eighteen-pointed base to it. This flower of light is held inside a crystal pine cone shape that moves down to earth and up and out to the universe, pulsating and vibrating to the rhythm of Mother Earth's heartbeat. You find yourself sitting in the centre of the crystal flower of light and ask to be healed of all disharmonies: physical, emotional, mental, and spiritual.

You feel your cells changing within your body, gently and slowly, as your DNA is subtly changing and quietly aligning you to the frequency of pure energy of our earth and this universe. You begin to feel whole again and know that something is changing within you. It is time to change and let go of the past. You feel renewed, revitalised, rejuvenated, and refreshed. It's time to move forward into yet even more light of love, peace, and balance.

Forgive all those around you and let go. Do not waste time being stressed; just let it go. Ask the universe to help you within your life, your work, your health, and your family. Feel the oneness of Mother Earth, the mountains, the oceans, and the land. We are one, a large family of one consciousness. Feel the support and love of the Divine Mother, holding you within her arms of love, golden light, and grace.

You are a wonderful, powerful being of love and light. You are a guardian to this planet. You are a co-creator of your life. Take your place within our universe now. You are greatly loved and cherished far more than you will ever know. Feel the Goddess love now. Feel grateful for the release of negative energy and for what you have experienced in the temple. Listen to your breathing and return to where you started. Stretch out your hands and your feet and smile.


**Meditation to Connect with the Temple of Golden Light in Paris, France**

This meditation will connect you to the Paris Temple of Golden Light. Sitting in your sacred space, please light a candle in front of you. If possible, you may like to hold a special crystal of your choice. Gently close your eyes. You find you are sitting in the most beautiful room.

You have personally chosen all the furnishings, flooring, curtains, pictures, paintings, mirrors, family photos, ornaments, flowers, and anything else you wish to have with you in your room.

Breathe in love and breathe out gold. Do this three times. I would like you to ground yourself, thinking of an old oak tree, tall and strong. Now splay out your roots and allow long, thick, golden roots to flow from the base of your feet through all the layers of the soil and rock through the crystalline grid and into Mother Earth's cosmic heart centre. As you do this, visualise a rose quartz crystal and a hematite crystal together. Rose quartz is for unconditional love, and hematite is for grounding. Wrap your roots around the crystals and place them in an area of water deep within the planetary core. Now begin to feel Mother Earth's loving, subtle energy flow upwards throughout the whole of your body, grounding you, healing you, and relaxing you.

You now find yourself sitting in the main hall of the temple placed in the etheric near the Sacré Coeur, Paris. Golden light is coming from source entering into your crown chakra. Allow this energy to flow to your heart centre. Feel your energy expanding into pure golden light, filling your aura with peace.

Rainbow angels are removing negativity from this lifetime and helping you to release past life issues at a cellular level. They help you with positive changes that create good relationships, feelings of abundance, and the energy to move forward, with a clear sense of purpose. Rainbow angels are special angels who can clear all of your chakras in one go—not one chakra at a time but all of your chakras together, healing, relaxing, and grounding you all at the same time. These angels are new to this planet. They appear with beautiful wings the colours of the rainbow. You are breathing in the rainbow angels' energy.

Your rainbow angel gently lifts you up in her rainbow wings, lifting you higher and higher, up through the sky. She gently places you on the rainbow. This feeling is magical. You start to dance on the rainbow, dancing through all of the colours. As each colour flows over you, you are aware of a different vibration. We are drawn to the colours needed to create balance in our lives—the goal in all healing. Colour is a frequency wavelength based on the seven basic rainbow colours we see as light. These seven colours are red, orange, yellow, green, blue, indigo, and violet. You marvel at the different colours. God has sent the rainbow angels to this planet because we are ready for their energy. God is colour, just as God is sound, God is nature, and God is all that there is.

With each major shift of our consciousness, the Divine showers us with new energies. The only qualities that are important are love and forgiveness. Focus on your heart chakra, releasing old stuck energy and sending love to all those who have hurt and upset you. See them now sending love back to you. Let rainbow angels repair any old damage to your heart centre.

Sit quietly for a few minutes and relish the knowledge of the healing that has taken place. Slowly make your way back to your sacred space. Stretch your fingers and toes and smile.

## Meditation to Connect with the Temple of Golden Light for Healing Animals in Sicily, Italy

First connect to the Temple of Golden Light in Istanbul, Turkey. Please find yourself sitting in the main hall of this beautiful temple. From here, we journey together to the very picturesque Temple of Golden Light in the etheric over Palermo, the capital of Sicily in Italy. This is the main animal healing temple. There are six animal healing temples, all overseen by St Francis of Assisi and filled with the love of Jesus Christ and Mother Mary.

You are introduced to St Francis of Assisi, an Italian saint well-known for being the patron saint of all animals as well as people. He is also known as an ambassador of peace. He was born and lived in the Italian town of peace called Assisi in Italy, near the town of Perugia, Umbria. He loved Jesus Christ so much that Francis himself received the stigmata on his hands, feet, and body. The following prayer is associated with him:

### *Prayer of St Francis*

Lord, make me an instrument of your peace.
Where there is hatred, let me sow love;
Where there is injury, pardon;

Where there is doubt, faith;
Where there is despair, hope;
Where there is darkness, light;
Where there is sadness, joy.
O Divine Master, grant that I may seek
not so much to be consoled, as to console,
to be understood, as to understand,
to be loved, as to love.
For it is in giving that we receive;
It is in pardoning that we are pardoned;
It is in dying that we are born to eternal life.

From St Francis of Assisi pours a constant flow of grace, love, and peace. This temple connects also to St Anthony of Padua, known in Italy as the patron saint of animals and children and as the saint of miracles. He started out as a Franciscan monk. The energy of this temple is filled with Christ consciousness and the Divine Mother. This animal healing temple is surrounded by four large protective king unicorns and is overseen by Pegasus the winged horse. The rainbow angels work in this temple helping to heal all the sick animals that come here.

You find yourself walking up the many golden steps leading to the golden front door of the temple. As the door opens, you are welcomed by St Francis of Assisi and St Anthony of Padua. You instantly feel their peace and love flowing towards you. St Francis of Assisi shows you around. He explains that all animals come from their own planet or star system and therefore have a right to live here and be free. They very often only become fearful due to human beings treating them badly.

Move through the temple, and when you find yourself in the main room, sit down and ask for healing for an animal that you know—any animal. See a miracle taking place and the animal being healed and full of health and vitality.

As you revel in the wondrous peace that you have experienced, it is time to leave. Bring your focus back to your breath, and find yourself back in your sacred space. Stretch out your hands and your feet and smile.

# Appendix I

Temples of Golden Light Placed Around the World

## Europe

1.  Istanbul, Turkey
2.  Bodrum, Turkey
3.  Glastonbury, England
4.  Stonehenge, England
5.  Snowdonia, Wales
6.  Edinburgh, Scotland
7.  Dublin, Ireland
8.  Paris, France
9.  Lourdes, France
10. Berlin, Germany
11. Cologne, Germany
12. Amsterdam, Netherlands
13. Madrid, Spain
14. Seville, Spain
15. Lisbon, Portugal
16. Rome, Italy
17. Venice, Italy
18. Sicily, Italy
19. Geneva, Switzerland
20. Zurich, Switzerland
21. Vienna, Austria
22. Salzburg, Austria
23. Savinja Alps, Slovenia

24. Budapest, Hungary
25. Oslo, Norway
26. Mo i Rana, Norway
27. Stockholm, Sweden
28. Helsinki, Finland
29. Tallinn, Estonia
30. Warsaw, Poland
31. Bratislava, Slovakia
32. Prague, Czech Republic
33. Zazanlak, Bulgaria
34. Zagreb, Croatia
35. Belgrade, Serbia
36. Athens, Greece
37. Crete, Greece
38. Paphos, Cyprus
39. Kiev, Ukraine

**The Americas**
*United States*

40. New York, New York
41. Mount Shasta, California
42. San Francisco, California
43. Sedona, Arizona
44. Phoenix, Arizona
45. Denver, Colorado
46. Salt Lake City, Utah
47. Idaho Falls, Idaho
48. Portland, Oregon
49. Omaha, Nebraska
50. Dallas, Texas
51. Little Rock, Arkansas
52. Nashville, Tennessee
53. Atlanta, Georgia
54. Indianapolis, Indiana
55. Minneapolis, Minnesota
56. Chicago, Illinois
57. Detroit, Michigan

58. Boston, Massachusetts
59. Kauai, Hawaii

## South America

60. Machu Picchu, Peru
61. Callao, Lima, Peru
62. La Paz, Bolivia
63. Rio de Janeiro, Brazil
64. Montevideo, Uruguay
65. Caracas, Venezuela
66. Santiago, Chile
67. Buenos Aires, Argentina
68. Havana, Cuba
69. San José, Costa Rica
70. Honduras
71. Mexico City, Mexico

## Canada

72. Ontario
73. Quebec
74. Lake Winnipeg, Manitoba
75. Vancouver
76. Great Bear Lake, Northwest Territories
77. Amundsen Gulf, Northwest Territories

## Australasia and Oceanic
### Australasia

78. Uluru, Australia
79. Margaret River, Perth, Australia
80. Brisbane, Gold Coast, Australia
81. Cairns, Australia
82. Sydney, Australia
83. South Island, New Zealand
84. Suva, Fiji

*Oceanic*

85. Pacific Ocean One, off the Hawaiian Islands, United States
86. Pacific Ocean Two, off La Paz, Bolivia, and Lima, Peru
87. Pacific Ocean Three, off Tokyo, Japan
88. Atlantic Ocean One, off Bermuda, outside the Bermuda Triangle
89. Atlantic Ocean Two, off Cape Verde, Gambia, Africa
90. Atlantic Ocean Three, off Rio de Janeiro, Brazil
91. Indian Ocean One, off Rockingham, Perth, Australia
92. Indian Ocean Two, off Colombo, Sri Lanka
93. Caspian Sea, off Azerbaijan
94. Arctic Ocean, off Spitsbergen, north of Norway
95. Mediterranean Sea, off Valencia, Spain
96. English Channel, off Dover, England

## Asia
*India, Pakistan, and the Himalayas*

97. Agra, India
98. Amritsar, India
99. Kolkata, India
100. Bangalore, India
101. Sri Lanka
102. Lahore, Pakistan
103. Hyderabad, Pakistan
104. Kathmandu, Nepal
105. Lhasa, Tibet
106. Thimphu, Bhutan

*China and Other Parts of Asia*

107. Hong Kong
108. Shanghai, China
109. Beijing, China
110. Changsha, Hunan Province, China
111. Yangtze River, Zhengzhou, China
112. Xianyang, China
113. Dandong, China

114. Gobi Desert, Mongolia
115. Atyrau, Kazakhstan
116. Tokyo, Japan
117. Padang, Singapore
118. Samar, Philippines
119. Hanoi, Vietnam
120. Ipoh, Malaysia
121. Bali, Indonesia

**Rest of the World**
*Antarctica, Arctic, Iceland, and Greenland*

122. Antarctica
123. Arctic
124. Reykjavik, Iceland
125. Ammassalik, Greenland

*Russia*

126. Moscow
127. St Petersburg
128. Siberia
129. Omsk
130. Ayan, Stanovoy Mountain Range

*Africa*

131. Cape Town, South Africa
132. Nairobi, Kenya
133. Lilongwe, Malawi
134. Huambo, Angola
135. Mogadishu, Somalia
136. Timbuktu, Mali
137. Casablanca, Morocco
138. Tunis, Tunisia
139. Cairo, Egypt

## Middle East

140. Beirut, Lebanon
141. Bethlehem, Israel
142. Jerusalem, Israel
143. Al Basrah, Iraq
144. Abu Dhabi, United Arab Emirates

# Appendix 2

Other Ways to Connect to the Temples of Golden Light

**Affirmation Creams**

I have produced a set of eighteen creams, each of which will connect you to the energy of an individual Temple of Golden Light. Each cream balances your chakra/energy centres, comes with a powerful affirmation, and contains a different blend of essential oils, creating a beautiful fragrance for you to enjoy. You can order and buy online from www.templesofgoldenlight.com

**Downloads/CDs**

I have recorded the following meditation CDs and MP3s to help you connect to the Temples of Golden Light.

- Temples of Golden Light Meditations
- Temples of Golden Light Meditations II
- Temples of Golden Light Meditations III
- Rainbow Angel Meditations
- Garden of Relaxation Meditations
- Unicorn Meditations

You will then be able to connect with at least eighteen Temples of Golden Light through my audio recordings of meditations. For more information, visit www.templesofgoldenlight.com

The 144 Temples of Golden Light act as a very powerful healing grid of energy working for the highest good of humanity and Mother Earth. Thirty-three of the temples are surrounded by cities of light, and you may visit these during your sleep-state or meditation. They are a gift from source. All of the temples perform specific healing functions, healing emotions, physical body disharmonies, heart issues, mind, children, and animals. They are surrounded by rainbow angels who can heal all of your chakras together at one time. They can be accessed and used by anyone, anywhere, and anytime.

> I love visiting the many different Temples of Golden Light in meditation. Whilst they are all filled with the most amazing light, as their name suggests, each one has a different appearance, and the energy provides different insights to me. With so many to choose from, there is always a new temple to explore or a familiar one to return to. And the effect after a visit is invariably the same: the Temples of Golden Light bring balance, healing, and a sense of peace and harmony to how I feel.—Sarah, researcher

> Since I joined the emissaries group for the Temples of Golden Light, my experience has been nothing short of phenomenal. I have found myself transported into a realm of peace and tranquillity where I have received healing which has balanced and centred me. I am in awe of them but also totally at home when working within the sacred space that they offer.—Christina, reconnective facilitator/healer

> Over the years that Linda has been channelling the 144 Temples of Golden Light, I have meditated with her and visited them in the etheric. In doing so, it has become very clear that the energies in the temples can be quite different and each brings its own type of comfort and healing. When I meditate alone, if I am uncertain which temple will help me the most, I simply ask for help and trust that I will be connected

to those that will benefit me most. I have no doubt in my mind that when I ask for healing, love, and support for my personal well-being, I am given what I need to help me face my challenges and lead a well-balanced life.—Julie, reiki master

The Temples of Golden Light are a gift from Source, to re-balance planet earth with Goddess energy, raising the vibration through ascension. As etheric temples each temple may be visited during meditation, contemplation or one's sleep state for healing, relaxation, peace, upliftment, grace, inspiration, cellular renewal, also for the release of any energy blocks stopping you from moving forward. The Temples will give you guidance and protection, they are filled with much love and total light. The Temples of Golden Light are sacred goddess temples of golden light. Three Goddesses over-light the temples, Lady Nada, twin flame of Jesus Christ, Goddess Jacinta she works with the Rainforests and Nature on planet Earth, and Goddess Lathinda who comes from another universe called the Universe of Golden Light. Surrounded by the Rainbow Angels who are able to heal all of your chakras at the same time, under the guidance of 2 New Archangels called Archangel Metaziel and his twin flame Archangel Honoriel.

The 144 Temples of Golden Light align to all of the pure energies within this wonderful Universe, and the Gods/Goddesses of Love and Light of Source. The Temples of Golden Light are surrounded by Four Universal Global Golden Seraphim Angels of the Highest Order representing north, south, east and west of our beautiful planet. Being a gift from source the temples may bring about Miracles. The aim of the Temples of Golden Light being to heal Humanity and Mother Earth herself bringing Peace and Harmony to a New Earth.

Linda Jarrett is an Author, Writer, Spiritual Teacher, Healer, Radio Host, Meditation Teacher and Clairvoyant. She is honoured to be the Ambassador for the 144 Temples of Golden Light. She has channeled this work to be able to help people to heal themselves. You can create a new positive, harmonious life by linking with the Temples of Golden Light this will bring about balance and peace. For more information on Linda's work please visit:
www.templesofgoldenlight.com

If you wish free distant healing please direct mail me via my Temple of Golden Light Facebook account @templesofgoldenlight

She has recorded 6 Meditation CDs/Downloads, Temples of Golden Light Meditations, Temples of Golden Light Meditations II, Temples of Golden Light Meditations III, Rainbow Angel Meditations, Unicorn Meditations, & Garden of Relaxation Meditations to listen and order: www.templesofgoldenlight.com

Affirmations Creams for Well Being available in 18 different Affirmation Creams: Balance, Believe, Abundance, Clarity, Unblock/Release, Tranquility, Earth Star, Enlightenment, Self-Confidence, Love, Harmony, Heart, Manifest, Empower, Joy, Forgive, Magical & Inner Peace. Each cream aligns to a different Temple of Golden Light bringing forward a powerful affirmation of your choice. You simply apply the cream to your wrists and say the affirmation at the same time twice daily. You will be amazed at how powerful the Affirmation Creams are, you can choose whichever well-being cream you wish to work with. To order visit: www.templesofgoldenlight.com

Printed in Great Britain
by Amazon